Harry Kalven, Jr. has been a member of the faculty at the University of Chicago Law School for over 20 years. He is director of the Ford Foundation-funded Jury Project at the University of Chicago, from which have come two watershed books: DELAY IN THE COURT (with Hans Zeisel and Bernard Buchholz) and THE AMERICAN JURY (with Zeisel). Constitutional law is another of Mr. Kalven's major interests, and his THE NEGRO AND THE FIRST AMENDMENT is considered a definitive work.

Contempt

Contempt

Transcript of the Contempt Citations, Sentences, and Responses of the Chicago Conspiracy 10

Foreword by RAMSEY CLARK, former Attorney General of the United States

Introduction by HARRY KALVEN, Jr., Professor of Law, University of Chicago

Including on-the-scene sketches by
BILL JONES, *Chicago Sun-Times*
JOHN DOWNS, *Chicago Daily News*
JAMES YEP, *Chicago Daily News*

THE SWALLOW PRESS INC.
CHICAGO

Published by
The Swallow Press Incorporated
1139 South Wabash Avenue
Chicago, Illinois 60605

LIBRARY OF CONGRESS CATALOG CARD NUMBER 70–120687

CONTENTS

PUBLISHER'S NOTE

Our intention in this book is to let the record speak for itself. Trite though the phrase sounds, it is of crucial importance that the record do precisely that. Ten men were cited for 175 separate incidents of contempt of court and sentenced to a total of 19 years, 3 months, and 3 days in jail. In the contempt proceedings, Judge Julius Hoffman presents *his* case: the specifications made, the sentences given, and the trial transcript portions chosen to document the contempt charges are all his own. In a genuine sense, then, this book is edited by Judge Hoffman; it is his version of the five-month trial in terms of the "deliberate and wilful attack upon the administration of justice."

The text of this book is taken from the official court reporter's typed transcript as follows: the Bobby Seale section, pages 5409-5484 of the transcript; and the remainder, pages 21445-21818. We present the contempt transcript with no deletions and without additions or changes except as noted. The chapter headings are ours. In a few cases we corrected obvious typographical or aural errors (e.g., we changed "fo" to "of," "seek" to "speak," "attempt" to "contempt," etc.). In nine places we inserted a word or an ellipsis to clarify the meaning of a sentence; these additions are in brackets. In making a contempt citation, Judge Hoffman almost always used the phrase *Specification* 3; a few times he said *Item* 3, but we changed Item to Specification for simple consistency. Other format and punctuation inconsistencies were retained. One final addition: In the original transcript the sentence (e.g., 7 days) for each contempt specification appears only once—at the end of each case, after Judge Hoffman has read all the specific charges and their supporting documentation and after the defendant has made his response to these. In order for the reader to more easily relate each sentence to its citation we have printed the sentence, in bold face, also immediately following each specification. All other text is left as is, even in a few instances where the sense was not clear but the alternatives were ambiguous. The asterisk ellipses were in the court reporter's transcript and indicate Judge Hoffman's editing as he compiled the contempt document from the trial transcript. Please note that THE COURT always indicates Judge Hoffman speaking and MR. HOFFMAN indicates defendant Abbott Hoffman speaking.

Two very special men, both lawyers, are in large part responsible for this book.

Mr. Bernard Weisberg of Chicago originated the idea and then arranged for us to obtain a copy of the official contempt transcript. Mr. Weisberg also led us to Professor Harry Kalven, Jr., author of the brilliant introduction to this book.

Mr. Landon Gerald Dowdey of Washington, D.C. really deserves a place on the title page of CONTEMPT. Without his encouragement, guidance, and research we would never have been able to complete work on the book in just four weeks. It was Mr. Dowdey who found what became our afterword, and who arranged for Mr. Ramsey Clark to provide his uncompromising foreword to this book.

To both these men go our sincere thanks and deep appreciation.

Durrett Wagner
Morton P. Weisman

FOREWORD

by Ramsey Clark

This book contains a concentrated dose of the raw stuff of our times. Do not expect to find much quiet, order, reason, dignity, art or faith, hope and charity. Such qualities are not totally lacking. They shine brightly from their turbulent setting, but their supply is desperately wanting. A handful of personalities—defendants, judge, prosecutors and defense attorneys, jurors, witnesses, clerks and spectators—participate in an intense little drama subjected to the full force of the major dynamics and emotions of the day. The strains and tensions of such powerful currents are clear.

This vital slice of distilled truth can tell us much about ourselves and our times—but like all important messages it is not easy to understand. A valuable case study for examination and thought, the reader must bring as much attention to the matter between the lines as to the printed word if he is to do more than observe a wild and sometimes seemingly bizarre episode.

Do not underestimate the prejudices you may bring to this book. They might be more than a preconception of the trial. They can reflect the values you hold from your total experience. Try to disenthral yourself.

Realize the principals came to court with their prejudices. Consider the impact of these on the trial. Suppose the defendants believed the trial was purely political—that there was neither the purpose nor the capability of sifting facts to find truth and applying clear and uniform rules of law to those facts. Suppose the judge, trained in law, religiously committed to respect for the system of law and the court as its highest priest, believed there was a deliberate, preconceived, continuing, and contumacious effort to humiliate by revolutionary forces? Might much of what happened flow from such attitudes? Add the sudden emotionalization from courtroom conduct appearing to confirm such prejudice and you may glimpse why what happened happened.

If there is to be a judicial process as we conceive it, there must be reason, objectivity, fairness of purpose, diligent preparation and presentation of evidence, clear, just rules, an orderly proceeding, and at least a modest efficiency. I know of no better way to seek justice in contests between the individual and the state. These elements are essential to the administration of courts as we have theorized them. But courts cannot operate in a vacuum. There is no way to check the action and passion of the times at the courthouse door. While we can strive to imbue the judicial process with special qualities of dignity and rationality we must recognize that issues and personalities come to court with antecedent history. The impact of that history is inescapable. Those who participate in writing it must be conscious of its meaning to judicial administration and justice. Compared to what is possible, even reasonably foreseeable, the Chicago Seven trial was sweet reason and placidity personified. Fifty trial days without even allegedly contemptuous conduct does not indicate an ardent and immutable intention to disrupt. We can bring desperate, irrational, uncontrollable emotion and cunning to the courtroom. Chains and gags can never contain it.

This test—the trial of the Chicago Eight, then Seven—which was relatively easy, was failed miserably. We should ask why. The capacity of the judicial system to cope with existing conditions is in question—and ultimately government by law. We must look deeply for the lessons of Chicago then and strive to avoid its mistakes.

The concerned reader of this record of torment should wonder as he reads:

Why this "Rap Brown" statute creating a new federal crime for 200 million Americans? Was its genesis only fear and hypocrisy? Is the trial the price we pay? Without the new law, only several months old in August, 1968, the conduct of defendants would have been judged by state laws as had always been the case theretofore.

Why no permit to speak, assemble, march, and petition for the protesters at the Democratic Convention? Soldiers Field stood empty as did a dozen other places. What of the Constitutional Rights of free speech and peaceful assembly? Were they violated? Had the permits been granted might violence have been avoided?

Why did a federal study refer to several episodes forming part of the basis for these indictments as "police riots"? Did civic leadership emotionalize police? Did the police violate the law? Could the defendants have believed they were victims of officially sanctioned repression?

Why did the State government not prosecute if defendants were guilty of acts of incitement to riot? Was this not a violation of state law? Did not the federal law recognize the primacy of state jurisdiction over riotous conduct?

Why was a federal prosecutor closely identified with Mayor Daley permitted to try the case? Must we not remove prosecutors personally involved, witnesses to parts of the activity complained of, from participation? How objective and fair might he seem to defendants?

Why were the cases brought? Was there really evidence giving probable cause to believe a crime was committed? Why these eight defendants out of scores who participated? Might the defendants feel persecuted?

Why was conspiracy alleged? Is it not enough to allege illegal acts of violence and incitement? Does acquittal of all defendants on the conspiracy count indicate it was a prosecution ploy? Had conspiracy not been alleged, this trial would never have occurred. The defendants would have been tried separately.

Why was Bobby Seale indicted? Did the defendants believe he had nothing to do with planning the protest? Had he attended only at the last moment and made speeches made thousands of times by scores of Black Militants and never a one indicted? Was it a sense of persecution and injustice that caused Bobby Seale to insist on his own lawyer? Was nearly all of the disruptive conduct in court caused by Bobby Seale's inclusion?

Why did the Court assign the case to Judge Julius Hoffman? Was the inherent volatility of the trial not apparent? Was he temperamentally suited for such a trial? Was there no one on the federal bench who could have tried the case better?

These are only some of the issues that may have contributed to shaping attitudes of contempt or respect for what happened in the courtroom. Respect does not come easily these days. It is not always accorded even when earned. But we must never value decorum over justice. If the rule of law is to prevail, it must proceed wisely, deliberately, fairly, and rationally. It must never react in emotion. If the system is so frail that it cannot cope with the events in Chicago, the days ahead will be turbulent indeed.

The failures at Chicago were failures of men and emotion. We cannot and should not judge the facts while the rights of the defendents remain before the courts. But even now we must see that Chicago offers no substantial evidence that our institutions of justice are inadequate. The principles of our judicial system will suffice if reason can conquer emotion.

At the very least the summary conviction of the defendants for contempt at the trial's end by the very judge involved and the cumulation of separate citations of contempt to impose sentences up to four years is impermissible by any standard of justice—or so far as I can see—law.

A special word about the author of the Introduction. You should not hold against him the fact that twenty years ago when I was his student he could have taught me law. He has been generally more successful. Even as a student I sensed he was exceptionally perceptive. Now I am quite sure. His Introduction here is only further evidence of the fact. A careful reading of Harry Kalven's sensitive essay will give the transcript far greater meaning. I commend it to you.

Washington, D.C.
March, 1970

INTRODUCTION

Confrontation and Contempt

by Harry Kalven, Jr.

This transcript of the contempt citations given by Judge Hoffman at the Chicago Conspiracy Trial makes a remarkable document. It provides a profound experience for the reader; it is at once irritating, powerful, alarming, unnerving, eloquent—and fascinating. It is in the nature of a public service to have published it, preserving the record and making it so widely available. The trial itself is already well on its way to becoming a legend in American law and politics; the controversies over the contempts which are here preserved will be a central part of that legend.

I

It may be well to begin with a few simple statements of fact. Eight individuals, Bobby Seale, David Dellinger, Tom Hayden, Rennie Davis, Abbie Hoffman, Jerry Rubin, John Froines, and Lee Weiner, all in varying degrees leaders in what has been called the "New Left," were indicted, under a recently enacted federal statute, for conspiring to cross state lines with an intent to incite a riot, and also for engaging in the same conduct as individuals. The riot in question was the nationally and internationally visible series of disturbances which took place in Chicago in August, 1968, at the time of the Democratic National Convention.

The trial began in the federal district court in Chicago before Judge Julius Hoffman on September 26, 1969, and lasted for five months, concluding on February 18, 1970. It received publicity which was extraordinary both in intensity and duration and became a national event and part of the popular culture.

After deliberating for over four days, the jury returned

a complex and interesting verdict. It acquitted two defendants, Weiner and Froines, in full. It acquitted all seven defendants of the conspiracy count—there were seven at the conclusion of the trial, Bobby Seale having been separated from the case in October by the order of the judge. And it convicted the remaining five defendants, Dellinger, Hayden, Davis, Rubin, and Hoffman on the individual counts of crossing state lines to incite a riot.

At the conclusion of the trial, while the jury was deliberating, Judge Hoffman, who had warned the defendants and their lawyers repeatedly during the trial, called them before him one at a time and adjudged them in contempt, sentencing them to periods ranging from two-and-a-half months to over four years. The drama of the contempt citations tended to overshadow in the public eye the verdicts themselves, and added an almost unprecedented dimension to the case. As he dealt with each party, Judge Hoffman read off a carefully documented series of citations specifying the event and placing it in the context of the trial transcript. The text of this book consists simply of these citations, the particular sentences for each offense, and the closing statements by the individuals and Judge Hoffman. The citations thus fall neatly into ten chapters, one for each of the contempt "histories."

In the case of the five defendants found guilty, Judge Hoffman made his contempt sentences run concurrently with the five-year sentences he gave to each for their violation of the statute. In these cases the contempts may thus not have any great practical significance unless the convictions under the statute are upset on appeal. In the other five cases—that of Seale who awaits trial, of Froines and Weiner who were acquitted, and of the two lawyers, William Kunstler and Leonard Weinglass—the contempts, unless upset on appeal, will have the result of placing them in jail not for violation of the riot statute, but for "crimes" committed in the course of defending during the trial.

The contempt sentences as well as the convictions are now on appeal. This book is not, therefore, the last word from the legal system on the matter of the contempts, and it is neither appropriate nor necessary to attempt an appraisal of their legality here.

II

These ten contempt histories provide an important, and quite possibly, the best way of getting a view of the Chicago trial. They have the great advantage of providing, on a reasonably neutral basis, *a sample* of the monstrously prolix trial transcript. On the one hand, they offer the distilled view of the trial judge as to what was distressing, obstructive, and contumacious in the tactics of the defense and hence provide a permanent memoir of the threat to the administration of justice; and on the other hand, they provide, from the vantage point of those who have not admired the way the judge and the prosecution handled matters, an equally permanent memoir of the imperfections of the legal system as it responded in this case.

This twin vision of the material is readily underscored by dipping into the transcript for a pair of quotations. The first is from Judge Hoffman at the end of a sharp colloquy with David Dellinger about which defendant had made a certain outburst in court: "I have never," said the judge, "sat in fifty years through a trial where a party to a law suit called the judge a liar." The second is from Lee Weiner as he addresses the judge prior to being sentenced for contempt: ". . . people must struggle in making their political revolution against a real world, not a fantasy world. You have helped educate people younger than ourselves as to what the real world is."

Perhaps the better way to put the point is this: the trial was a confrontation between two styles, the style of the legal order and the style of the new radicalism. It was in a sense an extended, if bizarre, dialogue between them. Because these participants are unusually articulate, the transcript carries odd echoes of the *Man For All Seasons,* or better, Shaw's *Saint Joan.* It was this, I suspect, rather than the precise charge or the details as to the anti-riot statute, that so steadily captured public attention. This book captures the essence of that dialogue.

Moreover, pushing law and politics to one side, there is the sheer human interest of the materials. We get a series of sharply etched profiles; we get a sense of the style, perhaps I should say offensive style, and quality of mind of each participant as he interacts with the process. And then, in more detail, there is that eleventh profile—the profile of Judge Hoffman as he duels with each "opponent."

The material can be read as a very modern morality play, a view of the trial that has seemed congenial to all participants in it, and for which all seemed to have been uncannily well cast. The problem may, in this instance, be to decide who are the guys with the white hats. But a virtue of the present endeavor is that it leaves that perception to each reader to make in the end for himself.

III

Nevertheless, given this format, some caveats are in order. Often the context will not be full enough to make intelligible exactly what was going on at the time. Judge Hoffman is, as a matter of style, often elliptical in his rulings and does not feel it necessary to explain. There is the chance always present, therefore, that any given episode read in the context of the full transcript would leave a somewhat different impression than we can garner here from the excerpt the judge has selected.

Moreover, the printed page cannot fully convey the flavor of the proceedings. We often will not get a sense of the tone, the loudness, the sarcasm, the demeanor, the murmuring, and the degree of disturbance that may have existed elsewhere in the courtroom. In brief, the trial may in fact have had a more unsettled air than these excerpts can suggest.

And again we must remind ourselves, as we examine Judge Hoffman's 175 individual citations, that he was understandably not trying to cite *all* instances of disturbance or offense. We can, however, feel secure that we have here a harvest of the strongest examples, the cream, as it were, of the contempt.

IV

As we have noted, the contempt citations are now on appeal, and the cases will serve to clarify important aspects of the law on contempt. Without attempting to predict the outcome of the appeals, it may be worthwhile to pause for a moment to reflect on this legal institution, the deep paradoxes of which were highlighted by the developments at the trial.

INTRODUCTION

At one of the unsettled moments during the trial, Judge Hoffman observes: "There comes a time when courtroom decorum must be observed." David Dellinger replies: "Decorum is more important than justice, I suppose." Dellinger's rhetorical question may prove in the end to be a real one, but the traditional answer has been that there is no conflict between decorum and justice, that decorum in the trial process is a rational value in the pursuit of justice. I have always thought the traditional answer was correct. And the contempt power has traditionally been viewed as an indispensable means to the preservation of order and decorum in the trial.

Yet there are anomalies. Because the contempt power carries penal sanctions, it marks, pragmatically viewed, a kind of crime. But as in the instant case, it is a crime which can be committed while one is in the process of being tried for some other crime. It may carry more serious penalties than the original crime with which one is charged. It may, as in the case of Froines and Weiner, still be a crime although the defendant is fully acquitted of the original charge. It may, as in the case of Kunstler and Weinglass, be a crime although one is involved in the proceedings simply as a lawyer. Or it may, as in the case of Seale, be a crime with serious penalties, although having been separated from the trial, he is still left to stand trial on the original charges.

Moreover, the contempt power has been summary, permitting the trial judge to proceed to adjudge men guilty of crime without any of the elaborate apparatus of the criminal law and procedure. There is no indictment, no time to prepare a defense, no jury; the judge is the witness, the prosecutor, and the judge; and he plays these roles at a time when he may well be vulnerable to anger.

Judge Hoffman did not, of course, invent the procedures he was using so vigorously. The contempt power, with all its anomalies, has a long history and is deeply embedded in Anglo-American legal traditions. Happily, there have not been many occasions for testing it under contemporary circumstances. The Chicago trial, if it does nothing else, may force us to recognize that the contempt power is a major part of our legal structure and as deserving of careful scrutiny in these days of dissent and unrest as are issues of speech and political freedom under the First Amendment.

The appeals of the contempts may pose an acute dilemma for the reviewing courts. The defense tactics may be read as the decisive proof that strong measures of discipline are needed if the trial process is not to be brought to its knees; Judge Hoffman's identifying and punishing 175 "crimes" committed during the trial may be read as equally strong proof that the exercise of the contempt power needs to be brought into line with the basic traditions of the legal system.

At the moment, our chief learning in these matters is the case of *Sacher v. United States,* decided by the United States Supreme Court in 1952, in which a divided court affirmed the summary exercise of the contempt power by the trial judge acting at the conclusion of a long trial. *Sacher,* too, was a case with political overtones. It involved prosecution of the leaders of the Communist Party for conspiring to teach and advocate the overthrow of the government of the United States. It resulted in a long (nine months), turbulent trial before Judge Harold Medina—a trial studded with sharp emotional clashes between judge and defense counsel. At the end of the trial, Judge Medina found the lawyers guilty of contempt, holding that, among other things, they had engaged in a conspiracy to destroy his health. He sentenced them each to six months in jail. The Supreme Court, splitting 5 to 3, upheld the sentences. Although it rejected the conspiracy theory of Judge Medina, it found enough individual acts of contempt to support the sentences.

The case is interesting to re-read in the present context. First, the examples cited by the court suggest that Judge Medina too had found it difficult to retain his composure under the pressure of the defense tactics. In any event, Judge Hoffman's performance here is entitled to be read against Judge Medina's performance there. Second, Judge Medina did not attempt to set out separate counts of contempt, but treated the total performance of counsel, over the length of the trial, as a contempt and gave a single sentence of six months for it. Third, the several opinions reflect deep concern about the institution.

Justice Jackson, writing for the majority in affirming

the need for a summary power in the judge, observes: "That contempt power over counsel, summary or otherwise, is capable of abuse is certain. Men who make their way to the bench sometimes exhibit vanity, irascibility, narrowness, arrogance, and other weaknesses to which human flesh is heir. Most judges, however, recognize and respect courageous, forthright lawyerly conduct. They rarely mistake over-zeal or heated words of a man fired with a desire to win, for the contemptuous conduct which defies rulings and deserves punishment."

He concludes his opinion with a passage heroically attempting to balance the conflicting values: "But that there may be no misunderstanding, we make clear that this Court if its aid be needed, will unhesitatingly protect counsel in fearless, vigorous and effective performance of every duty pertaining to the office of the advocate on behalf of any person whatsoever. But it will not equate contempt with courage or insults with independence. It will also protect the processes of orderly trial, which is the supreme object of the lawyer's calling."

The three dissenting justices, Black, Douglas, and Frankfurter, unite in a concern over the procedures used in contempt cases. Justices Black and Douglas would require jury trial; Justice Frankfurter, in a lengthy and careful opinion, would insist on trial before *another* judge, avoiding thereby violation of the basic principle that "no judge should sit in a case in which he is personally involved."

We will indulge in two further quotations. Justice Black, sensitive as always to political implications, states sharply: "I cannot reconcile this summary blasting of legal careers with a fair system of justice. Such a procedure constitutes an overhanging menace to every courtroom advocate in America. The menace is most ominous for lawyers who are obscure, unpopular or defenders of unpopular persons or unorthodox causes."

Justice Frankfurther, noted for his restraint, put his reactions to reading the long record of bickering between court and counsel thus: ". . . it is indubitably established that the judge felt deeply involved personally in the conduct for which he punished the defense lawyers. He was not merely a witness to an occurrence as would be a judge who observed a fist fight in his courtroom or brutal badgering of a witness or an impropriety toward the jury. The judge acted as the prosecuting witness; he thought of himself as such. His self-concern permeates the record; it could not humanly have been excluded from his judgment of contempt. Judges are human, and it is not suggested that any other judge could have been impervious to the abuse, had he been subjected to it. But precisely because a judge is human and, in common frailty or manliness, would interpret such conduct of lawyers as an attack on himself personally, he should not subsequently sit in judgment on his assailants, barring only instances where such extraordinary procedure is compellingly necessary in order that the trial may proceed and not be aborted."

On more than one occasion during the trial, Judge Hoffman admonished counsel to read the *Sacher* case and heed its message.

V

Cases subsequent to *Sacher* have intimated that where "serious" penalties were involved, the use of the contempt power would require a jury trial. The precise boundary line between serious and other offenses has yet to be set, but a common understanding has arisen among the lower courts that any penalty over six months requires a jury trial, or at least some procedure different from that used in the summary exercise of the contempt power.

We come then to what, to my mind, is the oddest feature of the Chicago contempts—the breaking of them down into individual crimes for each of which a punishment is assessed. The result is that we have a list of 175 offenses for each of which a precise penalty is set. In brief, we have an altogether remarkable Code of Hammurabi.

This strategy has three unfortunate consequences. First, and perhaps most important, Judge Hoffman is being unfair to himself and to his grievance. He cuts himself off from a general complaint that the whole trial was permeated by contumacious behavior of which these are some illustrations and for which this is the penalty; it would all then be part of a whole, and the illustrations would not be taken out of context, nor would we be tempted to ask: Is this all?

Second, as the press has already gleefully noted, the individual items with their solemn punishments, especially with participants as mercurial as these, necessarily verge on the absurd. The great instance, of course, is the record of the punishments assigned to the defendant Abbie Hoffman. We learn, for example, that blowing a kiss to the jury, holding up the *Berkeley Tribe* to the jury, refusing to rise when the judge leaves the courtroom are each offenses carrying sentences of one day; whereas, when the judge, who has just identified for the record that "the last statement was made by the defendant Abbie Hoffman," interrupting to observe: "I don't use that name any more," is an offense calling for seven days; and, again, laughing openly, conduct for which Hoffman was repeatedly cited, is an offense worth seven to fourteen days; on the other hand, when Judge Hoffman is observing to his New York visitor, Kunstler, that he, the judge, had practiced for years in the federal courts in New York, Abbie's interruption to suggest that it was "when it was under British control" earns him two days; and so it goes.

Finally, the procedure of detailing numerous individual offenses places an unbearable burden on the court to mete out punishments with an even hand. Here, again, I suspect Judge Hoffman is unfair to himself; the record is dotted with arresting inconsistencies, many of which must be the product simply of the time pressures and the elaborateness of the code he is forced to devise.

My own judgment is that Judge Hoffman has impeached unduly the rationality and fairness of his effort by his strategy of individualizing the contempts. I am inclined to find an element of poetic justice in all this. He appears to have been hoping thereby to avoid the procedural implications of the six month maximum which he reads as limiting the penalty he can give for any one count, but as not limiting the total penalty he may give any one individual for his conduct during the trial. Thus, in the cases of Seale and Kunstler, he can reach sentences of four years apiece without assigning more than six months for any one offense. The law is not altogether clear on the point and awaits clarification on appeal. My point bluntly comes then to this: Rather than surrender the power to punish for more than six months, Judge Hoffman has elected to risk the difficulties of particularizing the offenses. And if the particularization makes the enterprise look somewhat foolish, that, as I say, carries an element of poetic justice.

VI

The particularization of contempts does have its usefulness, however. It provides a perspective on the ebb and flow of disruptions during the trial. That is, one can plot the 175 citations on a calendar. I found the results interesting and surprising, although reading them is an avowedly subjective matter.

There are, for example, stretches of the trial during which few, if any, contempts arise. Thus, the five weeks from November 6 to December 10 show nine citations in all, six with penalties of less than seven days; they fall on five of the days and none of them involves Kunstler, Rubin, Hayden, and Froines. Conversely, certain events precipitate a rush of citable conduct. Thus, the troubles over Bobby Seale peak from October 28 to October 30 and, during this three-day interval, no less than fifty-four of all the contempts take place. Again, the thirteen-trial-day span between January 23 and February 7 accounts for another forty-eight contempts. Thus, over one hundred of the contempts have occurred within sixteen trial days of the five-month trial. Indeed, if we abstract the Seale episode, the trial proceeds from September 24 to January 8 in a relatively uneventful fashion, and there are some fifty trial days on which the judge has found no conduct worth citing.

Moreover, somewhat the same impression holds if we trace the individual participants. Hayden and Rubin each go through November and December without engaging in any conduct Judge Hoffman cites as contumacious. Weinglass goes from October 30 to January 13 without a contempt, and Kunstler has a five-week span from October 30 to December 9.

As I say, one could possibly extract a different message by playing further with the numbers, and it may be enough that during the five months there was the horrendous total of 175 contempts. Nevertheless, I am impressed, contrary to the impressions I had gotten from the press coverage, by the sense that the interruptions were in no sense random events and that two or three triggering events, such as the handling of Seale and the revocation of Dellinger's bond, account for the major part of the troubles. I am impressed because the incidence of unrest seems not easily compatible with the notion that the defendants and counsel relentlessly and steadily pursued a single-minded strategy of disturbing the trial process.

VII

The contempt transcript is so rich in incident and anecdote that one can only reluctantly bring an introduction to a close and get out of the reader's way. There is, however, one further aspect of the case which this transcript underscores. It is the part of the case that has most disturbed me. It is the handling of Bobby Seale.

It is true that Seale was separated from the trial a little before the full prosecution case was in, and we cannot thus be sure what other evidence there might have been about him. But given the jury verdict which officially rejected the government's conspiracy theory, the initial inclusion of Seale in the trial now seems extraordinary. If the others were not in a conspiracy, he, who hardly knew them, surely was not. Whatever problems may have been raised by his speech in Chicago, they surely could have been dealt with adequately without adding him to the federal case.

The consequences of including him are disastrous. First, as we have indicated, he proved an intractable participant and his treatment provided a chief occasion and stimulus for the trial disturbances. Second, the court felt forced at one point, as the whole world was told, to engage in the distasteful tactic of having him bound and gagged in court, thus furnishing to America and to the world a terrifying image of American justice. Third, whatever his crime during Convention Week may have been, he was able during the trial to commit a crime for which a sentence of four years was imposed. Fourth, his inclusion in the trial proved to be of no avail, and he was in the end separated and left to stand trial alone.

The Seale contempt transcript is a moving and disturbing document. No doubt he was more robustly defiant of the court and more deeply contemptuous of its rulings and procedures than anyone the judge had ever experienced. The judge persists in regarding him as singularly insulting, and throughout the trial, long after Seale has departed, refers to "the things that man said about me." If the transcript is accurate on this point, Seale appears to have actually said less in the way of epithets than Jerry Rubin or Abbie Hoffman.

Seale has a startling quickness and sense. The transcript is rich in exchanges. The judge says: "You are making it very difficult for me, Mr. Seale." Seale replies: "You are making it difficult for me, Judge Hoffman." On another occasion, Judge Hoffman says: "We are going to recess now, young man. If you keep this up. . . ." And Seale interrupts: "Look, old man, if you keep up denying me my constitutional rights you are being exposed to the public and the world. . . ." And once more. The court says: "Let the record show that the defendant Seale has refused to be quiet in the face of the admonition and direction of the Court." Seale says: "Let the record show that Bobby Seale speaks out in behalf of his constitutional rights to defend himself, his right to speak in behalf of himself in this courtroom."

No doubt Seale was being unequivocally defiant of the judge's orders and in that sense furnishing a literal obstruction to the progress of the trial on the judge's terms, and was thus posing a deep challenge to the trial process. The impasse was unmistakable, and on one view Judge Hoffman simply did what he had to do in order to proceed.

However, when one reads the transcript, competing impressions are generated. First, that Seale was not interrupting at random; he was not a madman out to make it impossible to have a trial. He was making a single point throughout, namely that he wanted to defend himself at least until his lawyer, Charles Garry, was available to represent him. He had raised the point before the trial proper had begun, and it provided each time the content and the occasion for his efforts to speak. Judge Hoffman ruled that Kunstler, who due to Garry's illness had filed an appearance for Seale, continued to represent Seale no matter what Seale or what Kunstler thought about it. The record we have here does not provide a sufficient basis for appraising the reasons for Judge Hoffman's ruling; perhaps there were persuasive ones. But whatever they were, two points stand out. The judge never during these innumerable colloquies states the reasons; he merely reiterates that Seale is irrevocably represented by Kunstler. Second, it must have been apparent that some adjustment of the problem of Seale's representation was called for; neither the judge nor the government, nor for that matter the defense, ever appear to have made any overtures. The judge thus appeared willing to leave matters on collision course even though the outcome quite predictably was almost literally to tear the trial apart.

The impasse produces one or two moments of grim comedy. At one point early in the trial, Kunstler is making a formal motion to withdraw as counsel for Seale. Seale asks if he may speak and is told no. When he asks why, Judge Hoffman says: "Because this is your lawyer's motion." Seale objects: "That ain't my lawyer." The judge replies: "This is not your motion. This is the motion of Mr. William Kunstler for leave to withdraw as your lawyer." A few more exchanges occur and this sequence of interruptions is later cited by the judge as contempt for which a sentence of three months is handed down.

Again at the end of Seale's stay in the trial, the judge has just read the sixteen citations which are to earn Seale a four-year sentence. He turns to Seale after Kunstler has understandably declined to speak for him and says:

THE COURT: Mr. Seale, you have a right to speak now. I will hear you.
SEALE: For myself?
THE COURT: In your own behalf, yes.
SEALE: How come I couldn't speak before?
THE COURT: This is a special occasion.

Then, there is the matter of the four-year sentence. Whatever the merits of Judge Hoffman's breaking down the conduct into separate contempts in the case of the others, it is hard to see Seale's behavior as involving anything other than the stubborn making of the single point that he does not recognize Kunstler as his lawyer, that he wishes to represent himself. Moreover, there is the circumstance that eight of the citations, each carrying a three-month sentence, fall within the three days from October 28 to October 30.

Finally, there is the puzzle as to why Judge Hoffman resorted to binding and gagging Seale. It is apparent that it was possible to separate him, since in fact that was done. Why, then, did the judge insist on going through the binding and gagging stage? Surely it was apparent it would not work and would greatly upset the trial. Why could he not have stated a few days earlier that it had become necessary to separate Seale since he had no alternatives other than to discontinue the trial or resort to the intolerable one of binding and gagging?

In retrospect, it is ironic that it was the Seale episode that attracted attention to the question of whether modern trials are viable. It is true that here is no easy solution to the problem of what to do with a party that is as adamantly defiant as Seale had become. Maybe he did represent a limit. But the Seale episode does not at all indicate that the trial process is yet faced with terrible choices. It was politically reckless and intrinsically unfair to have permitted matters to get to such an impasse.

VIII

Another reader of these materials might with equal warrant have devoted his attention principally to analysis and evaluation of the tactics of the defense. For several reasons I have not done so, although I find the prospect of confrontation tactics being moved from the streets and campuses to the courtroom a genuinely disturbing one, and I would echo Justice Jackson's fine phrase about protection of "the processes of orderly trial which is the supreme object of the lawyer's calling." The Chicago trial is so skewed by the mistakes in the handling of Bobby Seale that it is not at all apparent how it might have turned out absent that stimulus. Again, as we have noted, the ebb and flow of disturbances during the five months of the trial does not readily support the notion that the defense was pursuing a single-minded strategy of upsetting the trial. Further, the use of such serious contempt penalties affects judgment; the question is no longer whether the defense behaved well or whether they are deserving of censure; the question is whether in their conduct of the trial they committed serious crimes. Finally, I cannot escape an impression that the apparent collaboration among defendants in exploiting a particular incident is more like the improvising of a jazz group who are used to playing together than it is like a planned strategy.

At the moment my view would be that the defense moves, as enthusiastically exploited by the press, were more disturbing for the confrontations they *suggest* could happen in future trials than for what they actually achieved in this trial.

In any event, the tactics are varied. It is not clear that they ever reach the level of literal heckling making it impossible to proceed. At one extreme they consist of one-line jokes interjected quickly at the expense of the judge, the witness, or the prosecutors. At the other extreme, they involve an effort to turn the trial forum into a political forum, at least momentarily, as when they seek to stop the trial to read the names of the war dead. Occasionally, there is a gesture of civil disobedience as where in protest over Seale they refuse for those four days to rise for the judge. Ranging in between are two kinds of conduct: countless instances of caustic and, at times, insulting comments about the fairness of the trial and the judge, and countless remarks that are simply "out of order," in the sense of Roberts' Rules of Order.

The heightened sense of interruption that these tactics seem to have engendered is perhaps attributable to five factors. First, the gloss that the press, delighted with a new art form, insisted on placing on the events at the trial; second, the theatrical posture of the defense when outside the trial forum; third, the presence of the jury and the frequency with which the judge found it necessary to have the jury withdrawn, thus producing a sense of crisis after crisis; fourth, the presence of "a studio audience" which often interacted with the defense, producing applause or occasions on which spectators were ordered removed from the courtroom; and, finally, the propensity of Judge Hoffman, in his effort to control the flow of the proceedings, to use *direct orders,* which had the consequence of escalating many minor incidents into relatively major ones.

IX

Once again, then, this is an important document. The

reader can and should make his own evaluation of what it shows about contemporary tensions between decorum and justice. In view of our emphasis on the whole Seale episode as the key to so much that went wrong, we would end with a quotation from Judge Hoffman. He is replying to the speech Kunstler made after being sentenced for contempt. He is complaining that Kunstler did not make any effort to help the court when Seale was proving so disruptive. He says: "The only reason I mention the Seale episode is that I didn't want anyone here to get the impression that I was obtuse and didn't know what was going on. I didn't want anyone of the ladies and gentlemen of the press to get the impression that I didn't know what was really the time of day."

Chicago, Illinois
March, 1970

THE TRANSCRIPT

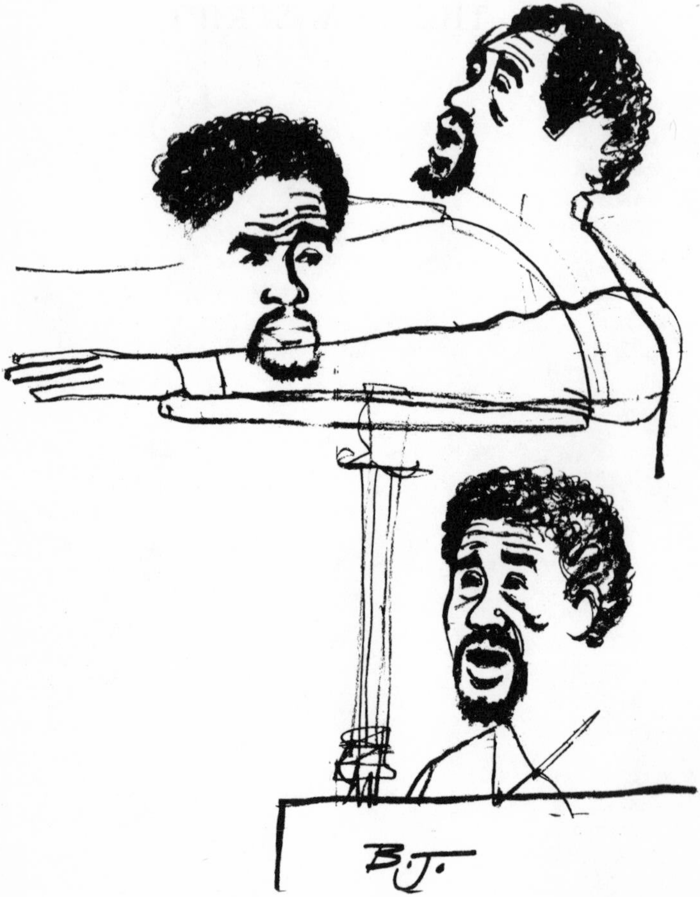
B.J.

SEALE

Wednesday, November 5, 1969, 2:00 P.M.

THE COURT: There is a matter that I wish to take up, gentlemen, before we proceed further with this trial.

I think, Mr. Witness, you may be excused and go into the witness room.

(Witness temporarily excused.)

THE COURT: As I think everyone who has attended the various sessions of this trial must if he is fair understand, the Court has done its best to prevent or [not] to have repeated efforts to delay and obstruct this trial which I think have been made for the purpose of causing such disorder and confusion as would prevent a verdict by a jury on the issues presented by the indictment and the pleas of not guilty thereto.

I must now, as I perceive my duty and obligation to, take proper steps to insure that the trial as it continues be conducted in an atmosphere of dignity, an atmosphere that the defendants and each of them are entitled to have prevail in the trial of this case. As we all know, the defendant Bobby G. Seale has been guilty of conduct in the presence of the court during this trial which is not only contumacious in character but his misconduct was of so grave a character as to continually disrupt the orderly administration of justice.

We have in the federal courts the Federal Rules of Criminal Procedure which together with Title 18 of the United States Code represent the rules that the Court must interpret and apply in the trial of criminal cases. In conformity with Rule 42(a) of the Federal Rules of Criminal Procedure and Title 18, United States Code, Section 401, I certify at this time that I saw and overheard the conduct of the defendant Bobby G. Seale to which I shall refer during these observations, which conduct took place in the actual presence of the court during the trial of this case which is entitled United States of America vs. David Dellinger and others, the case number being 69 CR 180.

The trial commenced on September 24, 1969, and has continued through this morning. I find not only from seeing and hearing the conduct to which I am about to refer, the conduct of the defendant Seale, but from reading the transcript of the proceedings that the acts, statements and conduct of the defendant Seale which I shall specify here each constitute a separate contempt of this Court; that each constituted a deliberate and wilful attack upon the administration of justice in an attempt to sabotage the functioning of the Federal Judicial System.

MR. SEALE: That is a lie. I stood up and spoke in behalf of myself. I stood up and spoke in behalf of myself and made motions and requests.

THE COURT: I don't permit anybody to speak while I am talking.

MR. SEALE: I stood up and walked to the lectern and demonstrated the fact I wanted to cross examine the witness. You allowed these men here and Tom Hayden to go all the way to California, to go all the way to California to see about my lawyer, which indicated, and I tried to persuade you again to recognize it. I was there no more than five minutes. You are talking about disrupting the proceedings of this trial? That's a lie. That's a lie.

THE COURT: You are making it very difficult for me, Mr. Seale.

MR. SEALE: You are making it difficult for me, Judge Hoffman.

THE COURT: I tried not to -- I have done my best. I have done my best.

MR. SEALE: I have a right to stand up and speak in my own behalf. I do. You know that.

THE COURT: You know you do not have a right to speak while the Judge is speaking.

MR. SEALE: I have a right to speak and make requests and make arguments to demonstrate the fact I want to cross examine. When you say I disrupt, I have never tried to strike anybody, I have never tried to hit anybody. I have never. You know that. And in my arguments and motions I called you a racist and a fascist and a pig, and that's what I consider you as, and my arguments and my motions will always carry that as long as my constitutional rights are being denied. So it is a lie, and you know it.

THE COURT: I find, I repeat, that the acts, statements and conduct of the defendant Seale to which I shall refer specifically each constitute a separate contempt of this Court; that each constituted a deliberate and wilful attack upon the administration of justice in an attempt to sabotage the functioning of the Federal Judicial System; that this misconduct was of so grave a character as to continually disrupt the orderly administration of justice.

To maintain the dignity of the Court and to preserve order in the courtroom under these circumstances has been a task of utmost difficulty. There were, accordingly, as the record shows clearly, repeated warnings and admonitions to the defendant Seale to cease this conduct and there were warnings that it would be dealt with accordingly at an appropriate time. However, his continued disruptive conduct made it necessary for the Court for the first time within the experience of this Court to physically and forcibly restrain him. Even these measures proved insufficient because of the potential effect that the continuation of these activities might have had in the future on the administration of justice.

In this case I find that it is necessary that I deal with his conduct at this time. I have tried—I have endeavored on many occasions—to make it clear to the defendant that his conduct was contumacious but I was not successful even right down to a few moments ago in persuading him to so conduct himself as we expect individuals to conduct themselves in the course of the Federal System.

As isolated excerpts from or references to the transcript can give but a partial view of the acts, statements and conduct to which I refer, I make the entire record part of these proceedings. The Court also notes that a reading of this record cannot and does not reflect the true intensity and extent of the disruption which in some instances were accompanied by a physical violence - -

MR. SEALE: That is a lie.

THE COURT: - - which occurred in the presence of the

Court.
MR. SEALE: That is a lie. I never attack anyone, and you know it. I never struck anyone and you know it.
THE COURT: Accordingly I adjudge - -
MR. SEALE: I will stand up in any court in America and say that.
THE COURT: Accordingly I adjudge the defendant Bobby Seale guilty of the several criminal contempts to which I shall refer. In citing these specific acts and statements of the defendant Seale as contemptuous, the Court has selected only the most flagrant acts.

Specification 1: On Friday, September 26, 1969, during the motion session prior to the time opening statements were made, the defendant Seale addressed the Court in the following manner, Transcript Page 3:

> "If I am consistently denied this right of legal defense counsel of my choice who is effective by the Judge of this Court, then I can only see the Judge as a blatant racist of the United States Court.
> "THE COURT: Just a minute. Just a minute.
> "MR. SEALE: With gross prejudicial error toward all defendants and myself.
> "THE COURT: Just a minute. What did you say?
> "Read that, Miss Reporter.
> "MR. SEALE: I said if my constitutional rights are denied as my constitutional rights have been denied in the past in the course of the trial, et cetera, then the tenor is the act of racism and me a black man, there seems to be a form of prejudice against me even to the other defendants on the part of the Judge." **3 months**

Specification 2: During the morning session on October 14, 1969, while the Court, Assistant United States Attorney Schultz, and defense counsel, Mr. Weinglass, were engaged in a colloquy, the defendant Seale interrupted Mr. Weinglass, and the following occurred: Transcript, Page 2206.

> "MR. SEALE: Hey, you don't speak for me. I would like to speak on behalf of my own self and have my counsel handle my case in behalf of myself. How come I can't speak in behalf of myself?

I am my own legal counsel. I don't want these lawyers to represent me.

"THE COURT: You have a lawyer of record, and he has been of record here for you since September 24.

"MR. SEALE: I have been arguing that before that jury heard one shred of evidence. I don't want these lawyers because I can take up my own legal defense, and my lawyer is Charles Garry.

"THE COURT: I direct you, sir, to remain quiet.

"MR. SEALE: And just be railroaded?

"THE COURT: Will you remain quiet?

"MR. SEALE: I want to defend myself, do you mind, please?

"THE COURT: Let the record show that the defendant Seale continued to speak after the court courteously requested him to remain quiet."

3 months

Specification 3: During the morning session on October 16, 1969, out of the presence of the jury, while the witness Oklepek, O-k-l-e-p-e-k, was testifying, a colloquy began between the court, a marshal, and Mr. Kunstler. After a marshal explained that three spectators who were asked to leave the court had been allowed to return, the defendant Seale stated to the Court:

"I think there is a bit of racism involved myself."

The transcript: 2700. **3 months**

Specification 4: During the afternoon session on October 20, 1969, out of the presence of the jury, the defendant Seale presented and extensively argued a motion to be permitted to defend himself. Transcript 3121 to 3145.

At the conclusion of the argument, the jury returned to the courtroom, and the following occurred: Transcript: 3145:

"THE COURT: Is there any cross examination of this witness?

"MR. SEALE: I would like to say, Judge, that you denied my motion to defend myself, and you know this jury is prejudiced against me.

"THE COURT: I will ask you to sit down.

"MR. SEALE: You know that. The jury can't go

home to their loved ones and their homes, and you know they have been made prejudiced against me.

"THE COURT: Ladies and gentlemen of the jury, you are excused."

The jury was then excused, and the following occurred: Transcript 3145 to 3149:

"MR. SEALE: They have been made prejudiced against me, I know. I should be allowed to defend myself. I should be allowed to speak so I can defend myself.

"THE MARSHAL: Be quiet.

"MR. SEALE: Don't tell me to shut up. I got a right to speak. I need to speak to defend myself.

"THE COURT: Mr. Seale, I must admonish you that any outburst such as you have just indulged in will be appropriately dealt with at the right time during this trial, and I must order you not to do it again.

"MR. SEALE: In other words, Judge - -

"THE COURT: If you do, you do it at your own risk, sir.

"MR. SEALE: In other words, you are saying you're going to put me in contempt of court for speaking on behalf of myself?

"THE COURT: I will not argue with you. Mr. Marshal - -

"MR. SEALE: Is that what you are saying to me? I mean, I want to be clear.

"THE COURT: Will you be quiet? That is all. You have a lawyer to speak for you.

"MR. SEALE: They don't speak for me. I want to represent myself. Charles R. Garry is not here in my service. I have explained to you in the past what the situation was. I was put in jail, and everything else. Now you are saying you are going to put me in jail. You are going to put me in jail. That's one thing. You are going to put me in contempt of court because I am speaking in behalf of myself.

"THE COURT: I didn't put you there, sir.

"MR. SEALE: Because I am speaking in behalf of myself, to have a right to defend myself.

"THE COURT: Yes, sir.

"MR. SCHULTZ: If the Court please, there's one thing that has not been stated.

"MR. SEALE: The jury is prejudiced against me, all right, and you know it because of those threatening letters. You know it, those so-called jive threatening letters, and you know it's a lie. How can that jury give me a fair trial?

"THE COURT: Mr. Marshal, will you go to that man and ask him to be quiet?

"MR. SEALE: I will speak for myself. They can [not] speak on behalf of myself. I still want to defend myself, and I know I have a right. I just want to let him know. That racist, that fascist. You know, the black man tries to get a fair trial in this country. The United States Government, huh. Nixon and the rest of them. Go ahead and continue. I'll watch and get railroaded.

"MR. SCHULTZ: If the Court please, there is one thing that has not been placed on the record, the fact that since the trial began, in fact, I think since September 24 so far as I know, and I think this is 100 percent accurate, whenever the defendants have wanted to meet with Mr. Seale and the lawyers, the marshals have made arrangements to bring them to a room where all of them could get together, where Mr. Seale and the defendants and the lawyers have all met and consulted at every occasion that they have so requested. It has been done on a regular basis since the trial did begin. I just thought that should be on the record.

"If there is any statement by defense counsel to the contrary, since I'm not at the meetings and I don't know how many times they have asked the marshals to meet, I think they should so state now.

"MR. SEALE: I would like to put something on the record. You weren't in that room unless you got a tape recorder in there - -

"THE MARSHAL: I am asking you to keep quiet.

"MR. SEALE: That man is lying on me.

"THE MARSHAL: All right.

"MR. SEALE: I met with these defendants and

argued with these so-called cats about so-called defending me. I want that for the record, too."

3 months

Specification 5: During the morning session on October 22, 1969, while argument on a motion of Attorney William Kunstler for leave to withdraw as counsel for the defendant Seale, the following occurred in open court, transcript 3534-3536.

"MR. SEALE: Can I speak on that and answer his argument?

"THE COURT: No. This is not your motion, sir. Your motion has been decided.

"MR. SEALE: In other words, I can't speak in behalf of myself?

"THE COURT: Not at this time, sir.

"MR. SEALE: Why not?

"THE COURT: Because this is your lawyer's motion.

"MR. SEALE: That ain't my lawyer.

"THE COURT: This is not your motion. This is the motion of Mr. William Kunstler for leave to withdraw as your lawyer.

"MR. SEALE: Well, this man has misconstrued a whole lot of things concerning my right to defend myself and he knows he did.

"They can jack you up and get you to sit up there and say rotten, crazy stuff concerning my right to defend myself.

"THE COURT: I would request the marshal to ask the young man to sit down.

"MR. SEALE: Well, I want my right to defend myself and this man knew, I indicated to him he was not my counsel at the very beginning when I first got here and arrived here and was in jail.

"THE COURT: That motion - - since you will not listen to the Court, you may sit down. Have him sit down, Mr. Marshal.

"MR. SEALE: I still want my right to defend myself. A railroad operation, and you know it, from Nixon on down. They got you running around here violating my constitutional rights." **3 months**

Specification 6: During the morning session on October 22, 1969, in the presence of the jury after the witness Carcerano had been excused, the Government attempted to offer Government's Exhibit No. 14 into evidence, and the following occurred, Transcript 3599-3601.

"MR. SCHULTZ: Your Honor, before the next witness testifies, would it be possible if the Court would permit the Government -- well, we haven't offered the picture, as a matter of fact. We have the picture of the boy with the black power symbol fist on his sweat shirt that was identified by Officer Tobin and Carcerano as the boy --

"THE COURT: Is that Government's Exhibit 14?

"MR. SCHULTZ: That's the one.

"THE COURT: For identification.

"MR. SCHULTZ: We are going to move to offer that exhibit in evidence at this time.

"THE COURT: Is that the number?

"MR. SCHULTZ: That's the number, your Honor. We would like to offer it at this time so that before the next witness takes the stand --

"THE COURT: Show it to counsel.

"MR. SEALE: That's not a black power sign. Somebody correct the Court on that. It's not the black power sign. It's the power to the people sign.

"THE COURT: Mr. Marshal, will you stop the talking, please.

"MR. SEALE: Yes, but that is still wrong, Judge Hoffman. It's not a black power sign. It's a power to the people sign, and he is deliberately distorting that and that's a racist technique.

"MR. SCHULTZ: If the Court please, this man has repeatedly called me a racist --

"MR. SEALE: Yes, you are. You are, Dick Schultz.

"MR. SCHULTZ: And called Mr. Foran a racist --

"THE COURT: Ladies and gentlemen of the jury, I will ask you to leave the court. Mr. Marshall, remove the ladies and gentlemen of the jury:

"(The following proceedings were had in open court, out of the presence and hearing of the jury:)

"THE COURT: Mr. Seale and Mr. Kunstler, your lawyer, I must admonish you that such outbursts are considered by the Court to be contemptuous, contumacious, and will be dealt with appropriately in the future.

"MR. KUNSTLER: Your Honor, the defendant was trying to defend himself, and I have already indicated my --

"THE COURT: The defendant was not defending himself.

"MR. SEALE: I was, too, defending myself. Any time anybody gives me the wrong symbol in this courtroom is deliberately --

"THE COURT: He is not addressing me with authority --

"MR. SEALE: -- distorting, and put it on the record.

"THE COURT: Instruct that man to keep quiet.

"MR. SEALE: I want to defend myself and ask him if he isn't lying, and he is going to put that lying crap on the record. No, siree—I am not going to sit here and get that on the record. I am going to at least get it be known—request that you understand that this man is erroneously representing symbols directly related to the party of which I am chairman." **3 months**

Specification 7: In the afternoon session on October 22, 1969, the Court informed the defendant Seale that the Court would supervise the decorum in the courtroom and the following occurred in open court, Transcript 3641-3642:

"MR. SEALE: They don't take orders from racist judges, but I can convey the orders for them and they will follow them.

"THE COURT: If you continue with that sort of thing, you may expect to be punished for it. I warned you right through this trial and I warn you again, sir. Bring in the jury.

"MR. SEALE: We protested our rights for four hundred years and we have been shot and killed and murdered and brutalized and oppressed for four hundred years because of --

"THE COURT: There is another instance, that

outburst may appear of record and it does. Did you get it, Miss Reporter?

"THE REPORTER: Yes, sir.

"MR. SEALE: I hope you got my part for the record, too, concerning that. Did you get that, ma'am?

"THE REPORTER: Yes, sir.

"MR. SEALE: Thank you.

"THE COURT: And that outburst also.

"MR. DELLINGER: I think you should understand we support Bobby Seale in this—at least I do.

"THE COURT: I haven't asked you for any advice here, sir.

"MR. SEALE: If you let me defend myself, you could instruct me on the proceedings that I can act, but I have to just - -

"THE COURT: You will have to be quiet.

"MR. SEALE: All I have to do is clear the record. I want to defend myself in behalf of my constitutional rights.

"THE COURT: Let the record show that the defendant Seale has refused to be quiet in the face of the admonition and direction of the Court.

"MR. SEALE: Let the record show that Bobby Seale speaks out in behalf of his constitutional rights, his right to defend himself, his right to speak in behalf of himself in this courtroom.

"THE COURT: Again let the record show that he has disobeyed the order of the Court. Bring in the jury, Mr. Marshal.

"MR. SEALE: Please do." **3 months**

Specification 8: At the opening of the morning session on October 27, 1969, the following occurred in open court, Transcript 4217-4222:

"THE COURT: Ladies and gentlemen of the jury, good morning.

"MR. SEALE: Good morning, ladies and gentlemen of the jury. As I said before, I hope you don't blame me for anything.

"THE COURT: Mr. Marshal, will you tell that man to sit down.

"THE MARSHAL: Take a seat, Mr. Seale.
"MR. SEALE: I know - -
"THE COURT: Mr. Marshal, I think Mr. Seale is saying something there.
"MR. SEALE: I know I am saying something. You know I am getting ready to speak out in behalf of my constitutional rights again, don't you?
"THE COURT: I will ask you to sit down, sir.
"THE MARSHAL: Sit down.
"MR. SEALE: You also know I am speaking out for the right to defend myself again, don't you, because I have that right as a defendant, don't I?
"THE COURT: I will have to ask you to sit down, sir.
"MR. SEALE: You know what I am going to say, don't you?
"THE COURT: No, I don't.
"MR. SEALE: Well, I said it before.
"THE COURT: I don't know what you are going to say and you have a very competent lawyer of record here.
"MR. SEALE: He is not my lawyer and you know I fired him before that jury was even picked and put together.
"THE COURT: Will you ask him to sit down, Mr. Marshal?
"THE MARSHAL: Sit down, Mr. Seale.
"MR. SEALE: What about my constitutional right to defend myself and have my lawyer?
"THE COURT: Your constitutional rights - -
"MR. SEALE: You are denying them. You have been denying them. Every other word you say is denied, denied, denied, denied, and you begin to oink in the faces of the masses of the people of this country. That is what you begin to represent, the corruptness of this rotten government, or four hundred years.
"THE MARSHAL: Mr. Seale, will you sit down.
"MR. SEALE: Why don't you knock me in the mouth? Try that.
"THE MARSHAL: Sit down.
"THE COURT: Ladies and gentlemen of the jury,

I regret that I will have to excuse you.
"MR. SEALE: I hope you don't blame me for anything and those false lying notes and letters that were sent that said the Black Panther Party threatened that jury, it's a lie, and you know it's a lie, and the government did it to taint the jury against me.

"(The following proceedings were had in open court, out of the presence and hearing of the jury:)
"MR. SEALE: You got that? This racist and fascist administrative government with its superman notions and comic book politics. We're hip to the fact that Super Man never saved no black people. You got that?
"MR. KUNSTLER: I might say, your Honor, you know that I have tried to withdraw from this and you know that Mr. Seale - -
"THE COURT: I don't know what you tried to do. I know your appearance is of record, and I know I have your assurance orally of record that you represent this man.
"MR. KUNSTLER: You have a withdrawal of that assurance, your Honor. You knew that on September 30, you knew that Mr. Seale had discharged me.
"THE COURT: You represent him and the record shows it.
"MR. KUNSTLER: Your Honor, you can't go on those semantics. This man wants to defend himself.
"THE COURT: This isn't semantics. I am not fooled by all of this business.
"MR. SEALE: I still demand the right to defend myself. You are not fooled? After you have walked over people's constitutional rights?
"THE MARSHAL: Sit down, Mr. Seale.
"MR. SEALE: After you done walked over people's constitutional rights, after you done walked over people's constitution rights, the Sixth Amendment, the Fifth Amendment, and the phoniness and the corruptness of this very trial, for people to have a right to speak out, freedom of speech, freedom of assembly, and et cetera. You have did everything you could with those jive lying witnesses up there

presented by these pig agents of the Government to lie and say and condone some rotten racists, fascist crap by racist cops and pigs that beat people's heads —and I demand my constitutional rights—demand —demand - -

"Call in the jury.

"THE COURT: Will the Marshal bring in the jury, please." **3 months**

Specification 9: During the direct examination of the witness William Frapolly on October 27, 1969, the following occurred, Transcript 4342-4346:

"MR. SEALE: I object to that because my lawyer is not here. I have been denied my right to defend myself in this courtroom. I object to this man's testimony against me because I have not been allowed my constitutional rights.

"THE COURT: I repeat to you, sir, you have a lawyer. Your lawyer is Mr. Kunstler, who represented to the Court that he represents you.

"MR. SEALE: He does not represent me.

"THE COURT: And he has filed an appearance. Ladies and gentlemen, I will excuse you.

"(The following proceedings were had in open court, out of the presence and hearing of the jury:)

"MR. KUNSTLER: May I say I have withdrawn or attempted to withdraw.

"MR. SEALE: The defense filed a motion before the jury ever heard any evidence, and I object to that testimony.

"THE COURT: For your information, sir, I do not hear parties to a case who are not represented by lawyers. You are represented by a lawyer.

"MR. SEALE: I am not represented by a lawyer. I am not represented by Charles Garry for your information.

"THE MARSHAL: Sit down, Mr. Seale.

"THE COURT: Now you just keep on this way and - -

"MR. SEALE: Keep on what? Keep on what?

"THE COURT: Just sit down.

"MR. SEALE: Keep on what? Keep on getting

denied my constitutional rights?

"THE COURT: Will you be quiet?

"MR. SEALE: I object to that man's -- can't I object to that man there sitting up there testifying against me and my constitutional rights denied to my lawyer being here?

"Now I still object. I object because you know it is wrong. You denied me my right to defend myself. You think black people don't have a mind. Well, we got big minds, good minds, and we know how to come forth with constitutional rights, the so-called constitutional rights. I am not going to be quiet. I am talking in behalf of my constitutional rights, man, in behalf of myself, that's my constitutional right to talk in behalf of my constitutional rights.

"THE COURT: Bring in the jury, Mr. Marshal.

"MR. SEALE: I still object to that man testifying against me without my lawyer being here, without me having a right to defend myself.

"Black people ain't supposed to have a mind? That's what you think. We got a body and a mind. I wonder, did you lose yours in the Superman syndrome comic book stories? You must have to deny us our constitutional rights.

"THE COURT: Are you getting all of this, Miss Reporter?

"MR. SEALE: I hope she gets it all.

"(The following proceedings were had in open court, within the presence and hearing of the jury:)

"MR. SEALE: Taint the jury against me, send them threatening letters that I never sent, that I never sent, and you know it's a lie, you keep them away from their homes and they blame me every time they come in this room because they are being kept away from their homes, and you did it.

"THE COURT: Are you going to stop, sir?

"MR. SEALE: I am going to talk in behalf of my constitutional rights.

"THE COURT: You may continue, sir, with the direct examination of this witness. And I note that your counsel has remained quiet during your dissertation.

"MR. SEALE: You know what? I have no counsel here. I fired that lawyer before that jury heard anything and you know it. That jury hasn't heard all of the motions you denied behind the scenes. How you tricked that juror out of that stand there by threatening her with that jive letter that you know darned well I didn't send, which is a lie. And they blame me every time they are being kept from their loved ones and their homes. They blame me every time they come in the room. And I never sent those letters, you know it.

"THE COURT: Please continue with the direct examination." **3 months**

Specification 10: On October 28, 1969, during the afternoon session, while the witness William Frapolly was testifying on cross examination, the following occurred in open court, Transcript 4607, et sequitur:

"THE COURT: Mr. Weinglass, do you want to cross examine this witness?

"MR. SEALE: I would like to request to cross examine the witness.

"THE COURT: You have a lawyer here.

"MR. SEALE: That man is not my lawyer. The man made statements against me. Furthermore, he violated Title 1892 of the United States. Well, you are still violating it.

"THE MARSHAL: Sit down, Mr. Seale.

"MR. SEALE: You violated the Code. You violated the United States laws against my rights.

"THE COURT: Mr. Marshal, will you ask Mr. Seale to sit down in his chair?

"MR. SEALE: You are violating Title 42, United States Criminal Code. You are violating it because it states that a black man cannot be discriminated against in his legal defense.

"THE COURT: Will you sit down, Mr. Seale?

"MR. SEALE: It is an old Reconstruction law and you won't recognize it. So I would like to cross examine the witness.

"THE COURT: Will you sit down, sir?

"MR. SEALE: I still want to cross examine the witness.

"THE COURT: You may not.

"A MARSHAL: May I remove the jury, please?

"THE COURT: Ladies and gentlemen of the jury, you may be excused."

After the jury was excused, the defendant Seale continued to refuse to obey the order of the Court to remain silent.

Thereupon the following occurred in open court, 4611 et sequitur:

"THE COURT: Let the record show that the defendant - -

"MR. SEALE: Let the record show you violated that and a black man cannot be discriminated against in relation to his legal defense and that is exactly what you have done. You know you have. Let the record show that.

"THE COURT: The record shows exactly to the contrary.

"MR. SEALE: The record shows that you are violating, that you violated my constitutional rights. I want to cross examine the witness. I want to cross examine the witness.

"THE COURT: Bring in the jury, Mr. Marshal, and we will let them go for this evening. I admonish you, sir, that you have a lot of contemptuous conduct against you.

"MR. SEALE: Admonish you. You are in contempt of people's constitutional rights. You are in contempt of the constitutional rights of the mass of the people of the United States. You are the one in contempt of people's constitutional rights. I am not in contempt of nothing. You are the one who is in contempt. The people of America need to admonish you and the whole Nixon administration.

"Let me cross examine the witness. You won't even let me read—you wouldn't even let me read my statement this morning, my motion this morning, concerning the fact that I wanted a copy of the transcript for my own legal defense.

"THE COURT: Bring in the jury. Is he getting the

jury?

"THE CLERK: Yes, your Honor.

"THE COURT: Tell him to just bring them before the box.

"MR. SEALE: I want to cross examine the witness.

"MR. HAYDEN: Let the record show the judge was laughing.

"MR. SEALE: Yes, he is laughing.

"THE COURT: Who made that remark?

"MR. FORAN: The defendant Hayden, your Honor, made the remark.

"MR. SEALE: And me.

"THE COURT: Let the record show that - -

"MR. SEALE: I still want to cross examine the witness to defend myself."

The jury was then returned to the courtroom to be excused for the day, during which time, the defendant Seale continued to speak. Thereafter, the following occurred in open court, transcript 4615, et sequitur.

"THE COURT: You may sit down. I must admonish the defendant and his counsel - -

"MR. SEALE: Counsel ain't got nothing to do with it. I'm my own counsel.

"THE COURT: You are not doing very well for yourself.

"MR. SEALE: Yes, that's because you violated my constitutional rights, Judge Hoffman. That's because you violated them overtly, deliberately, in a very racist manner. Somebody ought to point out the law to you. You don't want to investigate it to see whether the people get their constitutional rights. Sixty-eight thousand black men died in the Civil War for that right. That right was made during the Reconstruction period. They fought in that war and 68,000 of them died. That law was made for me to have my constitutional rights.

"THE COURT: Do you want to listen to me for a moment?

"MR. SEALE: Why should I continue to listen to you unless you are going to give me my constitutional rights. Let me defend myself.

THE COURT: I am warning you, sir, that the law - -

"MR. SEALE: Instead of warning, why don't you warn me I have got a right to defend myself, huh?
"THE COURT: I am warning you that the Court has the right to gag you. I don't want to do that. Under the law you may be gagged and chained to your chair.
"MR. SEALE: Gagged? I am being railroaded already. I am being railroaded already.
"THE COURT: The Court has that right and I - -
"MR. SEALE: The Court has no right whatsoever. The Court has no right to stop me from speaking out in behalf of my constitutional rights because it is denying me the constitutional rights to speak out in behalf of myself and my legal defense.
"THE COURT: The court will be in recess until tomorrow morning at ten o'clock.
"THE MARSHAL: Everyone will please rise.
"MR. SEALE: I am not rising. I am not rising until he recognizes my constitutional rights. Why should I rise for him? He is not recognizing - -
"THE COURT: Mr. Marshal - -
"MR. SEALE: I am not rising." **3 months**

Specification 11: On October 29, 1969, during the morning session, the following occurred in open court. Transcript 4632 et sequitur:

"MR. SCHULTZ: If the Court please, before you came into this courtroom, if the Court please, Bobby Seale stood up and addressed this group.
"MR. SEALE: That's right, brother.
"MR. SCHULTZ: And Bobby Seale said if he is - -
"MR. SEALE: I spoke on behalf of my constitutional rights. I have a right to speak in behalf of my constitutional rights. That's right.
"MR. SCHULTZ: And he told those people in his audience, if the Court please—and I want this on the record. It happened this morning—that if he's attacked, they know what to do.
"MR. SEALE: I can speak on behalf of my constitutional rights, too.
"MR. SCHULTZ: He was talking to these people about an attack by them.

"MR. SEALE: You're lying. Dirty liar. I told them to defend themselves. You are a rotten racist pig, fascist liar, that's what you are. You're a rotten liar. You're a rotten liar. You are a fascist pig liar.

"I said they had a right to defend themselves if they are attacked, and I hope that the record carries that, and I hope the record shows that tricky Dick Schultz, working for Richard Nixon and administration all understand that tricky Dick Schultz is a liar, and we have a right to defend ourselves, and if you attack me I will defend myself.

"SPECTATORS: Right on."

Mr. Marshal, - - I will direct the marshals to clear the courtroom in the event that laughter occurs again. Clear the courtroom of spectators if that occurs again. Let the record show now that there was loud laughter among the spectators.

"MR. SCHULTZ: If the Court please, that is what he said, just as he related it.

"MR. SEALE: You're darned right.

"MR. SCHULTZ: In terms of a physical attack by the people in this - -

"MR. SEALE: A physical attack by those damned marshals, that's what I said.

"THE COURT: Let - -

"MR. SEALE: And if they attack any people, they have a right to defend themselves, you lying pig.

"THE COURT: Let the record show the tone of Mr. Seale's voice was one shrieking and pounding on the table and shouting. That will be dealt with appropriately at some time in the future."

The defendant Seale then continued to speak after the jury entered the courtroom, and the Court then excused them. After the jury left, the defendant Seale made the following comment to the Court, transcript 4641:

"MR. SEALE: If a witness is on the stand and testifies against me and I stand up and speak out in behalf of my right to have my lawyer and to defend myself and you deny me that, I have a right to make those requests. I have a right to make those demands on my constitutional rights. I have a constitutional right to speak, and if you try to suppress my constitutional right to speak out in behalf of my constitutional rights, then I can only see you as a bigot, a racist, and a fascist, and I have said before and clearly indicated on the record." **3 months**

Specification 12: On October 29, 1969, during the morning session when the cross examination of the witness Frapolly was completed, the following occurred in open court: Transcript 4719, et seq.

"THE COURT: Is there any redirect examination?

"MR. SEALE: Before the redirect, I would like to request again—demand, that I be able to cross examine the witness. My lawyer is not here. I think I have a right to defend myself in this courtroom.

"THE COURT: Take the jury out, and they may go to lunch with the usual order.

"MR. SEALE: You have George Washington and Benjamin Franklin sitting in a picture behind you, and they were slave owners. That's what they were. They owned slaves. You are acting in the same manner, denying me my constitutional rights being able to cross examine this witness.

"(The following proceedings were had in open court, out of the presence and hearing of the jury:)

"MR. SEALE: You have had direct examination, we have cross examination by the other defendants' lawyers, and I have a right to cross examine the witness.

"THE COURT: Mr. Seale, I have admonished you previously - -

"MR. SEALE: I have a right to cross examine the witness.

"THE COURT: - - what might happen to you if you keep on talking.

"MR. SEALE: I still have the right to cross examine the witness. Why don't you recognize my constitutional rights.

"THE COURT: Mr. Kunstler has his appearance on record here as your attorney.

"MR. SEALE: He is not. He is not. He is not my lawyer, and you know that.

"THE COURT: He is. I don't know - -

"MR. SEALE: You know that.

"THE COURT: I know that he is, and I know this is just an entire device here - -

"MR. SEALE: He is not my lawyer. You have forced - - you have made your choice of who you think should represent me. That is not true. I made the choice of Charles R. Garry to represent me.

THE COURT: We are going to recess now, young man. If you keep this up - -

"MR. SEALE: Look, old man, if you keep up denying me my constitutional rights, you are being exposed to the public and the world that you do not care about people's constitutional rights to defend themselves.

"THE COURT: I will tell you that what I indicated yesterday might happen to you - -

"MR. SEALE: Happen to me? What can happen to me more than what Benjamin Franklin and George Washington did to black people in slavery? What can happen to me more than that?

"THE COURT: And I might add since it has been said here that all of the defendants support you in your position that I might conclude that they are bad risks for bail, and I say that to you, Mr. Kunstler, that if you can't control your client - -

"MR. SEALE: I still demand my constitutional rights as a defendant in this case to defend myself. I demand the right to be able to cross-examine this witness. He has made statements against me and I want my right to - -

"MR. SCHULTZ: May the record show, if the Court please, that while the marshals were seating Bobby Seale, pushing him in the chair, the defendant Dellinger physically attempted to interfere with the marshals by pushing them out of the way.

"MR. SEALE: I want my rights. I want my rights to defend myself. I want my right to defend myself in this trial. I want my rights recognized.

"THE COURT: Mr. Kunstler, I will address you if you will stand up.

"MR. KUNSTLER: I was going to address you,

your Honor, because you had made some remarks - -
"MR. SEALE: He doesn't represent me. You can address him all you want. He doesn't represent me. He doesn't represent me. You can address him all you want. They are the ones that's pushing me.
'MR. KUNSTLER: Your Honor, you made a threat about my - -
"THE COURT: I tell you that Mr. Dellinger—if that is his name—has said here that they support the performances of this man, the statements of this man.
"MR. KUNSTLER: They support his right to have a lawyer or to defend himself.
"THE COURT: You told me you were his lawyer.
"MR. KUNSTLER: Your Honor - -
"MR SEALE: He is not my lawyer.
"THE COURT: I have the transcript right here.
"MR. KUNSTLER: Your Honor, we have gone over that.
"MR. SEALE: I told you I fired him before the trial began.
"THE COURT: You haven't explained - -
"MR. KUNSTLER: I have explained it fully. I have been discharged - -
"THE COURT: No, you haven't, and you will.
"MR. KUNSTLER: I told you on the 27th and I told you on the 30th.
"THE COURT: I tell you some day you will have to explain it.
"MR. KUNSTLER: That is another threat to the lawyers your Honor. We have had so many that - -
"THE COURT: Now I will tell you this, that since it has been said here that all of the defendants support this man in what he is doing, I over the noon hour will reflect on whether they are good risks for bail and I shall give serious consideration to the termination of their bail if you can't control your clients, and you couldn't yesterday afternoon.
"MR. SEALE: I am not—I am not a defendant—he is not my lawyer. I want my right to defend myself. I want my right to defend myself.

"MR. KUNSTLER: Your Honor, they said this morning they supported fully his right to defend himself or have his lawyer of choice, and if that is the price of their bail, then I guess that will have to be the price of their bail.

"THE COURT: Let me tell you - -

"MR. SEALE: I have a right to defend myself. That's what you - -

"THE COURT: Will you, Mr. Marshal, have that man sit down.

"MR. SEALE: You trying to make jive bargaining operations and that's different from the right I have.

"I have a right to defend myself. I still have a right to defend myself whether you sit me down or not. I still got a right to defend myself. I got a right to speak on behalf of my defense. I have a right to speak out in behalf of my defense, and you know it. You know it. Why don't you recognize my right to defend myself?

"MR. SCHULTZ: May the record show that the defendant Dellinger did the same thing just now?

"THE COURT: I saw it myself.

"MR. KUNSTLER: Your Honor, he is trying to see what is happening.

"MR. SEALE: I want the constitutional right to defend myself. I want the right to cross-examine the witness, and why don't you recognize the law of this land and give me my constitutional right to defend myself?" **3 months**

Specification 13: At the beginning of the afternoon session on October 29, 1969, Court and counsel engaged in a lengthy colloquy during which the following occurred, Transcript 4752:

"MR. KUNSTLER: Your Honor, I would just like about two minutes to respond.

"MR. SEALE: Since he made all of these statements, can I say something to the Court?

"THE COURT: No, thank you.

"MR. SEALE: Why not?

"THE COURT: Because you have a lawyer and I

am not going to go through that again.

"MR. SEALE: He is not my lawyer. How come I can't say nothing? He had distorted everything, and it relates to the fact I have a right to defend myself.

"THE COURT: I ask you to sit down. If there has been any distortion by anybody, I am perfectly capable of understanding it.

"MR. SEALE: I don't think you will. See? I don't think you will. Your past actions of denying me the constitutional right to defend myself --

"THE COURT: Did you want to reply, Mr. Kunstler?

"MR. SEALE: Yes, I did. I wanted to reply.

"THE COURT: I was talking to Mr. Kunstler, if you don't mind."

The colloquy continued and the Court thereafter sent the jury into the jury room at which time the following occurred, Transcript 4762, et sequitur:

"MR. KUNSTLER: Then I have nothing further to say, your Honor.

"THE COURT: Bring in the jury, please.

"MR. SEALE: What about Section 1982, Title 42 of the Code where it says the black man cannot be discriminated against in my legal defense in any court in America?

"THE COURT: Mr. Seale, you do know what is going to happen to you --

"MR. SEALE: You just got through saying you observed the laws. That law protects my right not to be discriminated against in my legal defense. Why don't you recognize that? Let me defend myself. From the first time when I asked—when I attempted to make an opening statement, and you stopped me and denied me that right --

"THE COURT: I will not hear you now. I am asking you to be silent.

"MR. SEALE: I want to know will you—oh, look —it's a form of racism, racism is what stopped my argument.

"THE COURT: Hold the jury, Mr. Marshal.

"MR. SEALE: My argument is and I still argue

the point that you recognize my constitutional rights to defend myself.

"THE COURT: Mr. Seale, do you want to stop or do you want me to direct the marshal - -

"MR. SEALE: I want to argue the point about this so you can get an understanding of the facts. I have a right to defend myself.

"THE COURT: We will take a recess. Take that defendant into the room in there and deal with him as he should be dealt with in this circumstance.

"MR. SEALE: I still want to be represented. I want to represent myself.

"THE MARSHAL: Mr. Kunstler, will you instruct the defendants, sir, that it is the order of the Court that they will arise upon the recess?

"MR. KUNSTLER: If that is a direction of the Court, I certainly will pass it on.

"THE COURT: Let the record show none of the defendants have stood at this recess in response to the Marshal's request. The Court will be in recess for a few minutes.

"MR. SEALE: Let the record show that - -

"THE MARSHAL: This Court will take a brief recess.

"MR. SEALE: Let the record show - -"

In an attempt to maintain order in the courtroom, the Court thereupon ordered the defendant Seale removed from the courtroom, at which time he was forcibly restrained by binding and gagging.

The defendant Seale was then returned to the courtroom but continued to shout through the gag. The Court then ordered the Marshal to reinforce the gag. The gag was then reinforced and the defendant Seale was returned to the courtroom. Eventually the jury was allowed in the courtroom for the afternoon session. **3 months**

Specification 14: On October 30, 1969, at the opening of the morning session the court ordered the marshal to adjust the restraint on the defendant Seale after he had complained of discomfort. Thereupon the following occurred in open court, transcript 4814, et seq.

"THE COURT: If the marshal has concluded that

he needs assistance, of course.

"I will excuse you, ladies and gentlemen of the jury, with my usual orders.

"(The following proceedings were had in open court, out of the presence and hearing of the jury:)

"MR. KUNSTLER: Your Honor, are we going to stop this medieval torture that is going on in this courtroom? I think this is a disgrace.

"MR. RUBIN: This guy is putting his elbow in Bobby's mouth and it wasn't necessary at all.

"MR. KUNSTLER: This is no longer a court of order, your Honor; this is a medieval torture chamber. It is a disgrace. They are assaulting the other defendants also.

"MR. RUBIN: Don't hit me in my balls, mother fucker.

"MR. SEALE: This mother fucker is tight and it is stopping my blood.

"MR. KUNSTLER: Your Honor, this is an unholy disgrace to the law that is going on in this courtroom and I as an American lawyer feel a disgrace.

"MR. FORAN: Created by Mr. Kunstler.

"MR. KUNSTLER: Created by nothing other than what you have done to this man.

"MR. HOFFMAN: You come down here and watch it, Judge.

"MR. FORAN: May the record show that the outbursts are the defendant Rubin.

"MR. SEALE: You fascist dogs, you rotten, lowlife son-of-a-bitch."

MR. SEALE: That was right after I got hit in the testes by your marshals who attacked me.

"I am glad I said it about Washington used to have slaves, the first President - -

"MR. DELLINGER: Somebody go to protect him.

"MR. FORAN: Your Honor, may the record show that that is Mr. Dellinger saying someone go to protect him and the other comment is by Mr. Rubin.

"MR. RUBIN: And my statement, too.

"THE COURT: Everything you say will be taken down.

"MR. KUNSTLER: Your Honor, we would like the

names of the marshals. We are going to ask for a judicial investigation of the entire condition and the entire treatment of Bobby Seale.

"THE COURT: You ask for anything that you want. When you begin to keep your word around here that you gave the court perhaps things can be done.

"MR. KUNSTLER: If we are going to talk about words I am prepared to give you back your word about Mr. Ball yesterday and what he said you said to him. We have the transcript now.

"THE COURT: Don't point at me, sir, in that manner.

"MR. KUNSTLER: If we are going to talk about words, I'd like to exchange some.

"THE COURT: Don't point at me in that manner.

"MR. KUNSTLER: I just feel so utterly ashamed to be an American lawyer at this time.

"THE COURT: You should be ashamed of your conduct in this case, sir."

Thereafter, because of the chaos in the courtroom, the morning session of court recessed. **3 months**

Specification 15: During the afternoon session on Thursday, August 30, 1969, the following occurred, transcript 4930-4934:

"MR. SEALE: I would like to cross-examine the witness. I want to cross-examine the witness.

"THE COURT: Ladies and gentlemen of the jury, I will have to excuse you.

"MR. SEALE: My constitutional rights have been violated. The direct examination is over, cross-examination is over, I want to cross-examine the witness.

"THE COURT: Please be quiet, sir. I order you to be quiet.

"MR. SEALE: I have a right to cross-examine the witness. I want to cross-examine the witness at this time. I object to you not allowing me to cross-examine the witness. You know I have a right to do so.

"THE COURT: Ladies and gentlemen of the jury,

you are excused until tomorrow morning at ten o'clock. I must order you not to talk with anybody about this case, or let anybody speak with you about it, do not read the newspapers or any other journals. Do not listen to radio or television or look at television. If anybody attempts to communicate with you about this case in any manner, please get in touch with the United States Marshal who will in turn lay the matter before me. You are excused until tomorrow morning at ten o'clock. Mr. Witness, I direct you to return here tomorrow morning at ten o'clock.

"MR. SCHULTZ: If the Court please, I think the examination of the witness was completed.

"MR. WEINGLASS: No.

"MR. SCHULTZ: Oh, I am sorry. Mr. Weinglass was going to ask a question.

"THE COURT: He had another question, he said.

"I am sorry, I will have to direct you to return here tomorrow morning at ten o'clock.

"I must order you not to talk with anybody about this case or let anybody speak with you about it until you resume the stand.

"THE WITNESS: Yes, sir.

"THE COURT: Mr. Marshal, you may take the jury out.

"(The following proceedings were had in open court, out of the presence and hearing of the jury:)

"THE COURT: Now I want to tell you, Mr. Seale, again—I thought you were going to adhere to my directions. You sat there and did not during this afternoon intrude into the proceedings in an improper way.

"MR. SEALE: I never intruded until it was the proper time for me to ask and request and demand that I have a right to defend myself and I have a right to cross-examine the witness. I sit through other cross-examinations and after the cross-examinations were over, I request, demanded my right to cross-examine the witness, and in turn demanded my right to defend myself, since you cannot sit up here—you cannot sit up here and continue to deny me my constitutional rights to cross-examine the witness, my constitutional right to defend myself. I sit throughout other cross-examinations, I never said anything, and I am not attempting to disrupt this trial. I am attempting to get my rights to defend myself recognized by you.

"THE COURT: You have employed one of the most competent criminal lawyers I have ever seen.

"MR. SEALE: He is not employed by me. He is not, and you know Charles R. Garry is my only lawyer. He is not here.

"THE COURT: I have a written appearance here in his own handwriting.

"MR. SEALE: I fired him. He filed an appearance to see me in jail before the trial began. Mr. Charles Garry is the only one I ever agreed with that would be my trial counsel and you know that.

"THE COURT: I must tell you, sir, that time is running out. If you are going to persist in this sort of thing, the court will have to deal appropriately with your conduct.

"MR. SEALE: I have a right to object. I have a right - -

"THE COURT: Mr. Marshal, the court will be in recess.

"MR. SEALE: I have a right to my constitutional rights.

"THE MARSHAL: The court will be in recess until tomorrow morning at ten o'clock." **3 months**

Specification 16: On Wednesday, November 5, 1969, during the morning session, following the direct examination of the witness Ray, the following took place:

"MR. SEALE: I would like to approach the lectern.

"THE COURT: You may not cross-examine, sir.

"MR. SEALE: Well, I think I have a right to cross-examine.

"THE COURT: No, you have no right in the circumstances of this case.

"MR. SEALE: Why did you follow me, could you please tell me, Mr. Witness - -

"THE COURT: Mr. Seale --
"MR. SEALE: -- at the airport?
"THE COURT: Mr. Seale, I ask you to sit down.
"MR. SEALE: Have you ever killed a Black Panther Party member?
"THE COURT: Mr. Seale, I will have to ask you to sit down, please.
"MR. SEALE: Have you ever been on any raids in the Black Panther Party's offices or Black Panther Party members' homes?
"THE COURT: Mr. Seale, this is the third time I am asking you to sit down, as courteously as possible.
"MR. SEALE: Why don't you let me cross-examine the witness and defend myself.
"THE COURT: Because you are not entitled to. You have a lawyer of record who signed his appearance in his own handwriting.
"MR. SEALE: This man was fired. He was not my lawyer before the jury heard one shred of evidence, before one witness even raised his hand to be sworn in the trial. The trial had not started until that happened.
"THE COURT: You may not stand up --
"MR. SEALE: This man is not my counsel.
"THE COURT: Will you sit down, please.
"MR. SEALE: He is not the representative of me. I am trying to defend myself. I'm being railroaded.
"THE COURT: Will you sit down, sir.
"MR. SEALE: Why can't you see that I have a right to try and cross-examine witnesses, and I have a right to defend myself.
"THE COURT: I am saying that you do not have the right at this juncture, sir.
"MR. SEALE: Look there's 3500 material here that this here man is testifying against me. Somebody has to cross-examine him.
"THE COURT: But not you.
"MR. SEALE: Me, myself, my own person have no right to defend myself? This is erroneous. It is a complete, complete, overt, fascist attempt, fascist operation --

"THE COURT: Ladies and gentlemen of the jury - -
"MR. SEALE: - - of denying me my constitutional right.
"THE COURT: Ladies and gentlemen of the jury, I ask you to leave the courtroom.
"(Whereupon the following further proceedings were had herein, in open court, outside the presence and hearing of the jury:)
"MR. SEALE: How about that? You are talking about insulting you. You are the one that is insulting me, insulting the people of the world, insulting the people of America, and you know it.
"THE COURT: Gentlemen, we will recess until two o'clock." **3 months**

Accordingly, it is therefore ordered that pursuant to the authority vested in this Court by Rule 42(a) of the Federal Rules of Criminal Procedure and by Title 18, United States Code, Section 401, the defendant Bobby Seale be punished for contempt.

I will hear from you, Mr. Kunstler.

MR. KUNSTLER: Your Honor, I have already indicated that because I have been discharged I can say nothing for Mr. Seale. He wants to be his own attorney, as your Honor has read at least thirty or forty times from your own opinion, and I think that I would be derelict in my duty to my understanding of my right and liability as an attorney were I to speak for him now.

THE COURT: Mr. Seale, you have a right to speak now. I will hear you.

MR. SEALE: For myself?

THE COURT: In your own behalf, yes.

MR. SEALE: How come I couldn't speak before?

THE COURT: This is a special occasion.

MR. SEALE: Wait a minute. Now are you going to try to—you going to attempt to punish me for attempting to speak for myself before? Now after you punish me, you sit up and say something about you can speak? What kind of jive is that? I don't understand it. What kind of court is this? Is this a court? It must be a fascist operation like I see it in my mind, you know—I don't understand you.

THE COURT: I am calling on you --
MR. SEALE: You just read a complete record of me trying to persuade you, trying to show you, demonstrating my right, demonstrating to you the need, showing you all this stuff about my right to defend myself, my right to defend myself, history, slavery, et cetera; and you going to sit there and say something about, "OK, now you can speak"?

What am I supposed to speak about? I still haven't got the right to defend myself. I would like to speak about that. I would like to—since you let me stand up and speak, can I speak about in behalf of—can I defend myself?
THE COURT: You may speak to the matters I have discussed here today, matters dealing with your contemptuous conduct. The law obligates me to call on you to speak at this time.
MR. SEALE: About what? About the fact that I want a right to defend myself? That's all I am speaking about.
THE COURT: No, about possible punishment for contempt of this court.
MR. SEALE: Punishment? You've punished black people all your life. I mean, you, they even say you own a factory that produces raw materials to kill people in Viet Nam, you know, so it's nothing, death is nothing, I mean, if that is what you are talking about, or putting me in jail, or prison, or hanging people, and all that stuff. I have nothing to say about that. I have something to say about the fact that I want to defend myself still. I want my rights, to be able to stand up and cross-examine the witnesses. I want that, so I don't know what you're talking about.
THE COURT: I have tried to make it clear.
MR. SEALE: All you make clear to me is that you don't want me, you refuse to let me, you will not go by my persuasion, or my arguments, my motions, my requests to be, to the extent of even having to shout loud enough to get on that record for that record so that they can hear me half the time. You don't want to listen to me. You don't want to let a man stand up, contend to you that that man is not my lawyer, show you and point out to you that fact, in fact, made motions and told you that

I fired the man.

And to stand up here and say, "Look, I have the right to defend myself," continuously over and over, even to the point just recently on Friday you recognized that I did have only one lawyer by letting this man and Thomas Hayden to go and to talk to Charles R. Garry to see about coming out here for me, which begin to show me that I was beginning to persuade you to do something, at least allow somebody to investigate my situation. Now what are you talking about? Now all of a sudden on the record?

THE COURT: I want to make it clear. I don't want to be questioned any further. The law gives you the right to speak out now in respect to possible punishment for contempt of court, sir.

MR. SEALE: Well, the first thing, I'm not in no contempt of court. I know that. I know that I as a person and a human being have the right to stand up in a court and use his constitutional right to speak in behalf of his constitutional rights. That is very clear, I hope. That's all I have to say. I still want to cross-examine the witnesses, I make those requests. I make my motions, and I make those requests, and I will continue to make those requests, hoping that once in one way along this trial, you will recognize my rights as a human being, a black man living under the scope and influence of a racist decadent America where the Government of the United States does not recognize the black people's constitutional rights, and have never recognized them from 1867 to the Dred Scott case situation, in a period of slaves you never recognized them, and here you are, and all I can say is that you're probably acting in the same manner as Benjamin Franklin and George Washington. We are hep to that kind of business.

THE COURT: Oh, but you are mistaken about that.

MR. SEALE: Oh, yes, you're acting in the same manner as those courts acted in those periods of slavery history, and you know it. That's what you're doing.

If a black man stands up and speaks, if a black man asks for his rights, if a black man demands his rights, if a black man requests and argues his rights, what do you do? You're talking about punishing. If a black man gets up and speaks in behalf of the world - -

THE COURT: Are you addressing me, sir?

MR. SEALE: I'm talking. You can see I'm talking.

THE COURT: That's right, but if you address me, you'll have to stand.

MR. SEALE: Stand? Stand now. Now let's see, first you said that I couldn't stand. I got my suit. It's going to a higher court, possibly the highest court in America.

THE COURT: In conformity with the provision of Rule 42(a) of the Federal Rules of Criminal Procedure, I shall certify that the series of criminal contempts committed as described by the Court in its oral observations and specifications 1 to and including 16 were committed in actual presence of the Court, and were seen or heard by the Court during the trial of the case of United States of America vs. David T. Dellinger and others, 69 CR 180.

I find that the acts, statements, and conduct of the defendant Bobby Seale constituted a deliberate and wilful attack upon the administration of justice, an attempt to sabotage the functioning of the Federal Judiciary System, and misconduct of so grave a character as to make the mere imposition of a fine a futile gesture and a wholly insignificant punishment. Accordingly, I adjudge Bobby G. Seale guilty of each and every specification referred to in my oral observations, and the Court will impose—strike that—and the defendant Seale will be committed to the custody of the Attorney General of the United States or his authorized representative for imprisonment for a term of three months on each and every specification, the sentences to run consecutively.

I direct the United States Attorney to prepare from the oral remarks I made here a certificate of contempt for my signature together with a judgment and commitment order.

How soon—you will have to get the reporter to have that written up for you. How soon, Miss Reporter, will it be before it is written? I am glad I have got both of you here.

THE REPORTER: Six o'clock.

THE COURT: Get it to Mr. Foran as soon as you can, and I will ask Mr. Foran to get the certificate to me and the case will be continued until tomorrow morning. There will be an order in view of the disposition of this aspect of the case, there will be an order declaring a mistrial as to the defendant Bobby G. Seale and not as to any other defendants.

MR. SEALE: Wait a minute, I got a right—what's the cat trying to pull now? I'm leaving the [. . .] I can't stay?

THE COURT: The court will be continued until tomorrow morning at ten o'clock for signing the certificate of contempt and to continue with the trial in respect to the other seven defendants.

THE MARSHAL: Everyone please rise.

MR. SCHULTZ: If the Court please, we have the jury to inform.

THE COURT: Oh, yes, I'm glad you reminded me.

MR. SCHULTZ: Will your Honor set a trial date for the defendant Seale?

THE COURT: Yes. Yes.

MR. SEALE: I demand an immediate trial right now.

THE MARSHAL: Sit down, please. Come to order.

MR. SEALE: I demand an immediate trial right now.

THE COURT: Yes, we will give you a trial date.

MR. SEALE: I am talking about now. I don't want to be taken out. I have a right to go through this trial.

THE COURT: A mistrial has been declared with respect to you, sir. Your trial will be conducted on April 23, 1970, at ten o'clock in the morning.

MR. SEALE: I want it immediate, right now, though.

THE COURT: I am sorry, I can't try two cases at one time, sir.

(The following proceedings were had herein, in open court, within the presence and hearing of the jury:)

THE COURT: Ladies and gentlemen of the jury, I deeply regret having to keep you confined in the jury room this long, but there were matters that the Court had to consider with the parties and counsel out of your presence.

Since it is now nearly a quarter after four, we'll be in recess until ten o'clock tomorrow morning. The usual orders not to talk with anybody about this case, or let anybody speak with you about it. Do not discuss the case among yourselves. Do not read the newspapers or any other journals. Do not listen to radio or television or look at television. If anybody attempts to talk with you about this case, please communicate with the United States Marshal, who will in turn, lay the matter before me.

Mr. Marshal, the court will be in recess until ten o'clock tomorrow morning.

THE MARSHAL: Everyone will please rise.

MR. SEALE: I still want an immediate trial. You can't call it a mistrial. I'm put in jail for four years for nothing? I want my coat.

THE AUDIENCE: Free Bobby. Free Bobby.

(Whereupon an adjournment was had at 4:15 o'clock P.M. until the following day, November 6, 1969, at the hour of 10:00 o'clock A.M.)

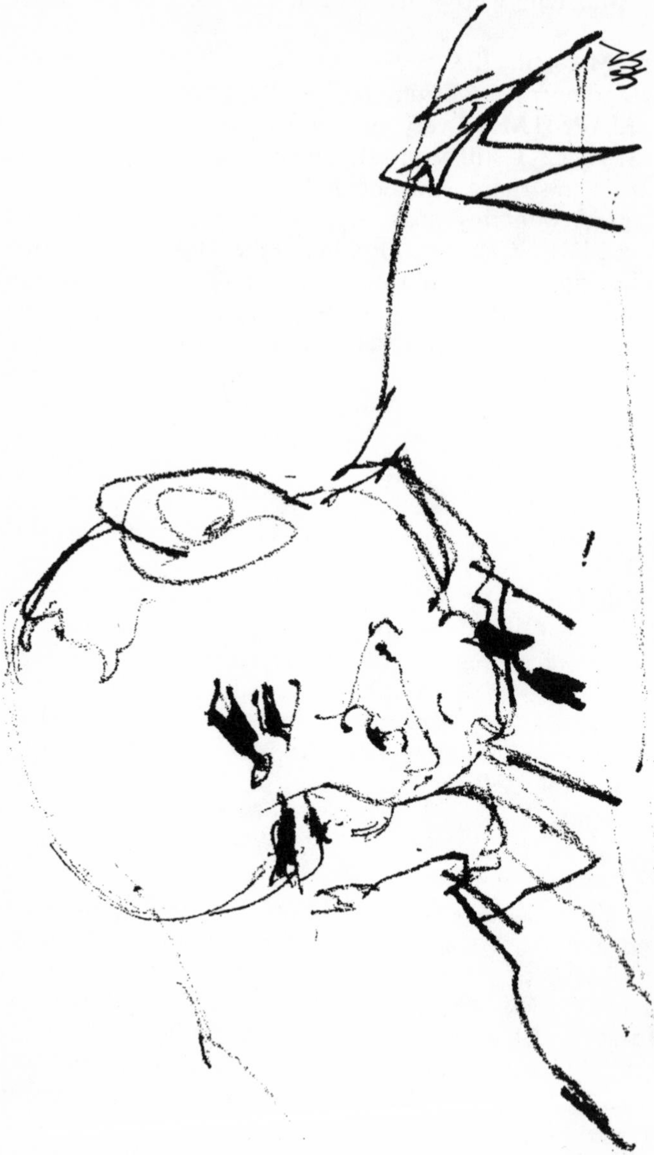

JUDGE HOFFMAN

Saturday, February 14, 1970, 9:30 A.M.

THE COURT: The court now has the responsibility of dealing appropriately with the contemptuous conduct that has pervaded this trial from the very beginning. Contempt by definition is any act calculated to hinder or disrupt the Court in the administration of justice and to lessen the Court's authority. Certainly no one would doubt that it is fundamental to not only our federal system but any state court legal system that the courts conduct their business in an untrammeled and undisrupted way. Therefore, misbehavior, misconduct which tends directly to prevent the discharge of judicial function is not and must not be overlooked.

I have tried right down to the very end without success to stop or put an end to that conduct, but as anyone who was in attendance here yesterday afternoon would know what happened—the record will show it.

The standard for determining whether conduct has impeded or obstructed the administration of justice is the reaction reasonably to be expected of those in the courtroom to words or acts under scrutiny. Parmelee Transportation Co. vs. Keeshin, 292 F. 2d 806, a case decided by the Seventh Circuit in 1961.

The United States Supreme Court has frequently taken the position that the courtroom is not the proper place for the disorderly expression of dissent and dissatisfaction with the law, with the orders and rulings of the court, regardless of a party's opinion as to the rulings of a trial judge.

Certainly I tried to make this clear both to the defendants and their counsel, even though I felt certain that they knew about the law.

Our legal system provides adequate and orderly means to challenge and test those rulings. Orderly procedures must be followed because the only alternative is anarchy, and we had during this trial such conduct.

The calculated use of contumacious conduct and the direct encouragement of disruptive outcries from spectators to express dissatisfaction or to intimidate the Court and the jurors are reprehensible and must be punished if our system of justice is to survive.

In ruling that orderly and unhindered courtroom proceedings are of paramount importance, Mr. Justice Goldberg once observed that the influence of a friendly or hostile mob upon the judicial process is repugnant to the very foundation of our constitutional democracy. Cox vs. Louisiana, 37 U.S. 559-62, 1965.

Knowingly and deliberately, I find, these defendants in this case and the lawyers have committed numerous acts which have evidenced a total disregard for the proper conduct of my trial. These acts of misbehavior occurred not infrequently in the presence of the jury. While the nature of the act does not rise to that of a felonious character, each act I find was deliberately disruptive and constituted an attempt to bring the Court and its process into disrepute. Upon many occasions such misbehavior required the removal of the jury. It was often necessary to admonish the jury to disregard misconduct occurring in their presence. Each and every act of misconduct constituted a separate and direct offense against this Court and our judicial system.

From the outset of the trial the Court admonished and warned the defendants and their counsel to refrain from such conduct, particularly when committed in the presence of the jury. They chose deliberately to disregard such admonition, right down through yesterday afternoon's hearing and have openly challenged and flaunted their contempt for both this Court and for the system of law it represents.

Particularly reprehensible was the conduct of counsel, who not only disregarded a duty to advise and direct their clients to observe the rules of this Court but participated with their clients in making a mockery of orderly procedure.

The Court warned the defendants and their counsel that their misconduct would be appropriately dealt with at a later time. They were advised that certainly their misbehavior would be punished when the defendant Seale was sentenced for various contemptuous acts early in the trial. Yet that conduct continued and intensified. Their misconduct continued and intensified.

The Court has withstood continual and repeated insults and interruptions from the defendants and their counsel during the course of the trial. The Court might have halted the the trial upon each instance of misbehavior and imposed punishment on the particular transgressor at that time. Other considerations, however, were more compelling. The disruption caused by each improper act or comment would have merely been compounded by an immediate contempt proceeding. The trial would have undergone even more substantial delay than those caused by the misconduct itself. Furthermore, the punishment of counsel for contumacious conduct might have interfered with the preparation and presentation of the defense and thereby impair the effectiveness of the defendants' right to counsel. Also some of the defendants and counsel have demonstrated complete lack of inhibition in bringing improper and prejudicial matter to the attention of the jury despite the admonition of the Court. Constant collateral contempt proceedings would merely have intensified the distractions which the conduct inflicted on the Court and jury.

No doubt cries of oppression would have greeted the Court if punishment were meted out during the course of the trial.

For these reasons the Court has waited until the close of the trial to deal with this problem. Such approach has been approved as the appropriate method to deal with this problem by appellate courts. United States against Schiffer, 361 F. 2d 91, Sixth Circuit, 1965; certiorari denied 384 U.S. 1003; United States vs. Galenti, 298 Fed. 2d 72, First Circuit, 1962.

The instances of misbehavior to be cited and punished are restricted to contemptuous conduct committed in the presence of the Court. The numerous instances of contemptuous conduct which occurred outside of the presence of the Court are not considered here. The transcript of this trial is replete with the contumacious conduct and comments of the defendants and their counsel. These offenses are matters of official record for which as a matter of law there is no defense. The misconduct was contemptuous per se since the record demonstrates that the misbehavior either disrupted the trial or brought improper matters to the attention of the jury and thereby was a direct affront to the administration of justice.

Congress has authorized summary punishment for misbehavior occurring in the actual presence of the Court. Rule 42(a), Federal Rules of Criminal Procedure, 18 U.S.C. Section 401-1.

The Supreme Court in Bloom vs. Illinois, 391 U.S. 194, at 209-10, 1968, recognized that direct contempt committed in the presence of the court are not suited to jury trials. The Bloom case, while holding that a jury trial is required on a charge that a serious or felonious contempt has been committed clearly indicated that direct contempt committed in the presence of the court generally should be punished by a light sentence. Such offenses do not require a jury trial. See also 82 Harvard Law Review, 153, 155, 1968.

There is nothing in Bloom which would preclude each contumacious act to be cited by the court. Each act was reprehensible and offensive to the administration of justice. No act in itself was so infamous as to require severe penalty and therefore a trial by jury. However, each act directly interfered with the trial and so requires discipline not unlike different offenses included in consecutive counts with one indictment or information.

Furthermore, as I have indicated, some of the offenders have engaged in such impudent repetition of their misconduct, that the court finds the imposition of consecutive sentences necessary. Even though the punishment imposed upon several of the offenders is grave, it is, nevertheless, based upon separate and distinct acts.

Once any party to a law suit has embarked upon a strategy of disruption such as that displayed in this case, rather than proceeding within the bounds of proper procedure, only cumulative sanctions can act as a restraint. Otherwise a first offense would offer immunity for further violations.

There is no reason in law barring cumulation of sentences for multiple offenses of this nature. It is, of course, impossible to know at this time whether or not the jury which is now deliberating will return a verdict of guilty as to any of the defendants on whom a sentence will be imposed. However, should that be the case, the defendants, shall, of course, not be precluded from presenting any appropriate motions later for concurrent sentences.

We come now to the specifications required under the Federal Rules of Criminal Procedure, particularly Rule 42(a) which deals with direct criminal contempt.

In conformity with Rule 42(a), Federal Rules of Criminal Procedure, 18 U.S.C., I hereby certify that the series of criminal contempts set forth below were committed in the actual presence of the court and were seen or heard by the court during the trial of the case of United States of America vs. David T. Dellinger, et al., 69 CR 180, which commenced on September 24, 1969.

This was a case marred by continual disruptive outbursts in direct defiance of judicial authority by the defendants and defense counsel. I will specify here the instances of conduct of record which I consider to have been contemptuous, but I also make the entire record of the case of United States of America vs. David T. Dellinger, et al., 69 CR 180, a part of this proceeding.

Much of the contemptuous conduct in this case does not show, of record. The constant murmurs and snickering emanating from the defense table were not captured on the printed page. No record, no matter how skillfully transcribed, can adequately portray the venom, sarcasm, and tone of voice employed by a speaker. No record, no matter how skillfully transcribed, can adequately reflect the applause, the guffaws, and other subtle tactics employed by these contemnors in an attempt to break up this trial. I have not focused on these cheap theatrics, histrionics, and affectations. I note them for the record lest my silence be construed as approval. But for the sake of the citations of contempt in this case, I limit myself to that conduct which is clearly and adequately portrayed in the record.

This was a long trial. The behavior of the defendants and defense counsel was prepared with direct and defiant contempt for the court and the Federal Judicial System as a whole. Here is a record of exceptional circumstances which were disruptive of the proceedings. It has been my considered judgment throughout this case that the behavior of the defendants was aimed at baiting the judge and inciting and harassing the U.S. Attorneys in an attempt to stop the trial. I would have been derelict in my duty as a Federal District Judge if I were to permit such base and unethical tactics to succeed. Consequently, I have waited until this trial was concluded before making a final determination of contempt. The exigencies of such a complex and difficult case compelled me to follow that course.

DELLINGER

I will first consider the conduct of the defendant David Dellinger.

Specification 1: On October 15 when the Judge entered the courtroom, Mr. Dellinger was standing and the following colloquy occurred:

"MR. DELLINGER: Mr. Hoffman, we are observing the moratorium.

THE COURT: I am Judge Hoffman, sir.

MR. DELLINGER: I believe in equality, sir, so I prefer to call people mister or by their first name.

THE COURT: Sit down. The clerk is about to call my cases.

MR. DELLINGER: I wanted to explain to you we are reading the names of the war dead.

THE MARSHAL: Sit down.

MR. DELLINGER: We were just reading the names of the dead from both sides.

THE MARSHAL: Sit down." Official Transcript, Page 2425A.

Subsequently the jury was brought into the room. When the jury was seated, the defendant Dellinger once more rose and the following colloquy occurred:

"DEFENDANT DELLINGER: Before the witness resumes the stand, we would like to propose --

MR. SCHULTZ: If the Court please --

MR. FORAN: Your Honor. If the Court please, may the marshal take that man into custody?

DEFENDANT DELLINGER: A moment of silence --

MR. SCHULTZ: Your Honor, this man --

THE COURT: Mr. Marshal, take out the jury.

(The following proceedings were had in open court, out of the presence and hearing of the jury:)

DEFENDANT DELLINGER: We only wanted a

moment of silence.

MR. FORAN: Your Honor, this man has announced this on the elevator coming up here that he was intending to do this.

DEFENDANT DELLINGER: I did not. It doesn't matter, I would have been glad to, but I did not.

MR. FORAN: Your Honor, I object to this man speaking out in court.

THE COURT: You needn't object. I forbid him to disrupt the proceedings. I note for the record that his name is - -

DEFENDANT DELLINGER: David Dellinger is my name.

THE COURT: You needn't interrupt my sentence for me.

DEFENDANT DELLINGER: You have been interrupting ours. I thought I might finish that sentence.

THE COURT: The name of this man who has attempted to disrupt the proceedings in this court is David Dellinger and the record will clearly indicate that, Miss Reporter, and I direct him and all of the others not to repeat such occurrences." Official Transcript Pages 2429-30. **6 months**

Specification 2: When the witness Salzberg left the witness box in order to identify the defendant Hayden, the defendant Dellinger said to him, in a voice loud enough for the jury to hear:

"MR. DELLINGER: Quite a let down. I am really disappointed in you." Page 3770. **1 month**

Specification 3: On October 22, after the defendant Seale had defied a judicial order by speaking out again and again, after being told to stop, the defendant Dellinger rose and addressed the Court:

"MR. DELLINGER: I think you should understand we support Bobby Seale in this—at least I do." Page 3642. **7 days**

Specification 4: On October 27, during the testimony of the witness Frapolly, the defendant Dellinger made the following comment:

"MR. DELLINGER: Mr. Foran, do you believe one word of that?
MR. FORAN: Your Honor, may the record show the comment from the defendant Dellinger, your Honor?
THE COURT: Yes. Mr. Dellinger has made several comments from time to time. The record may indeed show - - Did you get the comment of Mr. Dellinger?
MR. DELLINGER: Yes. I asked Mr. Foran if he could possibly believe one word of that. I don't believe the witness believes it. I don't believe Mr. Foran believes it.
THE COURT: And continue to take his words, and I admonish you, sir, not to interrupt this trial by your conversation or your remarks. You have a very competent lawyer representing you. You are not permitted to speak while he represents you." Page 4372.
3 months

Specification 5: On October 28, the following occurred:
"MR KUNSTLER: Your Honor, the defendants, with whom I have consulted, every one except Mr. Seale, have requested me to just make one question —ask one question of your Honor before they give me their decision, and the question would be: Is the price of my going the compromising or waiving by Mr. Seale of his constitutional assertion that I am not his lawyer and he wants to defend himself?
THE COURT: You don't expect me to answer a question put to me in that way, do you?
MR. DELLINGER: Why not? You expect us to answer a question." Page 4395. **7 days**

Specification 6: At the close of the court session on October 28, 1969, the defendant Dellinger refused to rise in the customary manner when the court left the room. Pages 4618-19. **1 day**

Specification 7: On October 28 in the afternoon session, after the Court had engaged in a colloquy with Mr. Seale concerning his right to cross-examine witnesses, Mr. Dellinger rose and stated the following:

> "MR. DELLINGER: And all the defendants support Bobby Seale's right to have a counsel of his choice here and affirm that he has been denied that right." Page 4638. **7 days**

Specification 8: On October 29 Mr. Dellinger engaged in a physical struggle with one of the marshals who was attempting to restrain the defendant Bobby Seale, and when the court called a recess, Mr. Dellinger refused to rise in the customary manner. Pages 4724-4729. **1 month**

Specification 9: On October 29 in the afternoon session, when the Court was compelled to call a recess, the defendant Dellinger again refused to rise in the customary manner. Page 4763. **1 day**

Specification 10: On October 30 at the beginning of the court session, the defendant Dellinger again refused to rise in the customary manner. Page 4801. **1 day**

Specification 11: On October 30 after the defendant Hayden had engaged in a colloquy with the Court, the defendant Dellinger commented aloud from the defense table:

> "MR. DELLINGER: What about the motion? There was a motion. The motion was for voir dire of the jury. He hasn't ruled." Page 4844. **7 days**

Specification 12: On October 30 when the Court again called a recess, Mr. Dellinger once more refused to rise in the customary manner. Page 4849. **1 day**

Specification 13: On November 12, during the direct examination of the witness Bock, the defendant Dellinger laughed at the Court as the Court made an observation and Mr. Dellinger said aloud so that the jury could hear:

> "MR. DELLINGER: We are not ashamed to laugh." Page 6258.

The conduct was repeated a few moments later during the testimony of Mr. Bock and the following occurred:

> "MR. SCHULTZ: Mr. Kunstler is laughing so he can influence the jury with the impression that this is

absurd. That is why he is laughing aloud because he—if Mr. Dellinger would stop talking when we are addressing the court - -

MR. DELLINGER: I am trying to tell something to my lawyer. It is absurd. It is—he is a vaudeville actor." Pages 6288-89. **2 days**

Specification 14: On November 19, during the cross-examination of the witness Bock, the following occurred:

"MR. SCHULTZ: Objection. That has no bearing, no probative—if Mr. Dellinger will stop talking to me when I am trying to address the court - -

MR. DELLINGER: I don't talk to you.

MR. SCHULTZ: And mumble to me every time I am trying to make an objection - -

MR. DELLINGER: Don't go making up things, Richard Schultz. I didn't talk to you. I don't mind your making all of these phony objections, but when you start lying about me too, I think that is disgusting.

THE COURT: Mr. Dellinger - -

MR. DELLINGER: I didn't say a word to him, Judge.

THE COURT: You just said enough to make me admonish you not to make any more remarks like that.

MR. KUNSTLER: Your Honor, you ought to admonish the U. S. Attorney not to make remarks - -

THE COURT: He may not speak out here. He has a lawyer.

MR. DELLINGER: He just lied about me.

MR. SCHULTZ: I am sitting next to Mr. Dellinger and he is mumbling under his breath to me. He has been doing this for the last - -

MR. DELLINGER: I said 'Ah' when he asked a bad question. I didn't say a word - -

THE COURT: You have competent lawyers to speak for you, sir, and I shall not permit you to speak for yourself.

MR. KUNSTLER: Then your Honor, I would ask your Honor to direct the U.S. Attorney not to take comments that are made here at the table to me or any other member of this table as remarks always addressed to him.

MR. FORAN: Your Honor, I was sitting here, too. I overheard the remark.

MR. DELLINGER: You're adding a lie to his lie, and I say that on my word.

THE COURT: I see that you are not accepting my admonition, sir, and I ask the reporter to make note of that." Pages 7341-43. **4 days**

Specification 15: On November 20, after the Court had made a ruling refusing to grant a writ of habeas corpus ad testificandum, the following colloquy took place:

"MR. DELLINGER: Aw Jesus—fascist - -

THE COURT: Who is that man talking, Mr. Marshal?

MR. DELLINGER: That is Mr. David Dellinger and he is saying that that is an arbitrary denial when you say who is key to our defense. We know who is key to our defense and we want to put on our key defense witness.

THE COURT: Mr. Marshal, ask that man to sit down.

THE MARSHAL: Sit down, Mr. Dellinger.

MR. DELLINGER: I think that is acting like a fascist court like Mr. Seale said when you make decisions of that kind and deprive us of our witnesses. Because he has already been persecuted in one court, now you are persecuting him and us in another court." Page 8078. **4 days**

Specification 16: On November 26, the day before Thanksgiving, after the Court determined that it would be unable to permit the sequestered jury to return home for the Thanksgiving Holiday, the following occurred:

"MR. DELLINGER: We move - -

MR. KUNSTLER: Your Honor, we move - -

MR. WEINGLASS: It's true. It's a true comment.

THE COURT: Who was that man who said he moved that is not a lawyer?

MR. DELLINGER: I am telling our lawyers we move the jury not have to be sequestered so they

can be home.
THE COURT: Mr. Marshal, will you have that man --
MR. DELLINGER: You asked about it, and I am telling you.
THE COURT: Let him sit down.
MR. DELLINGER: I was telling the lawyer before.
THE COURT: He has a lawyer." Page 8610. **3 days**

Specification 17: During the testimony of the witness Meyerding, the following occurred:

"THE COURT: I note for the record that certain of the defendants, Dellinger particularly --
MR. DELLINGER: I did not.
THE COURT: -- made noises.
MR. DELLINGER: I beg your pardon, I did not utter a single noise. When I have noises, I stand up and say so.
THE COURT: I heard you, sir.
MR. DELLINGER: I did not sigh; I did not utter a single noise, absolutely not.
THE COURT: And the man sitting next to you did also.
MR. DELLINGER: You mean to say you are calling me a liar? If so, you are a liar. I did not utter a single noise.
THE COURT: And make a note of that last statement.
MR. DELLINGER: I have called this a fascist court before and I think he is trying to prove it. It is absolutely irresponsible on your part.
THE COURT: Make a note of that last statement.
MR. DELLINGER: Absolutely irresponsible.
THE MARSHAL: Sit down, please.
MR. DELLINGER: And dishonest.
THE COURT: Make a note of that last statement. Miss Reporter, have you all of Mr. Dellinger's comments? Have you?
THE REPORTER: Yes." Official Transcript, Page 10,086-87. **6 days**

Specification 18: On December 11 during the cross-examination of the witness Ochs, the following occurred:

"MR. DELLINGER: He answered. You don't have to keep asking that.

MR. SCHULTZ: I don't know how many lawyers there are at that table.

MR. DELLINGER: I am consulting with my lawyer.

MR. SCHULTZ: I don't know whether an objection is being made or what?

THE COURT: The Court notes that - -

MR. KUNSTLER: Your Honor, Mr. Dellinger has made a remark to me that he doesn't have to keep asking the same question.

THE COURT: Will you let me finish my observation?

MR. KUNSTLER: Oh, go ahead. I thought you had.

THE COURT: Mr. Dellinger made a loud remark which provoked Mr. Schultz to say: 'I don't know how many lawyers there are,' and I think that was a good inquiry. Mr. Dellinger has done that sort of thing before and I merely wanted to identify the person, that is all, for the record." Page 10,628-29.

2 days

Specification 19: On December 15, when the Court was compelled to request the marshal to remove Mr. Stuart Ball, Jr., the following occurred:

"THE COURT: Mr. Marshal, take Mr. Ball out.

MR. DELLINGER: That is an injustice.

MR. KUNSTLER: That is a lawyer who is part of our defense team.

THE COURT: He is not a lawyer admitted to practice in this court.

MR. KUNSTLER: You are removing a lawyer from the defense table.

THE COURT: No, he is not a lawyer admitted to practice here.

MR. KUNSTLER: That doesn't matter, your Honor. He is - -

MR. DELLINGER: He wasn't laughing." Page 11,179-80.

A few moments later, the following colloquy occurred:

"MR. KUNSTLER: But he didn't laugh, your

Honor. If he laughed, that is one thing, perhaps, but two defendants have admitted laughing.
THE COURT: My eyesight is good and my hearing is good.
MR. KUNSTLER: You were wrong about Mr. Dellinger. You thought he made a noise. We have submitted an affidavit as to that.
THE COURT: I suppose I didn't hear him call me a liar in open court.
MR. KUNSTLER: That is a different matter, your Honor.
THE COURT: Oh - -
MR. DELLINGER: I said if you said I was talking that that was a lie, that you were calling me a liar.
THE COURT: You didn't—you said 'You are a liar.'
MR. KUNSTLER: No. Read the transcript.
MR. DELLINGER: You accused me of being a liar and I said that was a lie.
THE COURT: Will you sit down?
MR. DELLINGER: And you are very prejudiced and unfair and I state that in open court. It is not a fair trial and you have no intention of giving us a fair trial and when I speak throughout the country, I say that you are the assistant prosecutor or maybe the chief prosecutor and it is true and the people of this country will come to learn that about you and about some other judges in this court.
A SPECTATOR: Right on.
MR. DAVIS: That's why we were laughing."
(There was disorder in the courtroom.)
A SPECTATOR: Right on, boys.
MR. DAVIS: That's why we were laughing.
MR. HOFFMAN: You said you were doing it for us.
THE COURT: Have you got all those remarks, Miss Reporter?
MR. DELLINGER: Now one of our legal staff you have falsely accused and that is why I speak up.
THE COURT: Now, if you will permit me - -
MR. KUNSTLER: Your Honor, what is happening? The marshals are taking people out."

Just as they had to do now, I say parenthetically, and not

a part of these remarks, a regular part of these remarks.

"A SPECTATOR: Why don't you clear the whole courtroom?

THE COURT: Will you - -

MR. DELLINGER: You see, we are interested in the truth and you are not and the government is not and that is what the conflict is here." Official Transcript, Pages 11,182-85. **6 days**

Specification 20: On December 30, during the direct examination of the witness Hoffman, the following occurred:

"THE MARSHAL: Mr. Dellinger - -

MR. DELLINGER: I am a little upset by the dishonesty of the Court's process—yes, my name is David Dellinger.

THE COURT: That man's name is Dellinger, Miss Reporter.

MR. DELLINGER: They are not interested in the truth. They just want one side of things to go in, even made up things, but they won't allow the real things, the real truth.

THE COURT: Mr. Dellinger is continuing to speak, Miss Reporter.

MR. DELLINGER: Darned right. I hope the jury understands that, too.

MR. SCHULTZ: Your Honor, this is a deliberate attempt to make it appear - -

MR. DELLINGER: What do you - -

MR. SCHULTZ: - - that because the defendants don't follow - -

THE COURT: Mr. Schultz - -

MR. KUNSTLER: Oh, your Honor - - unfair to the government.

MR. DELLINGER: The government will go to jail for ten years, I suppose.

MR. SCHULTZ: Your Honor - -

THE COURT: Just a minute, sir. Now, Mr. Schultz, don't underestimate anybody's intelligence. Anyone knows that has been in a courtroom before that a defendant represented by counsel doesn't speak out.

MR. DELLINGER: Even when he's being railroaded he doesn't speak out.

THE COURT: I hope, Miss Reporter, you get those remarks.
MR. KUNSTLER: Your Honor, there comes a time when every human being feels the necessity to speak out and Mr. Dellinger - -
THE COURT: I didn't ask you to philosophize.
MR. KUNSTLER: I am not philosophizing, I am defending a client.
THE COURT: There comes a time when courtroom decorum must be observed.
MR. DELLINGER: Decorum is more important than justice, I suppose.
THE COURT: I have never sat in a trial over the many years where a defendant has spoken up on his own when - -
MR. FROINES: Perhaps you can give him four years like you gave Bobby Seale.
MR. DELLINGER: We just walk politely into jail."
Official Transcript, Page 12,913-16.

(And very slightly later:)

"THE COURT: And I direct you to sit down or I will have the marshal - -
MR. KUNSTLER: Mr. Schultz says - -
THE COURT: Please ask this lawyer to sit down.
MR. KUNSTLER: I have a right to stand and talk in defense of my client.
MR. DELLINGER: That's why we have to speak up, because you won't let our lawyers have a fair chance." Page 12,916. **4 days**

Specification 21: On January 9, after the court directed Mr. Rubin to remain in the courtroom and use the washroom facilities in the adjoining lock-up if he needed to go to the bathroom, the following colloquy occurred:

"MR. RUBIN: I want to go to the bathroom.
MR. DELLINGER: Convicted us already.
MR. DAVIS: Guilty until proven innocent." Page 14716. **3 days**

Specification 22: On January 9, when the Court reiterated its order concerning the use of the washroom facilities, the following occurred:

"THE MARSHAL: Mr. Dellinger - -
THE COURT: Let the record show that after I requested the Marshal to keep Mr. Dellinger quiet he laughed right out loud again. Out loud. The record may so indicate.
MR. DELLINGER: And he is laughing right now, too." Page 14,824. **3 days**

Specification 23: On January 12 the court made an evidentiary ruling and the following occurred:

"THE COURT: The objection of the government to Defendants' Exhibit 279 for identification will be sustained.
MR. DELLINGER: Oh, ridiculous.
THE COURT: Who said 'ridiculous'?
MR. DELLINGER: I did. It was ridiculous. I stand on that fact. You don't want us to have a defense.
THE COURT: I just wanted to know who said that.
MR. DELLINGER: You don't want us to have a defense. You are a hypocrite.
THE COURT: Did you get all those remarks?
MR. DELLINGER: I stand by them, too. You earned them. It really brings the whole system of justice under discredit when you act that way. What Mayor Daley and the police did for the electoral process in its present form you are now doing for the judicial process.
THE COURT: Mr. Marshal - -
MR. DAVIS: We want a fair trial.
MR. DELLINGER: You don't think it is a fair trial, do you?
THE MARSHAL: Just be quiet, Mr. Dellinger.
MR. DELLINGER: You are being paid by the same company but you ought to be able to think for yourself a little bit.
THE COURT: Bring in the jury.
MR. WEINGLASS: If your Honor please, before the jury comes in, I have a motion to make on behalf of the defendants. Prior to the jury leaving the court and while they were still here in the room and pursuant to my request for a five minute adjournment, your Honor made a statement in open court in the

presence of the jury that it was your attitude that this case should be 'gotten rid of.'
THE COURT: I didn't say that.
MR. DELLINGER: You did.
A DEFENDANT: You did so.
THE COURT: I said we shouldn't be wasting time. You got more than a five minute recess. I waited here.
MR. DELLINGER: You said 'get rid of the case.'
MR. WEINGLASS: As far as I'm concerned - -
THE COURT: Mr. Marshal, will you tell that man to remain quiet?
THE MARSHAL: Mr. Dellinger - -
MR. WEINGLASS: I most respectfully dispute the Court's recollection. Your Honor did use the words 'get rid of.'
THE COURT: Whether you are respectful or not, the evidence of the respect with which the Court is treated has been demonstrated by one of the defendants.
MR. DELLINGER: I didn't say anything you didn't deserve.
THE COURT: I will say to you, Mr. Weinglass - -
MR. DELLINGER: I only speak the truth." Official Transcript, Page 15,139-41. **5 days**

Specification 24: On January 14 the following occurred:
"THE COURT: Mr. Marshal, I am not here to be laughed at by these defendants, particularly Mr. Rubin.
THE MARSHAL: Mr. Dellinger, also, will you refrain from laughing?
MR. DELLINGER: That is a lie. And it wasn't Mr. Rubin. We laugh enough and you can catch us when we do but you just happened to get the wrong one.
MR. KUNSTLER: Your Honor, I don't think the record should constantly have these references to chuckles.
THE COURT: I think the record should show that and I see that the record does. I don't share your view.

MR. KUNSTLER: The Court has made a sally before and the room laughed and you didn't put that on the record.
THE COURT: I will not sit here—and you must know it by now, certainly—and have defendants laugh at my rulings, sir. And I will not hear you on that.
MR. KUNSTLER: You don't mind if they laugh at me or if they laugh at someone else.
THE COURT: I will ask you to sit down. Will you sit down? I saw Mr. Dellinger talking. If anybody else did - -
MR. DELLINGER: You did not see me talking. My lips were not moving. That is not the first time you have lied in this courtroom. My lips were not moving.
THE COURT: Did you get those last remarks?
MR. SCHULTZ: It was the defendant Hoffman.
MR. DELLINGER: If you can make an honest mistake, that's all right, but to lie about it afterwards and say you saw me talking when you didn't, that is different.
THE COURT: Will you ask that man to sit down.
MR. DELLINGER: You will go down in infamy in history for your obvious lies in this courtroom, of which that is only the most recent one.
THE MARSHAL: Sit down, sir.
MR. DELLINGER: It is absolutely true what I am saying.
THE MARSHAL: Will you - -
MR. DELLINGER: Absolutely true.
THE COURT: Mr. Marshal, will you ask that man to be quiet?
MR. DELLINGER: You will be ashamed of that for the rest of your life, if anything can shame you.
MR. SCHULTZ: Your Honor, it was the defendant Hoffman sitting immediately behind Dellinger who made those remarks.
THE COURT: Let the record show - -
MR. DELLINGER: Thanks for telling the truth, Mr. Schultz.
MR. KUNSTLER: Mr. Hoffman attempted to clarify the record. He was the one responsible. He took the

blame for it. It was not Mr. Dellinger or anyone else, or Mr. Rubin.
THE COURT: Oh, I heard Mr. Rubin and saw him.
MR. KUNSTLER: Your Honor - -
THE COURT: Will you please sit down? I will make the rulings here. The record will be what it is.
MR. KUNSTLER: I want the record - -
THE COURT: It can't be any more clear.
MR. DELLINGER: I want to make the record clear. Mr. Rubin did not laugh. You are standing there saying you heard it. That is why I called you a liar. He did not laugh. I was sitting next to him.
THE COURT: Mr. Marshal - -
MR. DELLINGER: And you made it up. It is about time this got out into the open so everyone could know what you are doing here. It is one thing to be prejudiced, it is another thing to be a liar.
THE COURT: Mr. Marshal, I ask you to restrain that man.
THE MARSHAL: Be quiet.
MR. KUNSTLER: He is trying to clarify the record.
THE COURT: He has got a lawyer.
MR. KUNSTLER: I am his lawyer and I represent - -
THE COURT: That is right, and we have had enough of this.
MR. KUNSTLER: But the record must be crystal clear that it was not Mr. Dellinger, it was not Mr. Rubin. Mr. Hoffman - -
THE COURT: Mr. Dellinger said enough.
MR. KUNSTLER: Mr. Hoffman has taken the blame.
THE COURT: I have never sat in fifty years through a trial where a party to a law suit called the judge a liar.
MR. DELLINGER: Maybe they were afraid to go to jail rather than tell the truth, but I would rather go to jail for however long you send me than to let you get away with that kind of thing and people not realize what you are doing.
THE COURT: Mr. Marshal, do I have to tell you

again, sir." Official Transcript, Pages 15,585-91.
6 months

Specification 25: Throughout the trial the defendant Dellinger has commented on the evidence and the witnesses presented by the prosecution. On January 16 during the cross-examination of the witness Goodwin the following incident occurred:

"MR. KUNSTLER: Then I think - -

MR. DELLINGER: Now he is going into his imagination.

MR. FORAN: Your Honor, there is testimony concerning this exact statement from Mr. Dellinger on August 28 between 10:30 and noon at 407 South Dearborn Street.

MR. DELLINGER: Yes, police agents, but you made it appear as if it was from my article. It is just Bill called the attention - -

THE COURT: Whose are those last words? Did you get the words of Mr. Dellinger, Miss Reporter?

THE REPORTER: Yes.

MR. KUNSTLER: He was just pointing out, your Honor, that there had been no shift from - -

THE COURT: I heard. I heard. I don't need your advice on that, Mr. Kunstler.

MR. FORAN: I shifted, your Honor, when Mr. Kunstler complained that I was talking about his article. I will go back and ask him another question." Official Transcript, Page 16,201. **7 days**

Specification 26: On January 23, during the direct examination of the witness Davis, the Court indicated that argument on a mistrial motion had been completed, and ordered Mr. Kunstler to sit down. After Mr. Kunstler flaunted the Court's orders and continued to argue, the defendant Dellinger rose from his place at the defense table, and the following incident ensued:

"MR. KUNSTLER: You haven't even heard the motion.

MR. RUBIN: You haven't heard it yet.

THE COURT: For a mistrial.

MR. KUNSTLER: Yes, but I would like to argue it.

THE COURT: Oh, there is no ground for a mistrial.

MR. KUNSTLER: Your Honor knows you have referred to the question of defendants' taking the stand. You have committed the cardinal error of a court with reference - -

THE COURT: I direct the marshal to have this man sit down.

MR. KUNSTLER: Every time I make a motion am I going to be thrown in my seat when I argue it?

THE COURT: You may sit down.

MR. DELLINGER: Force and violence.

MR. KUNSTLER: If that is the ruling of the court, that we cannot argue without being thrown in our seats - -

MR. DELLINGER: The judge is inciting a riot by asking the marshal to have him sit down.

THE COURT: That man's name is Dellinger.

MARSHAL JONESON: Will you be quiet, Mr. Dellinger.

MR. DELLINGER: After such hypocrisy I don't particularly feel like being quiet. I said before the judge was the chief prosecutor, and he's proved the point.

THE COURT: Will you remain quiet. Will you remain quiet, sir.

MR. DELLINGER: You let Foran give a foreign policy speech, but when he tries to answer it, you interrupt him and won't let him speak. There's no pretense of fairness in this court.

THE COURT: Mr. Marshal, will you go to that man and ask him to remain quiet.

MR. DELLINGER: No pretense of fairness. All you're doing is employing a riot—employing force and violence to try to keep me quiet - -

MARSHAL JONESON: Be quiet, sir.

MR. DELLINGER: - - just like you gagged Bobby Seale because you couldn't afford to listen to the truth that he was saying to you. You're accusing me. I'm a pacifist.

MARSHAL JONESON: Sit down, please, and be quiet.

MR. DELLINGER: I employ non-violence, and

you're accusing me of violence, and you have a man right here, backed up by guns, jails, and force and violence. That is the difference between us.

MARSHAL JONESON: Will you sit down.

(Applause.)

THE COURT: Will you continue, please, with the direct examination of this witness.

MR. DELLINGER: There goes the violence right there.

MR. KUNSTLER: That's the government in operation, your Honor, as it has been throughout this trial.

THE WITNESS: Your Honor, that's my sister they are taking out of the courtrom.

THE COURT: Even your sister - -

MR. KUNSTLER: Nobody but the government has employed violence in this courtroom—with Bobby Seale, with spectators." Official Transcript, Pages 17,371-17,373.

At this point, the marshals found it necessary to remove several of the spectators from the courtroom for disorderly conduct. Mr. Kunstler made some remarks about the removal of the spectators, and Mr. Foran rose to defend the way the trial was being conducted. This precipitated the following outburst from Mr. Dellinger:

"MR. FORAN: Your Honor, traditionally in American law cases are tried in a courtroom by the participants in the trial, not the audience, not spectators, not relatives of the defendants, but by witnesses and by the court and by the jury, not by shouting and screaming and voluntary statements from counsel or from the defendants shouting out in courtrooms, because that is the American judicial system, and it's worked very well for two hundred years, and it's not going to change now for these people.

MR. DELLINGER: Yes, kept the black people in slavery for two hundred years and wiped out the Indians and kept the poor people in problems and started the war in Viet Nam which is killing off at least a hundred Americans and a thousand Vietnamese every week, and we are trying to stop it.

MARSHAL JONESON: Sit down.

MR. DELLINGER: And you call that ranting and raving and screaming because we speak the truth.
MARSHAL JONESON: Mr. Dellinger, sit down, please.
MR. FORAN: Your Honor, in the American --
MR. DELLINGER: And that judge won't let that issue come into the trial, that's why we are here.
MR. FORAN: Your Honor, in the American system there is a proper way to raise such issues and to correct them.
MR. DELLINGER: That was the proper way with Fred Hampton, wasn't it?"

Mr. Kunstler made several more remarks, and Mr. Schultz rose to answer him, and Mr. Dellinger interjected a comment again:

"MR. SCHULTZ: We complied with the rules of this court. We have made no statements to the press, to any press, since this case was indicted. Mr. Kunstler, on a regular basis, has been falsifying, falsifying, to the press, violating the rules of the Court prohibiting every attorney in this case from making press conferences, and he has been doing it and he stands before this court and says the Government has.
MR. DELLINGER: And they have rules like that in Nazi Germany." Official Transcript, Pages 17374 through 375. **4 months**

Specification 27: On January 24, once more the testimony of the defendant Davis was interrupted. Mr. Foran was responding to an argument by Mr. Kunstler, when Mr. Dellinger interjected his remarks once more:

"MR. FORAN: In this case, your Honor, we have heard these people adopt or attempt to adopt Dr. King, attempt to adopt Senator McCarthy, Robert Kennedy, both of whom were better friends of mine than they ever were of theirs.
MR. DELLINGER: Oh, my God.
MR. FORAN: Mr. Kennedy appointed Mr. Schultz, your Honor.
MR. KUNSTLER: Oh, your Honor --
MR. DELLINGER: Reverend Abernathy was the co-chairman of the Mobilization and I worked in-

timately with Martin Luther King and Ralph Abernathy.

MR. FORAN: Robert Kennedy appointed this young man as an Assistant United States Attorney.

THE COURT: Mr. - - young man, will you have Mr. Dellinger sit down, and, Miss Reporter, did you get Mr. Dellinger's remarks?"

Mr. Dellinger did not sit down at the direction of the marshal and very slightly later the following ensued:

"THE COURT: Mr. Marshal, ask that man to sit down.

MR. DELLINGER: There has to be some way of speaking the truth. We have to speak the truth some way. If you won't allow it to come in other ways, we have to stand up and tell it because it is true.

THE COURT: Mr. Marshal - -

MR. DELLINGER: Ralph Abernathy was the co-chairman and close worker - -

THE COURT: Have that man sit down, Mr. Marshal, or do we have to have three marshals?" Official Transcript, Pages 17,808-17,811. **2 days**

Specification 28: At the end of the court session on January 24, while the Court was attempting to instruct the jury prior to recess, Mr. Dellinger made several loud remarks at the defense table, which were easily overheard throughout the courtroom. The incident is reported as follows:

"THE COURT: With that, Mr. Foran, I think we will recess tonight until Monday morning. Ladies and gentlemen - -

THE MARSHAL: Will you please keep quiet? Sit down. Sit down.

THE COURT: Ladies and gentlemen of the jury, we are about to recess until tomorrow morning.

MR. DELLINGER: - - hear a pig talk about civil disobedience - -"

DEFENDANT DELLINGER: I never used the word pig, your Honor. There is a mistake there.

"THE COURT: Mr. Marshal, will you - -

THE MARSHAL: Will you remain quiet, Mr. Dellinger?"

MR. DELLINGER: It is just a typographical error added

to your account.

"THE MARSHAL: Mr. Dellinger - -
MR. DELLINGER: I was just talking to my friend.
THE COURT: I will wait." Official Transcript, Page 17,860. **2 days**

Specification 29: On January 30, the court was required to instruct the marshals concerning the behavior of disorderly spectators. Mr. Dellinger made the following sarcastic comment after that instruction:

"THE COURT: I direct the jury to disregard the applause of each and every person who participated in it and the marshals will exclude from the courtroom any spectators who applauded after this witness left the stand.
MR. DELLINGER: Thanks, Pop. Thanks, fellows." Official Transcript, Page 19,032.

MR. KUNSTLER: Your Honor, the stenographer has admitted that that is not true, and that "pop" did not appear in the record. That was—it is not her fault but I have questioned her on that and I think if you question her - -
THE COURT: That is the way it appears here.
MR. KUNSTLER: I know it does. I saw it myself. I consulted with her and I think that is not the proper phrase.
THE REPORTER: It should be "Thanks a lot."
MR. KUNSTLER: "Thanks a lot" is the words to the witness. **7 days**

Specification 30: On February 4, the incident occurred which finally led the court to revoke Mr. Dellinger's bail. During the testimony of the witness Riordan, Mr. Dellinger rose from his place at the defense table and interjected the following remark:

"MR. DELLINGER: Oh, bull shit.
THE COURT: Did you get that, Miss Reporter?
MR. DELLINGER: That is an absolute lie.
THE COURT: Did you get that, Miss Reporter?
MR. DELLINGER: Let's argue about what I stand for and what you stand for, but let's not make up things like that.
THE COURT: All those remarks were made in the

presence of the Court and jury by Mr. Dellinger."

After a brief argument about the propriety of these remarks the Court determined to excuse the jury momentarily, and the following incident occurred:

"THE COURT: I will have to excuse you, ladies and gentlemen of the jury, with my usual orders.

MR. DELLINGER: You're a snake. We have to try to put you in jail for ten years for telling lies about us, Dick Schultz.

MARSHAL JONESON: Be quiet, Mr. Dellinger.

MR. DELLINGER: When it's all over, the judge will go to Florida, but if he has his way, we'll go to jail. That is what we're fighting for, not just for us, but for all the rest of the people in the country who are being oppressed.

A SPECTATOR: Damn right. Assert ourselves.

VOICES: Right on.

THE COURT: Take that man into custody. Mr. Marshal, take that man into custody.

VOICES: Right on, right on.

MR. SCHULTZ: Into custody.

THE COURT: Into custody.

VOICES: Right on.

MR. DAVIS: Go ahead, Dick Schultz, put everybody in jail.

MR. DELLINGER: Dick Schultz is a Nazi if I ever knew one.

MR. SCHULTZ: Your Honor, will you please tell Mr. Davis to walk away from me?

MR. DELLINGER: Put everybody in jail."

* * *

"MR. SCHULTZ: Your Honor, we have 3500 material. We have 3500 252-A-1 and 252-A-2.

THE COURT: I would like to make a note of those if you will go slowly, please.

MR. SCHULTZ: 3500 252-A-1 and 252-A-2. -A-1, your Honor, is the complete document.

MR. DELLINGER: It is completely false." Official Transcript, Pages 19,669 through 19,673.

5 months

Specification 31: On February 6, during the argument

of a motion to restore Mr. Dellinger's bail, Mr. Dellinger arose and inserted the following remarks into the record:

"THE COURT: Is there anything you want to say in reply to Mr. Schultz?

MR. DELLINGER: I would like to say that I have not - -

THE COURT: Not you, sir.

MR. DELLINGER: I would just like to say I have not screamed, and - -

THE COURT: I have asked your lawyer.

MR. DELLINGER: - - I have not used repeated vile or obscene language. That's untrue.

THE COURT: Please sit down." Official Transcript, Page 19,904. **7 days**

Specification 32: On February 7, the Court ruled against a special application on behalf of Mr. Dellinger concerning his confinement. At the close of the court session he made the following sarcastic remarks about the ruling:

"MR. DELLINGER: That wins respect.

THE COURT: Mr. Marshal, the Court will be in recess until Monday morning.

MARSHAL DOBROWSKI: Everyone please rise.

MR. DELLINGER: You now have my respect, Judge, I'm sure you know." Official Transcript, Pages 20,282-83.

We will take a recess here for thirty minutes until two o'clock and I direct all of the defendants to return with their counsel.

MR. SCHULTZ: Your Honor, about the exhibits, may we do those now?

THE COURT: Turn over the exhibits to the Marshal. The Marshal will deliver them to the jury. **7 days**

(Whereupon at 1:30 P.M. Court was recessed until 2:00 P.M. of the same day, February 14, 1970.)

Saturday, February 14, 1970, 2:00 P.M.

THE CLERK: 69 CR 180, United States of America vs. David T. Dellinger, et al.

THE COURT: The Court has concluded its reading of the record in respect to the defendant Dellinger. The Court

finds the defendant Dellinger guilty of direct contempt of court commited in the presence of the Court with respect to the following specifications enumerated by the Court in reading from the record this morning. Specification No. 1, the defendant will be committed—by the way, does counsel for Dellinger want to be heard before sentence is imposed?
MR. KUNSTLER: Your Honor, I have a legal argument on the power of the Court after trial and I would present the legal argument.
THE COURT: After trial - -
MR. KUNSTLER: - - to judge summary contempt after trial.
THE COURT: I am giving you the opportunity to be heard in respect to sentence. That is all now.
MR. KUNSTLER: Well, your Honor, there is—your Honor cited United States against Bloom as the authority for your action and you quoted from it.
THE COURT: That isn't it at all. I cited Bloom for certain statements made in Bloom, not for the authority. I have the inherent authority to punish anybody who is in direct contempt of court.
MR. KUNSTLER: Your Honor, but Bloom holds also that this power should not be exercised after trial; that summary contempt is only a method of preventing disturbance during trial and should be exercised during trial, but that after trial a man is entitled to a jury trial and also to all the requirements of 42(a).
THE COURT: I will not - -
MR. KUNSTLER: And that another judge should sit on it other than your Honor because it does involve what your Honor considers to be insults, et cetera, to you personally, and you should not be sitting in judgment on David Dellinger or anybody else with respect to that.

The only rationale of 42(a) is that the judge should have summary power so that he doesn't have to impanel a jury during the proceedings and stop the trial and should be able to punish summarily, but your Honor has read the opinion in Bloom where the Supreme Court says this should not be exercised after trial, that this is illegal and lacks all jurisdictional support, and I brought in Bloom, your Honor. I think it is proper here to indicate that in Bloom the Court says:

> "We hold that it is primarily because in terms of considerations which make the right of jury trial fundamental in criminal cases, there is no substantial difference between serious contempts and other serious crimes. Indeed, in contempt cases an even more compelling argument can be made for providing a right to jury trial as a protection against the arbitrary exercise of official power. Contempt conduct, though a public wrong, often strikes at the most vulnerable and human qualities of a judge's temperament, even when the contempt is not a direct insult to the court or the judge, it frequently represents a rejection of judicial authority or an interference with the judicial process or with the duties of officers of the court. We place little credence in the notion that the independence of the judiciary hangs on the power to try contempt summarily and are not persuaded that the additional time and expense possibly involved in submitting serious contempts to juries will seriously handicap the effective functioning of the courts. We do not deny that serious punishment must sometimes be imposed for contempt but we reject the contention that such punishment must be imposed without a right to jury trial."

Although Rule 42(a), the rule under which your Honor has alleged he is acting, is based in part on the premise that it is not necessary specially to present the facts of a contempt which occurred in the very presence of the judge, it also rests on the need to maintain order and the deliberative atmosphere in the courtroom. The power of a judge to quell disturbance cannot attend upon the impanelling of a jury.

There is, therefore, a strong temptation to make exception to the rule we establish today for disorders in the courtroom. We are convinced, however, that no special rule is needed and the only rationale for doing what your Honor is doing is to preserve order in the courtroom. Your Honor chose to wait, as you have explained in your lengthy preface, you chose to wait because you said it might delay the trial further to act then, but in choosing to wait you have to accept the consequences that 42(b) applies and not 42(a) because there is no rationale to 42(a) when it is delayed until the end because you are not quelling a disturbance here at all and therefore you are under 42(b) which requires notice and a hearing, and in those cases provided by law—and this is one of them—for a jury trial.

THE COURT: I have considered - -

MR. KUNSTLER: Just let me finish this one thing, your Honor.

- - because 42(b) says if the contempt charge involved disrespect to or criticism of a judge, that judge is disqualified from presiding at the trial or hearing except with the defendant's consent.

A VOICE: Right on.

MR. KUNSTLER: The defendants do not consent to your Honor sitting on their contempts and therefore I think your Honor is totally without jurisdiction to do what you are doing today and to sentence people from summary contempt after the trial is over.

You made that decision and I think you have to abide by the law after the decision.

And the Supreme Court has interpreted 42(a) and (b) as I have indicated. Bloom vs. Illinois, 88 Supreme Court, 1477, which is only last year, I believe, 1968—late 1968—a late 1968 decision. I also refer your Honor to Unger against Serafine, 84 Supreme Court 841, a 1964 decision, and I refer your Honor to Justice Frankfurter because in his dissent in Sacka, which is some years ago and which has been repudiated by Bloom, in Sacka the court says:

> "At the end of the trial the judge was not confronted with the alternatives of doing what he did or allowing the contempt to go unpunished. The question was not punishment but who should punish."

And the court goes on to say—or Mr. Justice Frankfurter says:

> "Whatever occasion may have existed during the trial for sitting in judgment upon claims of personal victimization, it ceased after the trial had terminated."

And I think, your Honor, the reasoning of Mr. Justice Frankfurter, which he states very clearly in that decision, he says:

> "Among the restrictions to be applied as a matter of course are two basic principles of our law that no

judge should sit in a case in which he is personally involved and that no criminal punishment should be meted out except upon notice and due hearing."

And I think your Honor is sitting in judgment in a case in which you are personally involved and that the rules of criminal procedure, Rule 42(a) and (b), and the Bloom decision preclude your Honor doing that.

So I think your Honor is acting without jurisdiction and should refer this matter on notice and hearing to another judge for a proper jury trial in this case.

THE COURT: I do not share your view. Mr. Dellinger, do you care to say anything?

DEFENDANT DELLINGER: Yes.

THE COURT: Not a legal argument.

DEFENDANT DELLINGER: No. I want to make a statement on the context - -

THE COURT: Only in respect to punishment. I will hear you.

MR. DELLINGER: Yes. I think it all relates—and I hope you will do me the courtesy not to interrupt me while I am talking.

THE COURT: I won't interrupt you as long as you are respectful.

MR. DELLINGER: Well, I will talk about the facts and the facts don't always encourage false respect.

Now I want to point out first of all that the first two contempts cited against me concerned, one, the moratorium action and, secondly, support of Bobby Seale, the war against Vietnam, the aggression against Vietnam, and racism in this country, the two issues that this country refuses to solve, refuses to take seriously.

THE COURT: I hope you will excuse me, sir. You are not speaking strictly to what I gave you the privilege of speaking to. I ask you to say what you want to say in respect to punishment.

MR. DELLINGER: I think this relates to the punishment.

THE COURT: Get to the subject of punishment and I will be glad to hear you. I don't want you to talk politics.

DEFENDANT DELLINGER: You see, that's one of the reasons I have needed to stand up and speak anyway, because you have tried to keep what you call politics, which means the truth, out of this courtroom, just as the prosecution has.

THE COURT: I will ask you to sit down.

DEFENDANT DELLINGER: Therefore it is necessary - -

THE COURT: I won't let you go on any further.

DEFENDANT DELLINGER: You want us to be like good Germans supporting the evils of our decade and then when we refused to be good Germans and came to Chicago and demonstrated, despite the threats and intimidations of the establishment, now you want us to be like good Jews, going quietly and politely to the concentration camps while you and this Court suppress freedom and the truth. And the fact is that I am not prepared to do that. You want us to stay in our place like black people were supposed to stay in their place - -

THE COURT: Mr. Marshal, I will ask you to have Mr. Dellinger sit down.

DEFENDANT DELLINGER: - - like poor people were supposed to stay in their place, like people without formal education are supposed to stay in their place, like women are supposed to stay in their place - -

THE COURT: I will ask you to sit down.

DEFENDANT DELLINGER: Like children are supposed to stay in their place, like lawyers—for whom I thank—I thank you—are supposed to stay in their places.

It is a travesty on justice and if you had any sense at all you would know that that record that you read condemns you and not us.

THE COURT: All right.

DEFENDANT DELLINGER: And it will be one of thousands and thousands of rallying points for a new generation of Americans who will not put up with tyranny, will not put up with a facade of democracy without the reality.

THE COURT: Mr. Marshal, will you please ask him to keep quiet?

THE MARSHAL: Be quiet, Mr. Dellinger.

DEFENDANT DELLINGER: You take an hour to read the contempt citation, you have the power to send me away for years, but you will not even give me one tenth the time to speak what is relevant by my deserts and by history's deserts as well. I sat here and heard that man Mr. Foran say evil, terrible, dishonest things that even he could not believe in—I heard him say that and you expect me to be quiet and accept that without speaking up.

People no longer will be quiet. People are going to speak up. I am an old man and I am just speaking feebly and not too well, but I reflect the spirit that will echo - -

THE COURT: Take him out - -

DEFENDANT DELLINGER: - - throughout the world - -

(Applause)

DEFENDANT DELLINGER - - comes from my children who came yesterday - -

(Complete disorder in the courtroom.)

DEFENDANT DELLINGER: Leave my daughter alone. Leave my daughter alone.

A VOICE: Tyrants. Tyrants.

MR. JACQUES LEVY: Leave her alone.

A VOICE: Leave that girl alone.

MR. KUNSTLER: What are you doing to us, your Honor?

A VOICE: Justice in the United States today.

A VOICE: That's what you have done, Judge Hoffman. That's what you have done.

A VOICE: That man up there. That man up there. It's his fault.

DEFENDANT RUBIN: Heil Hitler. Heil Hitler. Heil Hitler. Heil Hitler. I hope you're satisfied.

A VOICE: You mockie Hitler.

MR. KUNSTLER: My life has come to nothing, I am not anything any more. You destroyed me and everybody else. Put me in jail now, for God's sakes, and get me out of this place. Come to mine now. Come to mine now, Judge, please. Please. I beg you. Come to mine. Do me, too. I don't want to be out.

A VOICE: She's not going to yell out.

A VOICE: Leave her alone.

THE MARSHAL: Will the press sit down?

A VOICE: Get your fucking storm troopers out of here.

THE CLERK: Be seated, please. Be seated.

THE MARSHAL: All right, sit down. Have a seat.

DEFENDANT DELLINGER: Well, you preserved law and order here, Judge. The day will come when you'll take every one of us.

DEFENDANT RUBIN: Heil Hitler. That's how you should be greeted.

THE COURT: With respect to Specification No. 1 and all of the other specifications referred to by the Court this morning and now about to be referred to again, the Court finds the defendant Dellinger guilty of direct contempt in the presence of the Court. With respect to - -

DEFENDANT DELLINGER: I don't want to interrupt but there was one thing I wanted to say, namely, that the Court was in contempt of human life and dignity and truth and justice and if that's the way the punishment should be decided - -

THE COURT: If you don't, then don't.

With respect to Specification 1, the Court commits the defendant Dellinger to the custody of the Attorney General of the United States for imprisonment for a period of six months.

With respect to Specification 2, the Court commits the defendant Dellinger to the custody of the Attorney General of the United States or his authorized representative for a period of one month.

With respect to Specification 3, the Court commits the defendant Dellinger to the custody of the Attorney General of the United States or his authorized representative for imprisonmnt for a period of seven days.

With respect to Specification 4, the Court commits the defendant Dellinger to the custody of the Attorney General of the United States or his authorized representative for a term of three months.

With respect to Specification 5, the Court commits the defendant Dellinger to the custody of the Attorney General of the United States or his authorized representative for imprisonment for a period of seven days.

With respect to Specification 6, the Court commits the defendant Dellinger to the custody of the Attorney General of the United States or his authorized representative for imprisonment for a period of one day.

With respect to Specification 7, the Court commits the defendant Dellinger to the custody of the Attorney General of the United States or his authorized representative for imprisonment for a period of seven days.

With respect to Specification 8, the Court commits the defendant Dellinger to the custody of the Attorney General or his representative for imprisonment for a period of one month.

With respect to Specification 9, the Court commits the defendant Dellinger to the custody of the Attorney General or his representative for a period of one day.

With respect to Specification 10, the Court commits the defendant Dellinger to the custody of the Attorney General or his authorized representative for a period of one day.

With respect to Specification 11, the Court commits the defendant Dellinger to the custody of the Attorney General of the United States or his authorized representative for a period of seven days for imprisonment.

With respect to Specification 12, the Court commits the defendant Dellinger to the custody of the Attorney General or his authorized representative for a term of one day.

With respect to Specification 13, the Court commits the defendant Dellinger to the custody of the Attorney General of the United States or his authorized representative for a term of two days for imprisonment.

With respect to Specification 14, the Court commits the defendant Dellinger to the custody of the Attorney General of the United States or his authorized representative for a term of four days.

With respect to Specification 15, the Court commits the defendant Dellinger to the custody of the Attorney General of the United States or his authorized representative for a term of four days.

With respect to Specification 16, the Court commits the defendant Dellinger to the custody of the Attorney General of the United States or his authorized representative for a term of three days for imprisonment.

With respect to Specification 17, the Court commits the defendant Dellinger to the custody of the Attorney General of the United States or his authorized representative for imprisonment for a term of six days.

With respect to Specification 18, the Court commits the defendant Dellinger to the custody of the Attorney General of the United States or his authorized representative for a term of two days.

With respect to Specification 19, the Court commits the defendant Dellinger to the custody of the Attorney General of the United States or his authorized representative for imprisonment for a term of six days.

With respect to Specification 20, the Court commits the defendant Dellinger to the custody of the Attorney General or his authorized representative for a term of four days for imprisonment.

With respect to Specification 21, the Court commits the defendant Dellinger to the custody of the Attorney General of the United States or his authorized representative for a term of three days for imprisonment.

With respect to Specification 22, the Court commits the defendant Dellinger to the custody of the Attorney General of the United States or his authorized representative for imprisonment for a term of three days.

With respect to Specification 23, the Court commits the defendant Dellinger to the custody of the Attorney General of the United States or his authorized representative for imprisonment for a term of five days.

With respect to Specification 24, the Court commits the defendant Dellinger to the custody of the Attorney General of the United States or his authorized representative for a term of six months imprisonment.

With respect to Specification 25, the Court commits the defendant Dellinger to the custody of the Attorney General of the United States or his authorized representative for a term of seven days for imprisonment.

With respect to Specification 26, the Court commits the defendant Dellinger to the custody of the Attorney General of the United States for imprisonment for a term of four months.

That is 26?

THE CLERK: 26, yes, your Honor.

THE COURT: With respect to Specification No. 27, the Court commits the defendant Dellinger to the custody of the Attorney General of the United States for imprisonment for a term of two days.

With respect to Specification 28, the Court commits the defendant Dellinger to the custody of the Attorney General of the United States for imprisonment for a term of two days.

With respect to Specification 29, the Court commits the defendant Dellinger to the custody of the Attorney General of the United States for imprisonment for a term of seven days.

With respect to Specification 30, the Court commits the defendant Dellinger to the custody of the Attorney General of the United States for imprisonment for a term of five months.

With respect to Specification 31, the Court commits the defendant Dellinger to the custody of the Attorney General of the United States or his authorized representative for imprisonment for a term of seven days.

With respect to Specification 32, the Court commits the defendant Dellinger to the custody of the Attorney General of the United States for imprisonment for a term of seven days.

Mr. Marshal, the marshals will please remove Mr. Dellinger into custody. All of these sentences will run cumulatively and consecutively.

DEFENDANT DELLINGER: Right on, beautiful people, black people, Vietnamese, poor people, young people, everybody fighting for liberty and justices. Right on.

Not to mention Latin Americans.

MR. KUNSTLER: Your Honor, I would like to make a motion for bail pending appeal for Mr. Dellinger.

THE COURT: I would not bail anybody for contempt, direct contempt in the presence of the Court. It is not bailable.

MR. KUNSTLER: I would like your Honor to deny my motion on the record.

THE COURT: I deny your motion and in view of his conduct here, even if it were bailable, I certainly wouldn't do so.

Besides, I think to admit him to bail on appeal here would be frivolous in the opinion of the Court.

MR. KUNSTLER: Your Honor, I also move to set aside the contempt which you have just adjudged him guilty of on the grounds you lack the jurisdictional power pursuant to the Federal Rules of Criminal Procedure.

DEFENDANT DAVIS: You have just jailed one of the most beautiful and one of the most courageous men in the United States.

THE COURT: All right. Now we will talk about you, Mr. Davis.

I direct the United States Attorney to prepare the necessary documents in connection with these sentences—Mr. Schultz? I don't see Mr. Foran. There you are. Will you?

MR. FORAN: Yes, your Honor.

B. Jones

B. Jones
SEALE
CONSPIRACY 8
10-69

DAVIS

THE COURT: With respect to the defendant Rennard Davis, *Specification* 1: On October 22, the defendant Davis arrived in the courtroom 18 minutes after the start of the court session. The Court had denied a motion to permit the defendant to bring a cake into the courtroom. Upon arrival the defendant Davis announced in a loud voice:

> "MR. DAVIS: They arrested the cake, Bobby. They arrested it." Official Transcript Page 3,640. **2 days**

Specification 2: At the close of the court session on October 28, the defendant Davis refused to rise when the Court left the bench at the end of the session. Official Transcript Page 4,618-19. **1 day**

Specification 3: On October 29, at the conclusion of the morning session, the defendant Davis refused to rise when the Court left the bench. Official Transcript Pages 4,728-29. **1 day**

Specification 4: On October 29, when a recess was called during the afternoon session, the defendant Davis refused to rise when the Court left the bench. Official Transcript Page 4,763. **1 day**

Specification 5: At the beginning of the morning court session on October 30, the defendant Davis refused to rise at the direction of the marshal when the Court entered the chamber. Official Transcript Page 4,801. **1 day**

Specification 6. On October 30, when the jury returned to the courtroom, the defendant Davis rose from his seat at the defense table and made the following speech to the jury:

> "Ladies and gentlemen of the jury, I am trying

to say he was being tortured while you were out of this room by these marshals. They came and tortured him while you are out of the room. It is terrible what is happening. It is terrible what is happening." Official Transcript Page 4,845. **2 months**

Specification 7: On October 30, when the Court called a recess, the defendant Davis refused to rise as the Court left the bench. Official Transcript Page 4,849-50. **1 day**

Specification 8: On October 30, at the beginning of the afternoon session the defendant Davis refused to rise in response to the marshal's directions when the Court entered the room. Official Transcript Page 4,853. **1 day**

Specification 9: On November 26, when the Court requested Mr. Dellinger to sit down, the defendant Davis commented in a loud voice from his place at the table:

"MR. DAVIS: Why don't you gag all of us, Judge?
THE COURT: Who said that?
MR. DAVIS: Bobby Seale said that.
MR. SCHULTZ: The defendant Davis said that, your Honor.
THE COURT: The defendant Davis. Did you get that, Miss Reporter?" Official Transcript page 8,078. **14 days**

Specification 10: On December 15, Mr. Davis and other defendants laughed out loud at the Court while the Court was making a ruling on a motion. The defendant Davis acknowledged his laughter.

"MR. DAVIS: It was me that was laughing, your Honor." Official Transcript Page 11,179. **7 days**

Specification 11: On January 9, the defendant Davis commented out loud from the defense table:

"MR. DAVIS: Guilty until proven innocent." Official Transcript Page 14,716. **7 days**

Specification 12: On January 12, the Court refused to permit one of the attorneys to leave the room during the proceedings. Mr. Davis interrupted the orderly proceedings by rising and stating:

> "MR. DAVIS: Your Honor, my rights are being jeopardized by Mr. Weinglass not being able to leave the courtroom to interview witnesses.
>
> THE COURT: Will you sit down, sir.
>
> MR. DAVIS: If you want to protect my rights, I would kindly ask you to allow him to interview witnesses."

This outburst came in front of the jury. Official Transcript Page 15,074. **1 day**

Specification 13: On January 13, during the direct examination of the witness Bond, the defendant Davis stated from the defense table in a voice loud enough for the jury to hear:

> "MR. DAVIS: This is a joke." Official Transcript Page 15,364. **7 days**

Specification 14: On January 23, while the defendant Davis was on the stand as a witness on direct testimony, the Judge was required to make an evidentiary ruling. After the Court had considered a document and ruled that it could not come into evidence, Davis accused the Court of having ruled without reading the document.

> "THE COURT: I shall not take it in. In the presence of the jury I will sustain the objection of the Government.
>
> MR. WEINGLASS: Your Honor has read the document?
>
> THE COURT: I have looked it over.
>
> THE WITNESS: You never read it. I was watching you. You read two pages.
>
> THE COURT: Mr. Marshal, will you instruct that witness on the stand that he is not to address me. You, Mr. Marshal, you are closest to him.
>
> THE MARSHAL: Face this way.
>
> THE WITNESS: I will look at the Judge.
>
> THE COURT: Do you have what the witness said, Miss Reporter?
>
> THE REPORTER: Yes.
>
> MR. WEINGLASS: I didn't hear that.
>
> THE WITNESS: I said he didn't read the docu-

ment. I watched him. He never looked at it.

THE COURT: He said 'You never read it,' looking at me.

THE WITNESS: I meant the Judge did not read the document." Official Transcript, Page 17,443-44.
2 months

Specification 15: On January 23, the witness Davis falsely accused the Judge of sleeping during the proceedings.

"A. You are making me memorize them. If I can read them—is that admissible? The Judge is asleep.

THE COURT: What did he say?

THE WITNESS: I am sorry. I thought you had gone to sleep. I am sorry.

THE COURT: Oh, no. I am listening very carefully. I just wanted you to repeat. I wanted to be sure I heard what you said." Official Transcript, Page 17,542. **2 months**

Specification 16: During the time the witness Davis was being cross-examined by the Goverment Attorney, which is reported in the transcript, Page 17,820 through 18,245, Davis continually volunteered remarks and observations. He did not restrict his answer to the scope of the question posed. The Court was required to instruct him no less than 43 times to restrict his answers to the scope of the question posed. No sooner were these orders given than they were violated over and over and over again. This violation of 43 Court orders in the period of three days must be considered contemptuous. **6 months**

Specification 17: On January 28, the defendant Davis interrupted Mr. Schultz, the Assistant United States Attorney, to make the following remarks:

"MR. SCHULTZ: I wish Davis, who was such a gentle boy on the stand for the last couple of days, smiling at the jury and pretending he was just a little boy next door, would stop whispering and talking to me while I am talking.

MR. DAVIS: You are a disgrace, sir. I say you are

a disgrace. I really say you are a disgrace." Official Transcript, Page 18,397. **3 months**

Specification 18: On February 2, after an extended speech by Mr. Kunstler, there was an outburst of applause in the courtroom. Mr. Davis participated in that applause and admitted having done so. It is reported in the record as follows:

"THE COURT: Everyone of those applauders --
VOICES: Right on. Right on.
THE COURT: Out with those applauders.
MR. DAVIS: I applauded, too, your Honor. Throw me out." Official Transcript, Page 19,113.

14 days

Specification 19: On February 2, during the testimony of the witness Lynskey, Mr. Kunstler brought the Reverend Abernathy into the courtroom. The Court admonished him for this disruptive tactic and the following comment was made by the defendant Davis:

"MR. KUNSTLER: If it is disrupting to put a witness on the stand, I never heard of disrupting.
MR. DAVIS: I never heard of a case where you couldn't put a witness on the stand." Official Transcript, Page 19,160. **7 days**

Specification 20: On February 4, during the testimony of the witness Riordan, Mr. Dellinger spoke out. In the ensuing disturbance, Mr. Davis inserted the following remarks:

"THE COURT: Take that man into custody. Mr. Marshal, take that man into custody.
VOICES: Right on, right on.
MR. SCHULTZ: Into custody.
THE COURT: Into custody.
VOICES: Right on.
MR. DAVIS: Go ahead, Dick Schultz, put everybody in jail." Official Transcript, Page 19,671.

2 months

Specification 21: On February 4, when the Court announced that it had determined to revoke the defendant

Dellinger's bail, there was an outburst in the courtroom. Mr. Davis inserted the following remark:

"THE COURT: This isn't the first word, and I won't argue this.

MR. DAVIS: This Court is bull shit.

THE COURT: There he is saying the same words again.

MR. DAVIS: No, I say it."

* * *

"MR. RUBIN: Everything in this court is bull shit.

MR. DAVIS: I associate myself with Dave Dellinger completely 100 per cent. This is the most obscene court I have ever seen."

* * *

"MR. DAVIS: Mr. Rubin's wife they are now taking - -

MR. RUBIN: Keep your hands off her. You see them taking away my wife?

MR. DAVIS: Why don't you gag the press, too, and the attorneys, gag them." Official Transcript, Page 19,778-79. **5 months**

Specification 22: On February 5, after the Court had determined that it had heard sufficient argument it ordered Mr. Weinglass to discontinue arguing. The Court ruled. Mr. Davis then rose with the following statements:

"MR. WEINGLASS: Your Honor will not permit me to continue a legal argument?

THE COURT: You heard what I said. I deny the motion.

MR. DAVIS: May we defend ourselves if our lawyers can't?" Official Transcript, Page 19,800-01.

And slightly later, during the same argument:

"THE COURT: Have that man sit down. I will hear no further argument on this motion.

MR. DAVIS: Could I make a motion to defend myself since you won't let my lawyer represent me?" Official Transcript, Page 19,814. **14 days**

Specification 23: On February 7, at the conclusion of the government's rebuttal case, the defense moved for an early recess of the Saturday session. The purpose of this recess purportedly was to permit them to secure two additional witnesses and a certified copy of an Illinois court record. While the Court was discussing this request with Mr. Kunstler, there was a loud laugh from the defense table. The Court determined that there was no point in granting courtesies to parties unable to conduct themselves with a modicum of respect for the Court. Mr. Davis then made several comments to the Court:

"MR. DAVIS: Is it not possible to put on our defense?"

"MR. DAVIS: We can't put on our witnesses." Official Transcript Page 20270.

The jury returned, and the argument resumed in their presence. Mr. Davis, before the jury, interjected the following remark when Mr. Foran spoke in favor of the Court's ruling:

"MR. DAVIS: Save the Judge." Official Transcript Page 20276.

Shortly thereafter the Court ruled adversely to Mr. Dellinger on a special application concerning his confinement. Mr. Davis greeted this ruling with the following sarcastic comments:

"MR. DAVIS: That's fair. That's fair." Official Transcript, Page 20,282.

"MR. DAVIS: Have a good week-end, Judge." Official Transcript, Page 20,283. **1 month**

Which of you two lawyers represent Mr. Davis? You represent Mr. Davis, Mr. Weinglass? I will hear from you.

MR. WEINGLASS: I will be very brief, your Honor. Mr. Davis will speak in his own behalf. I do want to point out to the Court that I incorporate Mr. Kunstler's motion with respect to Mr. Dellinger. The court is proceeding without - -

THE COURT: I will consider that you have taken the same position with respect to the Bloom case.

MR. WEINGLASS: Yes, that the Court is proceeding without authority or jurisdiction. The Court has a limited authority to preserve in the midst of a proceeding but is without authority to usurp the function of a jury in imposing punishment for conduct, even conduct which is before the court.

Secondly, I want to point out to the Court that Specifications 2, 3, 4, 5, 7, and 8 all deal with failure to rise. Some of those specifications are at the close of the court session. Some are at the start of the court session.

Under a case, which the case name fails me just now; however, it was cited last year in the Seventh Circuit Court of Appeals—I believe it is United States v. Hall, although I might have the defendant's name wrong—in that opinion, the court found two spectators guilty of contempt for failure to rise. However, the court pointed out very carefully in its opinion that the obligations of a defendant are otherwise, and I assume by that the court indicated that a defendant has no obligation to rise when the court either enters the room or leaves the room.

The only reason why a spectator has the obligation and the defendant does not is because the failure of some spectators to rise might cause a disturbance among other spectators who might feel incensed over the fact that certain of their fellow spectators are not rising, and in that area, namely, in the spectators' section, there is potential for disruption. But at the defense, there is none, and for that reason, the defendants do not have the obligation, whereas the spectators do.

Second, that opinion also points out very clearly that there is a different rule at the end of the day than at the beginning because the failure to arise at the end of the day can in no effect be disruptive of anything, the court proceedings having already been terminated. So if the rule applies at all to defendants—I don't concede it does—it applies merely to the outset of the court's business and not to its conclusion.

Thirdly, your Honor has read the complete transcript against the defendant Davis. It has taken longer than twenty minutes, I believe it is twenty-two minutes.

Now in this five-month trial, the entire time, according to your Honor's own reading of it of disruption is a total of twenty-two minutes out of more than five months of trial time.

I want to point out to the Court that in not one single instance was it necessary for the Court to remove the jury from the room in any of these so-called 23 contempt citations.

Secondly, the Court did not distinguish, and I felt it should have, the contempt in the presence of the jury as opposed to those not in the presence of the jury. As your Honor knows, on the "arrest of the cake," the jury was not in the room, and that is one of the first.

The last remark, the remark of Mr. Davis in support of Mr. Dellinger, was not in the presence of the jury. I feel in any computation, approximately 50 percent of the so-called disruptive actions attributed to Mr. Davis were not at all disruptive because the jury was out of the room.

So those are my three main positions, legal positions, with respect to the point of sentence for contempt, and Mr. Davis will address himself to the factual portions of the contempt citation.

THE COURT: Mr. Davis, do you care to be heard?

MR. DAVIS: Yes. I am sorry I do not have the complete transcript with me so that I could report on each of the 23 counts in detail.

This morning you said that the only alternative to what I have done here in the courtroom is anarchy, and perhaps you are right. You have said as well that as a matter of law, there is no defense for what we have done, and I believe that there is a defense for what we have done.

I believe that what we have done is wholly defensible and I want to first of all put my 23 incidences in a general context of this trial, the context that motivated me to say what I did say, and then I would like to put the 23 incidences in the specific context at the time the words were uttered.

You may not believe this, but we came here to have a trial with a law that we regarded as unconstitutional and unfair and a jury that was inadequately selected.

We came here, nevertheless, to present our full case to this jury so that this jury might decide on whether or not our movement was just in coming to Chicago, or whether or not, as the government charged, we came here to incite a riot.

One of the first things that you did was to deny our right to have elementary questions asked of the jury, questions that would have determined whether or not the jury had an understanding of the nature of the case.

THE COURT: You are not speaking to the issue here.

MR. DAVIS: I am speaking to the issue here. I want to speak about the general context of unfairness in which this trial has proceeded.

THE COURT: That does not relate to these 23 specifications, sir.

MR. DAVIS: I think that it relates very specifically.

THE COURT: I don't think they do and I shall not hear you on anything except those I have outlined.

MR. DAVIS: All right.

Well, let me begin with the first incident, on October 22, when I was eighteen minutes late. We brought a birthday cake to this Courthouse for Bobby Seale, a man who was brought into this case simply because he was the Chairman of the Black Panther Party and is being railroaded to the electric chair for murder, alleged murder, in Connecticut, and a man whom the Nixon Administration has decided to keep in jail for the rest of his life if possible, and we thought it was a humane and decent thing to do, to join together with other people in celebrating his birthday.

We asked the marshals outside if it might not be possible for a little bit of time before the Court began without interrupting the time of this Court, if we might bring Bobby with us together so that we could have this birthday cake, and what happened outside in the corridor was that the marshals came up. There was a fight outside over a birthday cake, believe it or not. People were pushed and shoved. The cake was confiscated, and I came into the courtroom with Bobby Seale sitting here, and I said, out of the presence of the jury, "They have arrested your birthday cake, Bobby. They have arrested it."

On October 28, this whole incident—and you have several of them here—about the refusal to rise when you come into the room.

Let me just put that particular incident into context, if I may.

Bobby Seale that day was attempting once again to cross-examine a witness in this case, William Frapolly, because he did not have a lawyer here, a lawyer that has

represented him on many previous cases, a lawyer that he felt had to represent him here.
THE COURT: I will not hear you in that reference to Bobby Seale.
MR. DAVIS: I am putting the specific incidents in context.
THE COURT: I have heard enough about Bobby Seale and the lawyers he said he didn't have and the lawyers he did have. I don't want to hear about that.
MR. DAVIS: Just a matter of minutes before you cited me for the second count, Bobby Seale cited a Federal Code saying that he has a right to defend himself. Then you will recall the marshal ordered him into his chair.

Bobby then said from his chair, 'It's an old Reconstruction law, and you won't recognize it.'

THE COURT: I won't hear you about that, and if you persist in that, I will - -
MR. DAVIS: How am I to explain to you that what happened to Bobby Seale directly led to my feeling that I could not stand what you did to Bobby Seale at that moment.

Your refusal to allow him to cross-examine a witness and to have his elementary constitutional rights was the reason I did not stand for you at that time. Bobby Seale did not stand at that time.

THE COURT: In the first place, what you say is not accurate.
MR. DAVIS: I am reading from the record. I am reading from the record.
THE COURT: In the first place, before we ever got to the point of discussing his lawyer, you know what he called me.
MR. DAVIS: I do.
THE COURT: I wouldn't - -
MR. DAVIS: He called you a racist, a fascist, and a pig.
THE COURT: Several times.
MR. DAVIS: Many times, and not enough.
THE COURT: I will ask you to sit down.
MR. DAVIS: I have not completed my response.
THE COURT: I will ask you to sit down. I didn't ask you to get up here to further insult me.
MR. DAVIS: I have a right, I have a right to talk about

my intentions on each of these 23 incidences.

THE COURT: You have no right to make insulting remarks in your remarks. That has been the trouble with this whole trial.

MR. DAVIS: The trouble with the whole trial, Judge Hoffman - -

THE COURT: I will ask you to sit down, Mr. Davis.

MR. DAVIS: - - each and every time we attempt to make clear - -

THE COURT: Put that man in a chair.

MR. WEINGLASS: It is a fundamental right for a defendant to speak before he is sentenced.

THE COURT: It is not a fundamental right for any man to stand up and insult the trial judge. I won't take it.

MR. WEINGLASS: Your Honor - -

THE COURT: I have stood it for nearly five months, but I won't take it again.

MR. WEINGLASS: Your Honor, he has a right.

THE COURT: He has no right to do that.

MR. WEINGLASS: He has the right to place the allegations against him [in] a factual context, and that is what he is doing.

THE COURT: He has no right to say what he just said, and I won't permit it, and I won't permit you to argue it.

MR. DAVIS: Judge, you represent all that is old, ugly, bigoted, and repressive in this country, and I will tell you that the spirit at this defense table is going to devour your sickness in the next generation.

THE COURT: Mr. Clerk, with respect to the specification named hereafter, the defendant Davis will be committed to the custody of the Attorney General of the United States or his authorized representative for imprisonment for direct contempt committed in the presence of the Court as follows: *Specification* 1, 2 days; *Specification* 2, 1 day; *Specification* 3, 1 day; *Specification* 4, 1 day; *Specification* 5, 1 day; *Specification* 6, 2 months; *Specification* 7, 1 day; *Specification* 8, 1 day; *Specification* 9, 14 days; *Specification* 10, 7 days; *Specification* 11, 7 days; *Specification* 12, 1 day; *Specification* 13, 7 days; *Specification* 14, 2 days—or 2 months, rather, I beg your pardon; *Specification* 14, 2 months; *Specification* 15, 2 months; *Specification* 16, 6 months; *Specification* 17, 3 months; *Specification* 18, 14 months; *Specification* 19—wait a minute—14 days, pardon me; *Specification* 19, 7 days; *Specification* 20, 2 months; *Specification* 21, 5 months; *Specification* 22, 14 days; *Specification* 23, 1 month; The United States Attorney is directed to prepare the necessary papers in this connection. I direct the marshal to remove Mr. Davis to the custody of the Attorney General.

The sentences are consecutive.

MR. RUBIN: See you in jail.

MR. HOFFMAN: The whole country is in jail.

MR. WEINER: See you in jail, brother.

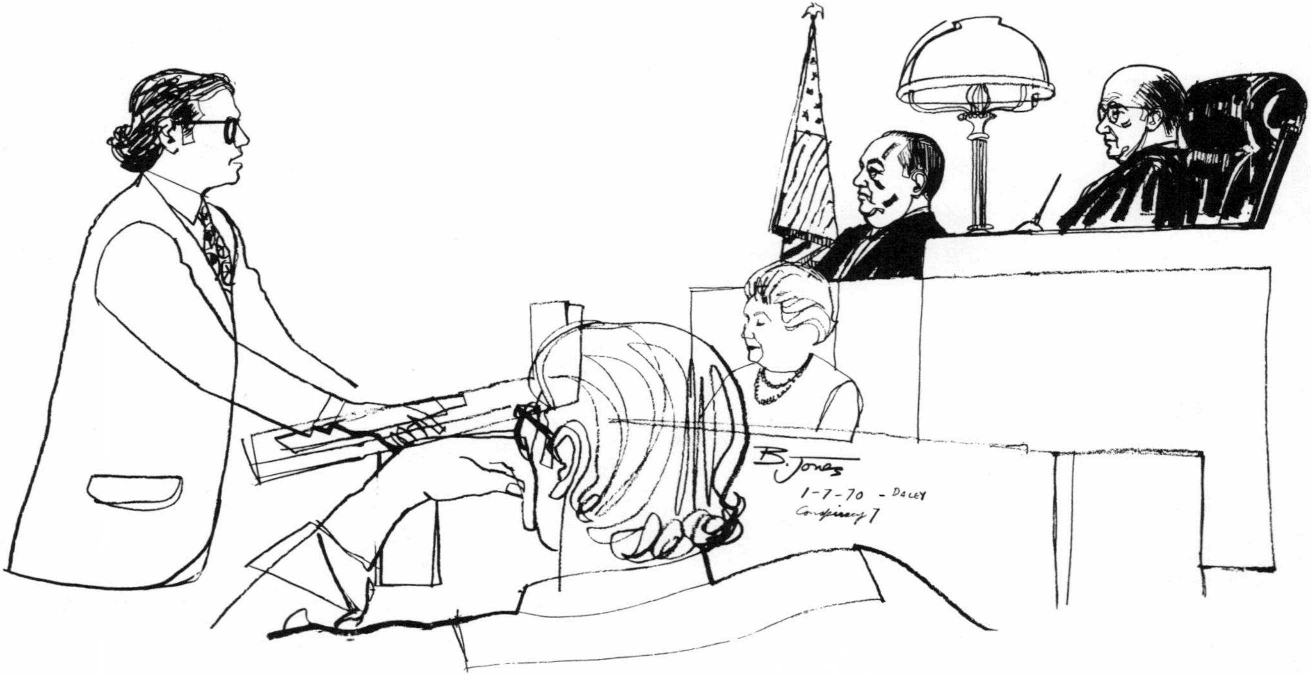
B. Jones
1-7-70 - DALEY
Conspiracy 7

HAYDEN

THE COURT: We come now to the consideration of the matter of Thomas Hayden.

Specification 1: On September 26, during opening remarks by Mr. Schultz, the defendant Hayden rose and shook his fist in the direction of the jurors. The following colloquy occurred:

> "THE COURT: This will be but a minute, Mr. Marshal. Who is the last defendant you named?
> MR. SCHULTZ: Mr. Hayden.
> THE COURT: Hayden. Who was the one before?
> MR. SCHULTZ: Davis, and prior to that was Dellinger.
> THE COURT: The one that shook his fist in the direction of the jury?
> MR. HAYDEN: That is my customary greeting, your Honor.
> THE COURT: It may be your customary greeting, but we do not allow shaking of fists in this courtroom. I made that clear.
> MR. HAYDEN: It implied no disrespect for the jury; it is my customary greeting.
> THE COURT: Regardless of what it implies, sir, there will be no fist shaking, and I caution you not to repeat it.
> MR. HAYDEN: May I use that gesture to my fellow defendants, my attorneys?
> THE COURT: That applies to all of the defendants. Mr. Marshal, bring the jury back." Official Transcript, Page 5. **2 days**

Specification 2: At the end of the afternoon session on October 28, the defendant Hayden refused to rise in the customary manner when directed to do so by the Marshal. Official Transcript, Page 4,618-19, **1 day**

Specification 3: On October 29, while the Court was engaged in a colloquy with Mr. Seale and Mr. Schultz, Mr. Hayden rose and made the following comment:

> "MR. SEALE: Will you please tell the Court the reason I am talking is because I didn't want a spontaneous response to any kind of activity that might go on. Will you please tell the Court I said to keep cool.
> MR. HAYDEN: They did nothing when Bobby Seale was physically attacked. They did nothing.
> THE COURT: Will you remain silent, you defendants, please. You have a lawyer.
> MR. HAYDEN: Just as he ordered them to.
> THE COURT: Mr. Marshal, bring in the jury."
> Official Transcript, Page 4,635. **1 month**

Specification 4: On October 29, at the close of the morning session, the defendant Hayden refused to rise in the customary manner when instructed to do so by the marshals. Official Transcript, Pages 4,728-29. **1 day**

Specification 5; During the afternoon session of October 29 when the Court was compelled to call a recess, the defendant Hayden refused to rise again, despite the instructions of the marshal. Page 4,763. **1 day**

Specification 6: On October 30, at the beginning of the morning session, the defendant Hayden refused to rise in the customary manner when the Judge entered the courtroom. Page 4,801. **1 day**

Specification 7: On October 30, when the Court was compelled to deal with Mr. Seale because of previous outbursts, Mr. Hayden indulged in the following rhetoric, rising to address the Court:

> "MR. HAYDEN: Your Honor, could I address you?
> THE COURT: No, you may not, sir. You have a lawyer. That is what lawyers are for. I am not permitted under the decisions of the Supreme Court to let you speak.
> MR. HAYDEN: All I want to say is that - -
> THE COURT: Sit down, please.

MR. HAYDEN: Bobby Seale should not be put in a position of slavery.
THE COURT: Mr. Marshal - -
MR. HAYDEN: He wants to defend himself.
THE COURT: Tell that man to sit down. What is his name?
MR. HAYDEN: My name is Tom Hayden, your Honor.
THE COURT: All right.
MR. HAYDEN: I would just like to - -
THE COURT: Let the record show that Mr. Tom Hayden rose and addressed the Court, persisted in speaking despite the Court's direction that he sit down.

Bring in the jury, Mr. Marshal." Pages 4843-44

3 months

Specification 8: On October 30, when the Court was compelled to direct the marshals to restrain Mr. Seale, the following incident occurred:

"MR. SEALE: The Judge is not—he is not trying to give you no fair trial. That's what you are. You are lying. You know exactly what you are.
MR. HAYDEN: Now they are going to beat him, they are going to beat him.
MR. HOFFMAN: You may as well kill him if you are going to gag him. It seems that way, doesn't it?
THE COURT: You are not permitted to address the Court, Mr. Hoffman. You have a lawyer.
MR. HOFFMAN: This isn't a court. This is a neon oven.
MR. FORAN: That was the defendant Hoffman who spoke.
THE COURT: Let the record show that the defendant Hoffman spoke.
MR. SCHULTZ: Prior to that it was Mr. Hayden who was addressing the jury while they were walking out of here.
MR. HAYDEN: I was not addressing the jury. I was trying to protect Mr. Seale. The man is supposed to be silent when he sees another man's nose being smashed?

MR. HOFFMAN: The disruption started when these guys got into overkill. It is the same exact thing as last year in Chicago, the same exact thing.
THE COURT: Mr. Hoffman, you are directed to refrain from speaking. You are ordered to refrain from speaking. It is clear that after this morning that I think we cannot go ahead. I would be glad to entertain first suggestions from the government and then from the defense as to whether or not this trial shouldn't be recessed until two o'clock. I am perfectly willing to try to continue and do my best to discharge the obligations of my office.
MR. FORAN: Your Honor, I would like to see if we couldn't continue.
THE COURT: What do you say?
MR. FORAN: I would like to see if we could continue.
THE COURT: All right. It will take some time to —then we will take a brief recess.
MR. HAYDEN: I thought you were going to ask the defendants.
MR. WEINGLASS: Are we part—weren't we being invited to participate in the dialogue between then - -
MR. SCHULTZ: It is they who are disrupting this trial and now they want to make the decision as to whether or not we should proceed. It is incredible. It is they who are fostering this and they want to advise the Court - -
THE COURT: I have ordered a recess.
MR. WEINGLASS: The Court invited it.
THE COURT: Let the record show that.
MR. HAYDEN: Stand up. Stand up. Don't let them have any pretext.
THE COURT: Let the record show that Mr. Hayden asked people - -
MR. HAYDEN: I ask the people there to do what they were told and they did it.
THE COURT: Mr. Hayden, do not try to fill my sentences out for me and you are not permitted to speak except as you may come to be a witness in this case. You are not permitted to speak out loud. You may, of course, consult with your lawyer."

Official Transcript, Pages 4846-49. **4 months**

Specification 9: On January 9, the defendant Hayden openly and blatantly laughed at the Court while the Court was attempting to make a ruling. Official Transcript, Page 14,824. **1 day**

Specification 10: On January 28, while the Assistant United States Attorney was making a statement to the Court, Mr. Hayden rose and said:

"MR. HAYDEN: That is not true. Official Transcript Page 18,439. **7 days**

Specification 11: On January 28 the Court ruled that the defendants would not be permitted to call former United States Attorney General Ramsey Clark to the stand as a witness. The Court entered the following order:

"THE COURT: I therefore sustain the objection of the government to having the defense call this witness, Attorney General Clark, before the jury, and I also order both counsel for the government and the defense not to refer to this hearing or the subject matter thereof before the jury after the jury is brought in.

MR. SCHULTZ: Does that include the defendants also, your Honor? They speak more than their attorneys sometimes.

THE COURT: Yes, yes.

MR. SCHULTZ: Would you direct them also?

THE COURT: I would order the defendants not to discuss that matter in the presence of the jury. It would not be fair to either side." Official Transcript, Pages 18,524-25.

The very next day Mr. Hayden directly and defiantly violated that order in the presence of the jury. The following occurred:

"MR. FORAN: Your Honor, the theatre is beginning again. May we have the jury excused, your Honor, since the government is unable to respond, since the government is bound to proper conduct in a courtroom?

MR. HAYDEN: Proper conduct? You wouldn't let

the former Attorney General of the United States testify.

THE COURT: Ladies and gentlemen, I direct you to disregard the statement of Mr. Kunstler and I will have to excuse you with my usual orders.

MR. KUNSTLER: I think the jury should hear the whole thing.

THE COURT: There are a lot of thoughts you have had here.

MR. FORAN: Your Honor, you will note, of course, that Mr. Hayden shouted out in the courtroom about the Attorney General not testifying before the jury after a direct and clear direction from the Court after the Attorney General had testified extensively on voir dire that it should not be mentioned before the jury. Mr. Hayden jumped to his feet, shouted that out while the jury was filing out of the room.

MR. WEINGLASS: The statement is as accurate as other statements made by Mr. Foran. This time it was done right in the presence of the Court. Your Honor must—your Honor does not have to be reminded that if there is a shout in the courtroom and I think the fact that Mr. Foran had to state it is proof of the fact that it didn't occur. The Court has never failed to note for the record when there was a disturbance in the courtroom.

MR. FORAN: Mr. Weinglass, honor and honesty are clearly demonstrated to the Court, I'm sure. Your Honor saw Mr. Hayden make that statement. It was very loudly said, clearly said for purposes of influencing the jury improperly.

MR. WEINGLASS: All right. Let's put it to the test of honesty. Did your Honor see Mr. Hayden jump up to his feet?

MR. SCHULTZ: It didn't jump to his feet, but Mr. Hayden .made the statement, Mr. Weinglass. Didn't Mr. Hayden make the statement, Mr. Weinglass? Did Mr. Hayden make the statement?

MR. DELLINGER: Save him, Dick.

THE COURT: The marshals will exclude from the courtroom anyone who is disorderly.

MR. SCHULTZ: Your Honor, would you inquire

> of Mr. Weinglass whether or not he heard Mr. Hayden make the statement?
> THE COURT: No. I will let the record determine that.
> MR. HAYDEN: Your Honor, I did make the statement. I did not intend to, as the government said. It came out because I lost my temper after listening to what Mr. Foran said. I am sorry that I did it. I did not intend it.
> THE COURT: You got the answer.
> MR. HAYDEN: I did not understand - -
> MR. WEINGLASS: He did not jump to his feet. He did not shout.
> THE COURT: That rather convicts you, doesn't it, by your own client?" Official Transcript, Pages 18,827-30. **6 months**

THE COURT: Who represents Mr. Hayden?
MR. WEINGLASS: I do, your Honor.
I make the same argument incorporating Mr. Kunstler's initial remarks about Mr. Dellinger that the court is without jurisdiction to make the citation or to impose punishment. I won't deal with the facts of each of the eleven citations. Mr. Hayden will do that.
THE COURT: Mr. Hayden.
MR. HAYDEN: Your Honor, in view of your ruling about Mr. Davis, I would like to just ask will I be able to go through the eleven citations and present what I think is my defense?
THE COURT: You speak to the specifications and I will hear you, Mr. Hayden.
MR. HAYDEN: If I feel I should not be punished for the eleven, am I allowed to go through the eleven as part of my statement?
THE COURT: I will let you speak to any observations I have made here with respect to the eleven specifications.
MR. HAYDEN: Well, I think that many of the eleven speak for themselves. In the ones that seemed to me the most serious, in almost every instance it had to do with, as in the case of greeting the jury, a spontaneous gesture which, for instance, Jesse Jackson made from the witness stand to your Honor and which he made to the defen-

dants when he left the witness stand. It is a customary gesture for people like myself, people around the table, and evidently for Jesse Jackson.

THE COURT: I don't know Mr. Jackson. I didn't notice that he made a gesture to me.

MR. HAYDEN: I think if it is in doubt, there is a lot of ways that that can be solved. I would be willing to present a number of witnesses if you give me a jury trial on just what that one - -

THE COURT: If Mr. Jackson made a gesture to me, I am not considering that right now.

MR. HAYDEN: It was when you commented on the church and he commented on the courtroom. He said, "You and I are going to get along fine." And he went like that (indicating) to your Honor.

THE COURT: Oh, I remember. I recall that incident. I do recall that incident.

MR. HAYDEN: But that would not be contempt of court on the part of Jesse Jackson, although if I make the same gesture on the first day of the trial, not knowing what is in contempt or not in contempt, and then I try to explain to your Honor that I implied no disrespect for the jury, I was greeting the jury, just as Mr. Jackson was greeting your Honor, you didn't regard him as being in contempt, and I didn't feel that I was in contempt of anything having to do with the jury. I even tried to explain it and I take it that it is contempt of court to greet people as they come in on the opening day of a trial in which you consider to be a customary way. And then when you learn it's not customary, it becomes contempt.

Several of the next citations flowed from my reactions to observing the conflict between your Honor and Bobby Seale and in particular between the marshals and Mr. Seale. I have spoken to marshals who regret very deeply what they had to do to Bobby Seale. They have extended apologies to ourselves and they have expressed very deep regrets that they were involved in the physical punishment —and that is a mild term compared to the terms that they told me—for what they did to Bobby Seale.

It does seem to me that - -

THE COURT: I would agree with the marshals.

MR. HAYDEN: I am only quoting your own marshals.
THE COURT: I deeply regret and I certainly waited a long time before I did what the law permitted me to do and had to do in order to quiet him. I could not continue to take the abuse and finally had to mistrial him out of the case, as you know. Nobody—there is no human being who would like to take the steps that we had to take in order to quiet Mr. Seale.
MR. HAYDEN: I am sorry, I was not speaking about your Honor's rulings about Mr. Seale. I think you probably know how we all feel about the rulings. I was speaking about the treatment administered by the marshals and the fact that marshals since that time have expressed regret over the way they treated Bobby Seale, which I think they meant by that that it was excessive force.

And I had the same feeling in watching that treatment and the series of citations here that have to do with feelings that just flowed out of me when I observed what was happening, and I thought—mistakenly, I guess, now, according to the law—that it might be possible to even say something to your Honor during that time, and I did, as your records note, but I think that a series of spontaneous remarks made when a man is in the midst of a physical struggle, where he is screaming in pain, hardly have to do with contempt of court as I understand it.

I don't think that those statements disrupted the orderly progress of the trial or the administration of justice. I don't think that the statements delayed the trial.

I would like to say something about the other substantive area and that has to do with your Honor's ruling that excluded Attorney General Ramsey Clark from the witness stand before the jury after the voir dire of Mr. Clark.

Now I was one of the people with John Froines and the attorneys who went to Mr. Clark's house. Stuart Ball was there. And I was surprised from the beginning at what happened at that house, and I think if I am able to try to argue against the punishment you are about to give for what I said about Ramsey Clark, that I would have to describe what happened from Sunday in his house until Tuesday when I made the remark.

As part of that defense, it was a spontaneous remark but it came out of experiences that I had gone through for three days.

We were at the former Attorney General's house and we were met there by two agents of the Justice Department, Mr. Morrill—and I forget the other person's name —who said that they were there to be the eyes and ears, they were there to make sure that the Attorney General was not going to be stained by our presence. They had come before at other meetings and I think, though, that we did have—our staff did have meetings with Ramsey Clark and not in their presence, but at those meetings he said that for this formal occasion it might be a good thing to have representatives of the Justice Department there because he felt that he wanted to testify to the truth and not be partisan to either side.

One of the Justice Department agents, Mr. Morrill, who was sitting here on Tuesday in the courtroom, is a person who claimed that he had seen me many times before and I think he had seen me in Mississippi when he was working for an agency of the government there, and I think he had been in court against Mr. Kunstler on civil rights matters in Mississippi.

I said that he said that he had been following me for a long time. I took that as a remark that I had better not respond to because I thought he was serious about being the eyes and ears and I didn't know what he meant by that. So I sat and listened silently to the interview.

Ramsey Clark said a great many things. I think that you know what he said. His feelings have been made clear about this law, about this court, about this trial, about Mr. Foran and Mr. Schultz, so I won't go into that.

But after we left that day, I spoke to one of our attorneys, Mr. Kunstler, later. Mr. Kunstler related to me a conversation that he had that is very important in understanding my motivation.

He said that after we left and after he stepped out of the room to make a phone call and to go to the bathroom at Ramsey Clark's house, he came back in and he found the Attorney General, the former Attorney General, standing by the fireplace against the wall with two agents of the Justice Department speaking to him, trying very vigorously to persuade him not to testify. You can ask Mr. Kunstler for the details. You can ask them. You can ask Ramsey Clark. They were persuading him that if he testified it would be a stain on himself and a stain on law and order because he would simply be used by people like ourselves, people who Mr. Foran described as evil five or six times yesterday; that for him to be associated with us would be to the dishonor of the United States, we would use him to have a press conference, that we would do things of that kind.

He asked Mr. Kunstler a few questions when Mr. Kunstler returned to the room and he finally volunteered to testify. He said that he thought he had a duty to the system to testify, as Mr. Kunstler recounted to me, at any rate. Then he arrived in our witness room and who was with him in the witness room? Mr. Morrill. No chance for private conversation with Ramsey Clark. Mr. Morrill is there protecting him, he says. No way to talk to him about what is going on in the courtroom or what we wanted to ask him any more without Mr. Morrill being there. It would be as if we were able to have our staff go with the jury as we proposed earlier so that not just the marshals would be with the jury. The government staff is with our witnesses. And what are they with the witnesses for? Well, I don't know what ominous final reason they are with Ramsey Clark, but I know that Mr. Morrill came in this courtroom and sat behind Mr. Schultz and whispered to Mr. Schultz and then Mr. Schultz got up and made a motion out of the presence of the jury that they had information that we were about to present a witness, Ramsey Clark, who had nothing to say that was relevant or material to the case. There was some possibility, I think Mr. Schultz even said, that we were just going to use him and use our circus antics or use some kind of antics and the net result, I guess, of our using these antics would be to increase our prestige with the jury because Ramsey Clark would be on the stand and even though he had nothing to say that was relevant, we would put him on the stand in order to bask in his light, in order—Ramsey Clark is the man who was working for the Democratic Party, he was the Attorney General of the United

States when all of us were engaged in resistance against the draft, resistance against the war in Vietnam. He indicted Dr. Spock. We don't think of him as a prestigious person who shares our views. We don't think of him as a close friend of the defense. But we do think that what happened in Chicago had to do with one arm of the government, one arm of the Democratic Party deciding to crack down on dissenters and another arm extending from the Attorney General's office trying to restrain the police. Mr. Foran - -

THE COURT: If I may interrupt to suggest this, Mr. Hayden: You are getting a little away from the point.

MR. HAYDEN: Your Honor, I am just about to get to the citations - -

THE COURT: You must understand that my ruling with respect to Mr. Clark's testimony was made and was based on a matter of law as well as the point made by the government—made by the government as was developed on voir dire that he could not contribute anything by way of testimony to the case. But for a former Attorney General, the chief law officer of the government, to take the witness stand presumably—I don't know what he would have testified to—his father and I are old friends and I certainly didn't like to take the position that he had no right as a matter of law to testify—that was my view then and it is my view now, and it was the obligation of everybody in this case to follow the order of the court. You can't pick—I know you would like to but you can't pick out the orders of the court that you want to abide by any more than I can pick out orders of court higher than this one to abide by and disobey others. You are not privileged to do that. This trial would have gone very smoothly if only the people concerned, some of the people concerned, were respectful and were not insulting, did not use vituperative language, which I never heard any place, let alone in the United States District Court room - - I just never had.

Now regardless of what you may think of how Mr. Clark might have contributed to your case, I exhausted the possibility by permitting a voir dire examination and I made my ruling as a matter of law. Now that was a ruling that you and everybody in this case was bound to accept. And even as recently as yesterday afternoon a young woman ran out of this courtroom or was taken out of the courtroom and shouted in a large voice in the presence of the jury "Why didn't you let - -" —or words to this effect— "- - Ramsey Clark testify?"

It is the spirit of rebellion against the orders of the Court. I know you don't like courts, but you are going to have to like them or deal with them and you had better decide to just respect them. If you don't want to, that is, [of] course, your privilege, but you are going to have to somewhere along the line take the consequences. That is all.

Now I know I don't get any contact with your mind in saying these things. I say them only because in one or two newspapers I read that I frivolously and without giving—or capriciously is a better word—denied him the right to testify. That wasn't true at all. There were two basic reasons: One was, as you remember, the Department of Justice regulation. One was a matter of ethics. One was a matter of his inability to make a contribution to the evidence in this case. And I don't think that a judge making a ruling with basic reasons like that should have abuse heaped on him and I want to tell you that you would have had a happier time around me, you and all of your friends, if you had just agreed to do it conventionally, and even though you didn't approve of me or my rulings, I learned early in my career that it doesn't pay to fight the judge on every little thing that he does.

There was scarcely a day that I came out here that I wasn't the subject of at least some sarcasm and it went all the way from sarcasm to awful invective. I just don't stand for that kind of treatment and I don't get it from anybody. I have tried some of the most highly and widely publicized criminal cases in the United States. I have never had, but never have I been treated in any of those cases as I have been treated here. And all I was asking for was respect, the same kind of respect that I would extend to any litigant or any lawyer who comes in here.

To be characterized as a racist was an absolute absurdity. There is nothing here that shows me a racist.

Is there now? Now is there anything that shows me a racist? You think I disciplined Mr. Seale because of his color? It's what he said and what he did. And a white man would have been disciplined in the same way.

It will interest you to know—and I have said this before; you heard it—I have never in the years I have sat on the state court bench—I am getting to be like you are, making speeches—I never had in the state court or the federal court ever sentenced any person but one and that was a thing that was easily disposed of—for contempt of court—never. That may come, unless you heard me say that some time ago, and that was some time ago—that may come as a surprise to you.

That is why we have upper courts. If a lower court doesn't rule properly and an upper court or a reviewing court is persuaded of it, that is where we go under the American system which some of the parties to this case don't seem to like. Well, I can't help it. I have to work under it. I have to work under the Federal Rules as they are.

That is my explanation to you of my ruling in the case of Mr. Clark. He was given every chance to testify. It wasn't true that he was, as one newspaper said, refused the privilege of testifying. We did what the law said we had to do. We permitted a voir dire. And it was a comprehensive voir dire. And I don't think I deserved the abuse that came from that. I just don't think I did.

MR. HAYDEN: I would like to respond to that but I would like to - -

THE COURT: I didn't want to get into a controversy about it. I was merely trying to make one point to you, sir, on that. I am not always right, and if I am wrong, there are at least two courts that a litigant can go to to try to demonstrate that.

MR. HAYDEN: There is something - -

THE COURT: You don't shout obscenities—I say you—one doesn't shout obscenities at the trial judge who has been in this work as long as I have. I just don't deserve that from anybody. And I don't get it here ever—I never had it. I never have. Oh, sometimes lawyers get worked up, enthusiastic, a little too enthusiastic about his case, but nothing has ever occurred that has occurred during this trial.

No, Mr. Clark got full fair treatment. If it comes to pass that my ruling there is thought to be erroneous, that is the way to do it. That is the way to do it, to preserve it in the record, and it is in the record. If it is an error, that can be assigned. And I looked into the matter very carefully. Now is there anything else? We will go from the Clark matter.

MR. HAYDEN: I am still on it, yes. There is -- I am still on the park incident and I was just about to sort of sum it up.

There is something I would like to say about the two upper courts and the higher system of appeals but I would like to say that towards the end of it, or I would like to first go through these incidents.

What I was saying about Ramsey Clark is that my understanding of our interview with him was quite different from that of Mr. Morrill, the man I met in Mississippi and met at Mr. Clark's house, and I think that Mr. Schultz was acting on Mr. Morrill's report of the conversation when he first described how it was immaterial and irrelevant, and there were whole sections of the Clark interview that were left out of what Mr. Schultz presented to your Honor, at least from my notes, and I was so astounded by it I said "That's not true," and I said it to Richard Schultz. And his reaction I thought was interesting. He said it was true and he pointed to Morrill, and Morrill stood up and I started to get up and we were going to argue with each other about the notes. We even tried to have it arranged that we both take the witness stand and go through the notes of the interview to see what was correct. And then maybe have Ramsey Clark verify it. It ended in a moment because everybody knew it wasn't going to happen. But Morrill was up saying things, disrupting the orderly proceeding of the court, I suppose—I don't know. He sat back down again. I didn't even stand up. I mean, it seemed like a very peculiar incident at the moment. I let it go.

Then came Ramsey Clark to the stand and off he went, not allowed to speak.

THE COURT: Not that quickly. Not that quickly.

MR. HAYDEN: No, you are right. He was there for --

THE COURT: He didn't come on and go off.
MR. HAYDEN: - - for half an hour.
THE COURT: He was given a respectful hearing. I have great respect for men who occupy the most important legal position on government for a while.
MR. HAYDEN: If I might go to my own motivation, this doesn't have to do with questioning your Honor's ruling, it has to do with explaining my motivation.

When I saw—from what I saw from Sunday to Tuesday was the Attorney General of the United States, Ramsey Clark, former Attorney General, tell us that he thought he could testify, that there were things that he could testify about, then Mr. Schultz, a junior person in the Department, tried to imply to him in questions that it would be against his own regulations for him to testify about certain matters—and in his understated way, Mr. Clark disagreed. We could go back to the transcript and show what Mr. Clark said to Mr. Schultz. And if you want to bring Mr. Clark in here, or, if the press wants to ask him what he feels about Mr. Schultz' statements about that regulation book which Mr. Clark supervised, was in charge of, you can do it, but I thought it was bizarre and shocking that the former Attorney General of the United States would be told by an Assistant United States Attorney that the rules which he operated under when he was Attorney General prohibited him from testifying about things that he thought he could testify about. That shook me. It also shook me that there should be a ruling that the Attorney General's testimony was immaterial and could not go before the jury and that he could not testify as a witness called by the defense. Mr. Kunstler said that was an unprecedented act. I don't know the legal history of the country as well as you and Mr. Kunstler, but it seemed unprecedented, it seemed like a very strange and unfair atmosphere had developed in the courtroom up to that time, and that this was kind of a high point in the development of this kind of situation; that if anything demonstrated that there is no just one thing as the law, we are outside the law and everybody else is inside it, the thing that seemed most clearly to me was not just the fact that Bobby Seale could draw on Reconstruction Statutes, but that a former

Attorney General of the United States would not be allowed to be a defense witness when he thought that he could be—evidently the man who was the chief law enforcement officer of the United States—I'm only talking about my feelings—the man who administered the system of law in the United States—it struck me that more than anything else this demonstrated that there was more than one understanding of the law that a person could have.

THE COURT: Well, I was the one that had responsibility for ruling and I did. And I ruled after careful consideration.

MR. HAYDEN: I know you did. I want to speak to that later, though, the question of the Court's authority. What I want to do is explain my feeling about each incident.

THE COURT: All right. You have explained. Go to something else now because I think we have -- if you have anything else --

MR. HAYDEN: All that finally happened was that in the midst of an attack on us by Mr. Foran, I responded while the jury was going out of the room to the effect that you wouldn't even allow the Attorney General to testify. Then I stood and said that I had done it because of Mr. Foran. I sat down. That's why I did it.

The other -- I said I didn't wish to lose my temper.

The other incidents have to do with three counts of refusal to rise. My understanding as I was sitting there not rising, and I don't even know if it was really three because I am not sure that Dorothy could see who was rising or who wasn't, but my understanding of that at the time from the law is that it is no impediment to the progress of the trial, it is no obstruction of the machinery of the trial for a person not to stand. I thought it was a protest that was legitimate and within the law because it did not in any way obstruct the administration of justice.

I had to be found in contempt before I could discover that it was illegal. In other words, there is no prior statement that I understood that it would be illegal not to rise. I thought that it was at the discretion of the marshal. Your Honor often said

THE COURT: It would have --

DEFENDANT HAYDEN: The discretion of the marshal

is not the law.

THE COURT: It would have been so much easier to rise, wouldn't it? Why assume a rebellious attitude about something of a relatively simple matter? In other words, fight the judge - -

MR. HAYDEN: Why find someone in contempt for a relatively simple matter?

THE COURT: Fight the judge all the way up from not rising to much more important decisions. That has been the attitude.

All I can say to you is that I don't think it worked to the advantage of yourself and the other defendants.

I am ready to - - I can't say much about rising. I am an informal person. I may sound a little starchy up here but I don't insist on deference that some other judges do off the bench.

But I do believe—and I know you men don't—that the dignity and decorum are important in the conduct of a lawsuit. I think that it makes for fairness for all litigants. And if we are going to have a table of defendants, several defendants, each one privileged to speak out whenever the spirit moves them, we won't have an orderly trial and there never will be one.

And I don't think even if the great—I don't even know the reforms you're suggesting but I don't think that the Federal Courts of our country are ever going to be anything other than as dignified as we can make them. Now dignity doesn't mean unfairness. You know the Solicitor General of the United States when he argues before the Supreme Court puts on a—this is rather a humorous observation in the light of the tailoring in this case—he is obligated under the rule of court to wear a cutaway, a morning coat and striped trousers.

Now some people think that is a little stiff but we can get in between.

Thank you for your observations.

MR. HAYDEN: Well, I was not really—I wanted to say something - -

THE COURT: Well, I - -

MR. HAYDEN: I wanted to say two things, one about my feelings about punishment and the other was just - - if you would allow me to say something about what you were commenting on, I thought that you sort of invited a comment about the system of the courts and the appeals courts. I think there is something I could say about that. It is not related necessarily to my punishment but it explains a lot of why people find it very difficult to wait for the appeals court.

The Attorney General Ramsey Clark said that the decision to prosecute in this case was a signal of political repression because under his administration they did not find that there was any evidence worth a prosecution.

So before the trial began, many of us felt that this was a political trial, that it signaled not just a change of political direction but a change in the direction that the courts would be moving. And one reason it is difficult to have confidence in the higher court is easily found by reading Life Magazine or the Atlantic Monthly or any other magazine that simply interviews Attorney General Mitchell, Deputy Attorney General Kleindeist who calls us ideological criminals, or read the writings of men who are putting justices like Judge Carswell on the Supreme Court, on the higher court.

It doesn't seem to me likely that a man who has fought against outside agitators - -

THE COURT: Don't you go adding to Judge Carswell's troubles here. Your words might be spoken on the floor of the United States Senate.

MR. HAYDEN: By Abbie perhaps, but - -

THE COURT: No, I - -

MR. HAYDEN: The point I am trying to make, your Honor, is just that if you put into office on the highest court of the land men who have a record that we feel runs strongly against outside agitators and against what we consider to be social justice, then I would doubt that such a man would be in a position to overturn any rulings here because he is, if anything, a very, very powerful defender of a status quo that is supported by fewer and fewer people.

Therefore, for a lot of people who feel the way I do, we are in the movie "Z," I mean there is not going to be a higher court.

THE COURT: You are going to shout them down right here at the trial level, is that right?

MR. HAYDEN: I am not raising my voice. But I find this is the only place I may have or I may in the next two years be allowed to speak to these people, to them and to the press. But the point that I wanted to make about punishment is that the problem that I think people have who want to punish us—Mr. Foran who calls us evil, people who want to punish us, is that what must cause a great problem for the understanding of people like that is why the punishment does not seem to have effect. Even as the elder Dellinger is taken off for two years, a younger Dellinger fights back.

THE COURT: If you call him elder, what do you call me?

MR. HAYDEN: I call you "Your Honor."

Even as the elder Dellinger is taken off, older than myself—I am ten years—

THE COURT: I won't tell him that you called him that.

MR. HAYDEN: He knows it.

THE COURT: You will have to - -

MR. HAYDEN: We will have plenty of time to speak about it.

THE COURT: You will have to resign from the lodge here. You might lose your place at the table.

MR. HAYDEN: I am 22 years younger than Dellinger, a generation older than the daughter who fought back and was dragged out, and I don't know how many generations I am older than the 14-year-old daughter who is here being filled with rage at what she sees done to her father.

So, your Honor, before your eyes you see the most vital ingredient of your system collapsing because the system does not hold together.

THE COURT: Oh, don't be so pessimistic. Our system isn't collapsing. Fellows as smart as you could do awfully well under this system. I am not trying to convert you, mind you.

DEFENDANT HOFFMAN: We don't want a place in the regiment, Julie.

THE COURT: What did you say? Your turn's coming up.

DEFENDANT HOFFMAN: I am being patient, Julie.

THE COURT: Well, I don't - - you see? There is the sort of thing, this familiar - - he thinks that annoys me by addressing me by a name - - he doesn't know that years ago when I was his age or younger, that's what my friends called me.

DEFENDANT HOFFMAN: My turn will come later.

Why don't you save it? Save it, Julie. I'm coming next.
THE COURT: But you are going to have to abide by the system, the rules of the system, the Federal System, when you get into trouble. And you might as well stay out of trouble. You haven't decided - - you don't want to stay in trouble. I have literally beseeched these defendants and the lawyers, begged them to refrain from continuing what I regarded as contemptuous conduct. And I couldn't ever get any contact with the minds of the defendants or the lawyers. Not once. Not once.
MR. HAYDEN: I was trying to give at least a personal explanation of why that failure might exist. In my own case.
THE COURT: Oh, we really have one or two judges, Mr. Hayden—and you try to work up a system to improve the Federal System. I suppose it can be improved. But we have some really great judges on the Federal Bench.
MR. HAYDEN: I think the difficulty is trying to try people for political crimes or crimes of consciousness or ideological crimes. That is what brings politics and consciousness into the courtroom. But I just wanted to say for myself that I was trying to think of what about punishment I most regretted or how could I argue why I would be upset or opposed to your punishing me which I guess is the purpose of these remarks, and I thought very carefully, and in thinking about it I think I realized why punishment is so ineffective, because - -
THE COURT: Oh, I can't get into that with you. I know there have been some judges on the bench who think nothing of the deterrent effect of punishment, otherwise excellent judges. I won't argue that with you. There are some people who think we ought to burn every prison in the land. If they do, they would save me a lot of cases such as I have just gone through here. We wouldn't have any indictments and I wouldn't have to listen to all this erudition of the two brilliant lawyers that conducted the defense of the defendants.
MR. HAYDEN: If I could just say one or two final sentences - -
THE COURT: Yes, I hope those two sentences aren't like a lawyer's two sentences.
MR. HAYDEN: I will try to follow in the tradition of Mr. Kunstler and Mr. Weinglass, with one or two sentences.

The point I was trying to make is that I was trying to think about what I regretted about punishment. I can only state one thing that affected my feelings, my own feelings, and that is that I would like to have child.
THE COURT: There is where the Federal System can do you no good.
MR. HAYDEN: Because the Federal System can do you no good in trying to prevent the birth of a new world.
VOICES: Right on. Right on.
THE COURT: Mr. Clerk, with respect to the defendant Hayden, he will be found guilty of direct contempt committed in the presence of the Court on eleven different occasions.

With respect to *Specification* 1, he will be committed to the custody of the Attorney General of the United States for imprisonment for a period of two days; *Specification* 2, one day; *Specification* 3, one month; *Specification* 4, one day; *Specification* 5, one day; *Specification* 6, one day; *Specification* 7, three months; *Specification* 8, four months; *Specification* 9, one day; *Specification* 10, seven days; *Specification* 11, six months; and I direct the United States Attorney to prepare the proper papers reflecting the views of the Court, and the sentence will be cumulative and consecutive.

B.J.

HOFFMAN

Next, Abbott Hoffman. Will the marshals take care of Mr. Hayden.
MR. FROINES: See you in jail.
THE COURT: We will now deal with the defendant Hoffman.

Specification 1: On September 26, during the opening statement by the Government, defendant Hoffman rose and blew a kiss to the jurors. Official Transcript, Page 9. **1 day**

Specification 2: On October 23, well after the date of the Court's order sequestering the jury and ordering the jury that they may see no newspapers, the defendant Hoffman held up a newspaper so the jurors might see the headline in the courtroom. The following colloquy occurred:

> "MR. SCHULTZ: If the Court please - -
> MR. KUNSTLER: I would rather be directed.
> MR. SCHULTZ: Before you direct him, if you are going to direct Mr. Kunstler, I would like to make one observation for the record. At 12:30 this morning or 12:30 early this afternoon, when the jury was adjourned, after the jury stood up, defendant Hoffman - - in fact, he had the same article that he has in front of him there - -
> MR. HOFFMAN: Yes, I was going to show it to - -
> MR. SCHULTZ: He held up the newspaper for them to see and - -
> MR. HOFFMAN: It ain't a newspaper. It is the Berkeley Tribe and doesn't tell lies, so it isn't a newspaper.
> THE COURT: I wonder if you would ask your client - - you know, when I was out there trying cases, if my clients started to talk when another lawyer was speaking, Mr. Kunstler, I told him to remain quiet.

Now, I can direct him to remain quiet. The United States Attorney was speaking to the Court. He is entitled to be heard just as you are entitled to be heard. We are not running a circus. This happens to be a court—even though there are those who don't share views.

MR. KUNSTLER: I would suggest, your Honor, then, that Mr Hoffman be permitted to respond and not be interrupted - -

THE COURT: I will not hear from your clients.

MR. HOFFMAN: I was just trying to be helpful, your Honor.

THE COURT: I will not hear from your client. I will let Mr. Schultz finish his observation." Official Transcript, Pages 3,866-67. **7 days**

Specification 3: On October 28, at the close of the session, the defendant Hoffman refused to rise in the customary manner when directed to do so by the marshal. Official Transcript, Pages 4,618-19. **1 day**

Specification 4: On October 29, the following colloquy occurred:

"THE COURT: I will ask you to sit down, sir. You have a lawyer to speak for you. I haven't been told that you represent all of these defendants, either.

MR. HOFFMAN: We have been told that they are defendants, too.

MR. FORAN: May the record show that that was the defendant Hoffman who made that - -

THE COURT: Yes; yes.

MR. FORAN: The previous statement was made by the defendant Dellinger.

THE COURT: The last statement was made by the defendant Abbie Hoffman.

MR. HOFFMAN: I don't use that last name anymore."

THE COURT: That grieved me sorely, I say, off the record, when he said that. I didn't think I deserved that so early in this case.

"THE COURT: Will you remain quiet." Official Transcript, Page 4,639. **7 days**

Specification 5: "At the close of the morning session on October 29, the defendant Hoffman refused to rise in the customary manner. Official Transcript, Pages 4,728-29. **1 day**

Specification 6: On October 29, when the Court was compelled to call a recess during the afternoon session, the defendant Hoffman once more refused to rise in the customary manner. Official Transcript, Page 4,763. **1 day**

Specification 7: On October 30, at the beginning of the court session, the defendant Hoffman refused to rise in response to the marshal's direction. Official Transcript, Page 4,801. **1 day**

Specification 8: On October 30, when the Court was compelled to deal appropriately with Mr. Seale, Mr. Hoffman engaged in the following:

> "MR. SEALE: The Judge is not—he is not trying to give you no fair trial. That's what you are. You are lying. You know exactly what you are.
>
> MR. HAYDEN: Now they are going to beat him, they are going to beat him.
>
> MR. HOFFMAN: You may as well kill him if you are going to gag him. It seems that way, doesn't it?
>
> THE COURT: You are not permitted to address the Court, Mr. Hoffman. You have a lawyer.
>
> MR. HOFFMAN: This isn't a court. This is a neon oven.
>
> MR. FORAN: That was the defendant Hoffman who spoke.
>
> THE COURT: Let the record show that the defendant Hoffman spoke." Official Transcript, Page 4,846.

And very shortly thereafter he continued in the following interchange:

> "MR. HAYDEN: I was not addressing the jury. I was trying to protect Mr. Seale. The man is supposed to be silent when he sees another man's nose being smashed?
>
> MR. HOFFMAN: The disruption started when these guys got into overkill. It is the same thing as last year in Chicago, the same exact thing.

THE COURT: Mr. Hoffman, you are directed to refrain from speaking. You are ordered to refrain from speaking." Official Transcript, Page 4,847.

After this interchange the Court determined that a recess would be appropriate. When the Court left the bench the defendant Hoffman refused to rise in the customary manner. Official Transcript, Page 4,849. **2 months**

Specification 9: On October 30, after a brief recess the Judge returned to the bench in the afternoon and the defendant Hoffman again refused to rise in the customary manner. Official Transcript, Page 4,853. **1 day**

Specification 10: On November 12, the defendant Hoffman and the other defendants openly laughed at the Judge while he was making a ruling. The following colloquy occurred:

"THE COURT: That observation will remain on the record and this loud laughter has got to cease.

MR. HOFFMAN: Mr. Weinglass, how many years do you have to laugh at?

MR. WEINGLASS: I would further want to - -

MR. HOFFMAN: I am talking to my lawyer." Official Transcript, Pages 6,257-59. **7 days**

Specification 11: On November 26, after the Court made a ruling the following colloquy occurred:

"THE COURT: I decide each motion on its own papers, sir, and I am not aware of any witnesses that the Government has sought to bring here. I don't know whether - -

MR. HOFFMAN: We are very confused about this. Is the Government going to present our defense as well as our prosecution?

THE COURT: Have you gotten that - - what is the name of that defendant speaking?

MR. HOFFMAN: Just Abbie. I don't have a last name, Judge. I lost it. We can't respect the law when it's tyranny.

THE COURT: Are you able to hear the defendant Hoffman speaking?

MR. HOFFMAN: Abbie.

THE REPORTER: Yes, sir." Official Transcript,

Page 8,081. **1 month**

Specification 12: On December 15, the defendant Hoffman openly laughed at the Court during its ruling on a motion, and admitted it.

"MR. HOFFMAN: I was laughing." Official Transcript, Page 11,181. **14 days**

Specification 13: On December 30, while the defendant Hoffman was testifying on cross-examination, the following colloquy occurred:

"THE COURT: I will admonish the jury -- the United States Attorney --

THE WITNESS: Wait until you see the movie.

THE COURT: -- if it is required that he be admonished.

THE WITNESS: Wait until you see the movie.

THE COURT: And you be quiet.

THE WITNESS: Well -- the movie's going to be better.

THE COURT: Did you get that last, Miss Reporter?

THE REPORTER: Yes, sir.

THE COURT: The last words spoken by the witness on the stand." Official Transcript, Page 13,013. **14 days**

Specification 14: On January 9, the defendant Hoffman openly laughed at the Court again. The following colloquy occurred:

"MR. KUNSTLER: Oh, your Honor, there is a certain amount of humor when talking about a bathroom --

THE COURT: Oh, I know that is your favorite reply.

MR. HOFFMAN: I laughed, too." Official Transcript, Page 14,824. **7 days**

Specification 15: On January 14, there was again an excessive and obnoxious outburst of laughter from the table of the defendants. The following colloquy occurred:

"MR. KUNSTLER: I just don't want to get thrown in my chair by the marshals so I will have to sit

down, but I just don't think it is fair to do that.
MR. HOFFMAN: I laughed anyway.
THE COURT: Will you be quiet, Mr. - -
MR. HOFFMAN: I laughed. It wasn't Jerry, it was me.
THE COURT: Did you get that, Miss Reporter?
MR. HOFFMAN: At that ruling. I laughed. He didn't.
THE COURT: That was Mr. Dellinger.
MR. KUNSTLER: That was not Mr. Dellinger.
MR. SCHULTZ: Your Honor, that was Mr. Hoffman.
MR. KUNSTLER: Your Honor - -
MR. SCHULTZ: That was the defendant Hoffman speaking.
MR. HOFFMAN: I was him." Official Transcript, Page 15,587. **1 day**

Specification 16: On January 16, the defendant Hoffman interjected the following comment into the proceedings, in an attempt to make a mockery of the Court:

"THE COURT: I won't ask you to do it. Move the lectern over, Mr. Marshal. I didn't ask you to do it. I asked the marshal to do it. We don't punish a man before he is punishable.
MR. HOFFMAN: We don't either. We don't either. We don't either." Official Transcript, Page 16,263.
[See page 128] **Withdrawn**

Specification 17: On January 21, the defendants were conducting a conference with one of their staff "members" at the defense table, while Mr. Foran was attempting to speak. The co-conference was loud enough to cause the following disturbance:

"THE MARSHAL: Excuse me, Mr. Foran. Will you take your seat at the table, please.
MR. HOFFMAN: We're organizing the defense.
THE MARSHAL: Take your seat. Now. come on.
MR. HOFFMAN: She's on the staff.
THE MARSHAL: Mr. Kunstler, talking is not - - I'm asking him to take his seat.
MR. KUNSTLER: I don't know what he was doing.

He said he was talking to his wife.
MR. HOFFMAN: We are talking in a low voice. He didn't even hear.
THE COURT: The defendant's place at the trial is at the defendants' table.
MR. HOFFMAN: We were talking - -
A DEFENDANT: Let our staff sit at the table, everything would be all right.
MR. KUNSTLER: Your Honor, he was sitting, just talking quietly with his wife, who is part of our staff.
THE COURT: I know. I know what he's doing. I require - - the rule of this court is that the defendants sit at the defendants' table.
MR. HOFFMAN: How do we organize the trial?
THE COURT: I order Mr. Hoffman to sit at the defendants' table.
MR. HOFFMAN: OK. We can just talk from here. Why don't you go out and talk to Paul Krassner and get the defense together.

I don't see how we can prepare the defense. We have to sit here seven days - -" Official Transcript, Pages 16,791-92. **42 days**

Specification 18: On January 23, while Mr. Foran and Mr. Dellinger were engaged in a colloquy, Mr. Hoffman inserted the following remarks:

"MR. FORAN: Your Honor, in the American system there is a proper way to raise such issues and to correct them.
MR. DELLINGER: That was the proper way with Fred Hampton, wasn't it?
MR. FORAN: And correct them, your Honor, by the proper governmental system, and there is a proper way to do that.
MR. HOFFMAN: Correction the way you handled the war in Viet Nam, the same proper - -" Official Transcript, Page 17,376.

Shortly thereafter during the same incident a discussion ensued concerning the propriety of Mr. Kunstler's press conferences. Mr. Hoffman again interjected his comments. It's reported as follows:

"THE COURT: Yes, there is a law against a lawyer

participating - -
MR. KUNSTLER: No, there isn't. The rule is quite clear, and we know what it is.
THE COURT: There is a law against - -
MR. HOFFMAN: The Judge had an interview in Time Magazine.
THE COURT: A lawyer on television discussing the case.
MR. KUNSTLER: Let's have what I said that was false. That was the accusation.
THE COURT: I will ask you both to sit down.
MR. HOFFMAN: The Judge gave an interview to Time Magazine.
THE COURT: And I will instruct Mr. Weinglass to continue with the direct examination of this witness."
Official Transcript, Page 17,379. **14 days**

Specification 19: On January 30, at the conclusion of the court's session, the Court asked the parties and attorneys to stay after the jury had been excused. The Court then broached the subject of the propriety of the public speeches given by the defendants. While this discussion was going on Mr. Hoffman again inserted his remarks gratuitously. The incident is reported as follows:

"THE COURT: I am not going to be put on the griddle about it. Now you are the lawyer. You are one of the lawyers for the defendants. And I think it is wholly inappropriate for defendants in a criminal case to make the kind of speech that was made and the matter of bail goes beyond mere protection for the Government that the defendant appear. Read the book.
MR. WEINGLASS: But I do not think the matter of bail should be held over their heads in order to reduce the amount of public speaking they are doing.
THE COURT: Oh, I don't - -
MR. HOFFMAN: I will be in Miami on Sunday afternoon with the same speech.
THE COURT: That expression - - did you hear that? I haven't heard either lawyer for the defendants try to quiet their clients during this trial when they spoke out, not once in four and a half months, not

once." Official Transcript, Page 19,094-19,095. **7 days**

Specification 20: On April 2, the Court had determined that argument on a particular question had been completed. The Court admonished Mr. Kunstler several times to sit down and desist arguing. The Court had previously ordered the defendants and their attorneys not to mention the fact that the former Attorney General of the United States, Ramsey Clark, had been excluded by order of the Court. Mr. Hoffman made several comments after the Court had indicated argument was completed, and he violated the Court's order concerning the Attorney General. The record states:

"THE COURT: You sit down, sir, or we will arrange to have you put down.

MR. HOFFMAN: Are you going to gag the lawyers, too?

A VOICE: Chained to the chair - -

MR. HOFFMAN: You don't have to gag the jury, because they haven't been able to see our witnesses.

THE COURT: That was Mr. Hoffman that made that remark, Miss Reporter.

MR. HOFFMAN: The past Attorney General of the United States, Ramsey Clark - -" Official Transcript, Page 19,159.

Later in the day, the defendant Hoffman interrupted the Court to make the following sarcastic remark:

"THE COURT: All I have to repeat to you, Mr. Kunstler, is that I know you practice in the Southern District of New York. I have practiced there a lot as a lawyer before all of the then District Judges. I never saw - -

MR. HOFFMAN: When it was under British control." Official Transcript, Page 19,199-200. **2 days**

Specification 21: On April 4, during the cross-examination of the witness Phillips, Mr. Kunstler was examining the witness concerning the witness' concept of how hippies dress. During that incident, Mr. Hoffman got up and danced around, lifting his shirt and baring his body to the jury, and engaged in antics designed to make light of the testimony of the witness. The incident is reported as follows:

"Q You are the first one that hasn't identified him. (Hoffman.) This is Mr. Hoffman over here.

(There was laughter in the courtroom.)

THE COURT: Let the record show that Mr. Hoffman stood up, lifted his shirt up, and bared his body in the presence of the jury - -

MR. KUNSTLER: Your Honor, that is Mr. Hoffman's way.

THE COURT: - - dancing around.

(There was laughter in the courtroom.)

MR. KUNSTLER: Your Honor, that is Mr. Hoffman's way.

THE COURT: It is a bad way in a courtroom."

* * *

"Q Mr. Phillips, my question before we had the little colloquy had to do with - -

THE COURT: It was not a little colloquy, that was taking Mr. Hoffman to task for improper conduct in the courtroom.

BY MR. KUNSTLER:

Q Before Mr. Hoffman was taken to task for improper conduct in the courtroom, I asked you whether he was in hippie dress.

MR. HOFFMAN: That would make it hippie dress, naked." Official Transcript, Page 19,622-24. **4 days**

Specification 22: On April 4, at the end of the session, the Court indicated that it had determined to revoke the bail of the defendant Dellinger. In the uproar which followed this decision, Mr. Hoffman made the following remarks:
MR. SCHULTZ: Excuse me, your Honor, you are saying "April." I think you mean "February."
THE COURT: We will begin with 22.
MR. SCHULTZ: And the prior charge as well. I think you erroneously used the month April instead of February. Also in No. 21.
THE COURT: I have February 4 in each case.
MR. SCHULTZ: No. 20 also. I believe your Honor used April.
THE COURT: I don't know how that happened.
MR. SCHULTZ: I think you used April inadvertently.

THE COURT: No. 20 was February 2.
MR. SCHULTZ: Thank you, sir.
THE COURT: No. 21 was February 4. We have covered that. It refers to February 4.

> "Q Mr. Phillips, my question before we had the little colloquy - -" - - we have gone over that.
>
> "MR. HOFFMAN: That would make it hippie dress, naked." That was the end of that Official Transcript, Page 19,622-24.

I'm going to go back to Item 22 here. On February 4, at the end of the session, the Court indicated that it had determined to revoke the bail of the defendant Dellinger. In the uproar which followed this decision Mr. Hoffman made the following remarks:

> "MR. HOFFMAN: You are a disgrace to the Jews. You would have served Hitler better. Dig it."
>
> * * *
>
> "MR. HOFFMAN: I heard you haven't let anybody free in four years. That's right, stop me."
>
> * * *
>
> "MR. HOFFMAN: They are all our cases. We are bailing that guy out and every guy that gets arrested.
>
> * * *
>
> "MR. HOFFMAN: No spectators while they put them in jail." Official Transcript, Pages 19,781-82.

5 days

Specification 23: On February 5, after the Court had decided not to reinstate Mr. Dellinger's bail, Mr. Hoffman made the following remarks in the outburst which ensued:

> "MR. HOFFMAN: Your idea of justice is the only obscenity in the room. You schtunk."

S-c-h-t-u-n-k. I can't understand the following words. They are spelled as follows:

> "MR. HOFFMAN: Vo den? Shanda fur de goyem? Huh."

I can understand the last.

> "MR. HOFFMAN: Obviously it was a provocation. That's why it has gone on here today because you threatened him with the cutting of his freedom of speech in the speech he gave in Milwaukee.
>
> THE COURT: Mr. Marshal, will you ask the de-

fendant Hoffman to - -

MR. HOFFMAN: This ain't the Standard Club.

THE MARSHAL: Mr. Hoffman - -

MR. HOFFMAN: Oh, tell him to stick it up his bowling ball. How is your war stock doing, Julie? You don't have any power. They didn't have any power in the Third Reich either.

THE COURT: Will you ask him to sit down, Mr. Marshal?

THE MARSHAL: Mr. Hoffman, I am asking you again to shut up.

MR. RUBIN: Gestapo.

MR. HOFFMAN: Show him your .45. Show him a .45. He ain't never seen a gun." Official Transcript, Pages 19,801-02.

"MR. HOFFMAN: Mies van der Rohe was a Kraut, too." Official Transcript, Page 19,803.

"MR. HOFFMAN: You know you cannot win the fucking case. The only way you can is to [put] us away for contempt. We have contempt for this court, and for you, Schultz, and for this whole rotten system. That's the only justice. That is why they want this because they can't prove this fucking case." Official Transcript, Pages 19,803-4.

* * *

"MR. HOFFMAN: You put him in jail because you lost faith in the jury system. I hear you haven't lost a case before a jury in 24 tries. Only the Krebiozen people got away. We're going to get away, too. That's why you're throwing us in jail now this way.

Contempt is a tyranny of the court, and you are a tyrant. That's why we don't respect it. It's a tyrant." Official Transcript, Page 19,814.

"MR. HOFFMAN: The judges in Nazi Germany ordered sterilization. Why don't you do that, Judge Hoffman?" Official Transcript, Page 19,815.

* * *

"MR. HOFFMAN: We should have done this long ago when you chained and gagged Bobby Seale. Mafia controlled pigs. Racist." Official Transcript, Page 19,816.

* * *

> "MR. HOFFMAN: No, I won't shut up, I ain't an automaton like you. I don't want to be a tyrant and I don't care for a tyrannical system. Best friend the blacks ever had, huh. How many blacks are in the Drake Towers? How many are in the Standard Club? How many own stock in Brunswick Corporation? Official Transcript, Pages 19,816-17.

And later in the day Mr. Hoffman, at the end of the session, made the additional comment:

> "MR. HOFFMAN: It was every man. We'll see you at the Standard Club, Julie." Official Transcript, Page 19,877. **6 days**

Specification 24: On February 6, the defendant Hoffman attempted to hold the court up to ridicule by entering the courtroom in judicial robes. Official Transcript Page 19,888.

While the transcript does not reflect it, he remained in those robes for a considerable period of time before the jury. Later, he removed the robes, threw them on the floor of the courtroom, and wiped his feet on them. **7 days**

The court finds - -

Does any lawyer want to speak for Mr. Hoffman?

MR. WEINGLASS: If the Court please, I repeat the motion with respect to lack of jurisdiction and lack of authority.

THE COURT: I will consider that you made the same point.

MR. WEINGLASS: The only other matter which I want to point out to the court deals with Item No. 16 and I point it out for one very specific but limited purpose.

In this particular incident the Court noted that on January 16 a marshal was attempting to move this lectern, I think a movie was being set up, and Mr. Hoffman at that time rose from his chair and attempted to assist the marshal in moving the lectern. The Court advised Mr. Hoffman he didn't have to do that because - - I think the direct quote is "We don't punish a man in the court until he is punishable."

And I think the Court was engaging there in a witticism. I remember I myself laughed. I thought it was a quite funny remark.

When the Court made that funny remark, I think every one in the courtroom laughed and then Mr. Hoffman replied to that witticism in kind for he said, I believe—something to the effect that "We don't either."

Now for the Court's humor which got a laughing response there was, of course, no punishment. For Mr. Hoffman's response to the Court's humor he will have to, of course, serve time in jail, and I think this incident more than any indicates how the Court can pluck out of this transcript items which have occurred where in this one particular case the Court itself was involved together with Abbie Hoffman in doing something that I think we have all tried to do in the course of this trial which lasted over five months and that is at times inject humor. Your Honor has done it. You have gotten laughing responses. I have laughed. Other people have laughed.

When Abbie Hoffman attempts even while the laughter for the Court is dying down to inject his own humor, he is going to be sent to jail and punished for it. And I just point it out.

THE COURT: While I do not agree with your interpretation of Item 16, I will take it out.

I will hear from Mr. Hoffman if he wants to be heard.

DEFENDANT HOFFMAN: Well, I think - -

THE COURT: If you will be respectful.

DEFENDANT HOFFMAN: Respectful? My six-year-old daughter yesterday sent me a note. She said perhaps when the judge changes his glasses he doesn't have a pair that enables him to see what the defendants are all about.

The use of the word "respect" is quite different to me. I called this place a neon oven. A neon oven in a stainless steel cuckoo nest, designed by your friend Mies van der Rohe. I might add he died right after he built this, it kind of killed him, building a building in which he had to put men away in prison and perhaps into death houses.

THE COURT: I will let you speak to the specifications, sir.

DEFENDANT HOFFMAN: You have always referred to—they were my remarks—you said that we did not pay tribute to the highest court in the land, but to us the Federal Court is not the highest court in the land.

THE COURT: I didn't hear myself say that.

DEFENDANT HOFFMAN: Oh, yes, you did. You always call it the highest court in the land. Sure.
THE COURT: The Supreme Court is.
DEFENDANT HOFFMAN: The defendants have no respect for the highest court in the land. It ain't high.
THE COURT: I will have to ask you to sit down.
DEFENDANT HOFFMAN: I ain't going to sit down. I ain't going to sit down. I am going to fight for my right to speak in the same way that I fought for my right to speak and assemble in Lincoln Park.
THE COURT: You are not going to continue your insults and besides you are making statements - -
DEFENDANT HOFFMAN: We don't consider it the highest. We consider the people the highest court in the land.
THE COURT: You may speak to these specifications.
DEFENDANT HOFFMAN: You have said repeatedly - - you have said this afternoon that we do not respect the dignity and decorum of this court.
THE COURT: That is right.
DEFENDANT HOFFMAN: But when the decorum is oppression, the only dignity that free men have is the right to speak out. Furthermore, you said we do not honor your authority, but we recognize that authority as illegitimate in the same way that the authority that decided the political decisions in that heavy week in August in 1968 was illegitimate and did not represent the will and the desire of the people.

So we cannot respect an authority that we regard as illegitimate. We can only offer resistance to such illegitimate authority.

What are you guys getting nervous about?

Furthermore, you have asked us to respect the law but this is a law - - I sat there on the witness stand and Mr. Schultz said, "What were you wondering?" as he quoted from my book and speeches. "What were you wondering that night when you stood before a building?"

And I said, "Wonder? Wonder? I have never been on trial for wondering. Is that like a dream?"

He said, "Yes, that's like a dream."

And I have never been on trial for my dreams before. How can I respect the highest court in the land or a federal

government that puts people on trial for their dreams. I can show it no respect.
THE COURT: You took the Fifth Amendment, though, didn't you? You took the privilege of the Fifth Amendment?
DEFENDANT HOFFMAN: Which Fifth Amendment? Where did I take the Fifth? No, I didn't. I didn't take it because I wasn't ashamed and that's why we put on all of those witnesses that Mr. Foran said -- oh, evil people -- running for pope.
THE COURT: Oh, that is right. You decided to answer the question. I guess that was it.
DEFENDANT HOFFMAN: And I said --
THE COURT: Have you got anything more to say with regard to the specifications?
DEFENDANT HOFFMAN: No. 18 where I said we cannot respect when we wanted to bring John Sinclair in here, a man who is right now serving ten years for two cigarets of marijuana. I said that we cannot respect a law, a law that is tyranny, and a law that is trying us, and the courts are in a conspiracy of tyranny, and when the law is in tyranny, the only order is insurrection and disrespect, and that's what we showed, and that's what all honorable men of free will will show. That's it.
A VOICE: Right on.
THE COURT: Mr. Clerk, the court finds the defendant Hoffman guilty of direct contempt in the presence of --
DEFENDANT HOFFMAN: I didn't say -- I might say that a lot of those statements I didn't say, but maybe some of the other people that said them said it, but it's O.K., it don't matter.
THE COURT: Direct contempt --
DEFENDANT HOFFMAN: We are proud of what we say.
THE COURT: -- direct contempt of the court with respect to the specifications mentioned.
DEFENDANT HOFFMAN: You forgot that I wiped my feet on the robes because I didn't see a black robe of justice. I saw a white robe with a hood on it.
THE COURT: Will you sit down. Yes, I was kind to you. I said you put the robe on the floor.
DEFENDANT HOFFMAN: You're kind to us. You said

you were kind to Bobby Seale when you chained and gagged him. You said, "I am doing this for your own good, Mr. Seale, in order to insure a fair and proper trial for you and the other defendants."

THE COURT: Mr. Marshal, have that man sit down.

DEFENDANT HOFFMAN: Sure. I can say it seated.

THE COURT: Mr. Clerk, as I said before, the court finds the defendant Hoffman guilty of direct contempt in the presence of the court and in respect to the specifications which I shall mention here and designate the punishment in connection with each item:

Specification 1, 1 day in the custody of the Attorney General of the United States or his authorized representative; Specification 2, the defendant will be committed to the custody of the Attorney General of the United States or his authorized representative for a period of 7 days; Specification 3, 1 day; Specification 4, 7 days; Specification 5, 1 day; Specification 6, 1 day; Specification 7, 1 day; Specification 8, 2 months; Specification 9, 1 day; Specification 10, 7 days; Specification 11, 1 month; Specification 12, 14 days; Specification 13, 14 days; Specification 14, 7 days; Specification 15, 1 day; Specification 17, 42 days; Specification 18, 14 days; Specification 19, 7 days; Specification 20, 2 days; Specification 21, 4 days; Specification 22, 5 days; Specification 23, 6 days; Specification 24, 7 days. All these sentences are to be cumulative and consecutive for the defendant Hoffman.

MR. WEINGLASS: Your Honor, at this time - - I haven't done it before, but I would like to ask bail pending appeal of contempt for not only Mr. Hoffman but the other two defendants, Mr. Davis and Mr. Hayden.

THE COURT: It will be denied because these are direct contempts in the presence of the court and any appeal would be in the opinion of the court frivolous.

The remaining matters here involving Mr. Rubin, Mr. Weiner, Mr. Froines, Mr. Kunstler and Mr. Weinglass will be disposed of tomorrow morning.

DEFENDANT RUBIN: Could we do it now? I don't want to be separated from my brothers.

MR. FORAN: Oh, no.

THE COURT: Tomorrow morning at ten o'clock. I expect the defendants will be around here. The jury is, you know, deliberating.

You don't want to ask a favor of Mr. Hitler, do you, Mr. Rubin?

DEFENDANT RUBIN: Well, Hitler gives his punishment like you do, so let's give it right now. I am ready for it.

THE COURT: I don't think you have much right to ask any sort of courtesy when you talk with a judge the way you have right down to today, to this very afternoon.

These matters of contempt will be considered at ten o'clock tomorrow morning. The court will recess until the return of the jury.

THE MARSHAL: Recess into chambers awaiting the jury?

THE COURT: Yes.

MR. KUNSTLER: Your Honor, does that mean we wait in the Courthouse or could we have - -

THE COURT: I would say you have got a counsel room. If you want to enter into a stipulation for a sealed verdict - -

MR. KUNSTLER: No, no. We don't have a counsel room. They have taken away our room.

THE COURT: If you don't have it, I can't do anything about it. If you will stipulate for a sealed verdict, you may go until tomorrow morning. I have no alternative the other way.

MR. KUNSTLER: Could we be on ten minutes call?

THE COURT: No. I won't do it that way. The defendants will have to wait.

MISS LEANER: Are you going to stay here?

MR. FROINES. Until how long?

THE COURT: All right. I will wait.

MR. WEINER: What do you mean all right?

MISS LEANER: Thanks, Judge.

(Court adjourned.)

RUBIN

February 15, 1970, 10:00 A.M.

THE CLERK: 69 CR 180, United States of America vs. David T. Dellinger, et al.; case on trial.

Your Honor, the defendants are not here. Mr. Weinglass isn't here.

THE COURT: We will have to wait for Mr. Weinglass and Mr. Rubin and any others.

THE CLERK: Everybody is here, your Honor.

THE COURT: I come now to deal with the conduct of Jerry Rubin during this trial.

Specification 1: At the conclusion of the afternoon session on October 28, the defendant Rubin refused to rise in the traditional manner at the direction of the United States Marshals. Official Transcript, Page 4,618-4,619. **1 day**

Specification 2: At the conclusion of the morning session on October 29, the defendant Rubin once more refused to stand at the urging of the Marshal. Official Transcript, Page 4,728-29. **1 day**

Specification 3: When the Court was compelled to call a recess during the afternoon session on October 29, the defendant Rubin once more refused to rise in the traditional manner. Official Transcript, Page 4,763. **1 day**

Specification 4: On October 30 at the beginning of the morning session the defendant Rubin once more refused to rise in the traditional manner. 5. Prior to 5, Miss Reporter, Official Transcript Page 4,801. **1 day**

Specification 5: On October 30, when the Court was required to employ the marshals to physically restrain the defendant Seale, the following colloquy took place:

"MR. KUNSTLER: Your Honor, are we going to stop this medieval torture that is going on in this courtroom? I think this is a disgrace.

MR. RUBIN: This guy is putting his elbow in Bobby's mouth and it wasn't necessary at all.

MR. KUNSTLER: This is no longer a court of order, your Honor; this is a medieval torture chamber. It is a disgrace. They are assaulting the other defendants also.

MR. RUBIN: Don't hit me in the - -"

b-a-l-l-s, Miss Reporter; after that word comes the word mother f-u-c-k-e-r.

"MR. SEALE: This - -"

m-f . . . Fill in the words, Miss Reporter (mother fucker).

"MR. SEALE: - - is tight and it is stopping my blood.

MR. KUNSTLER: Your Honor, this is an unholy disgrace to the law that is going on in this courtroom and I as an American lawyer feel a disgrace.

MR. FORAN: Created by Mr. Kunstler.

MR. KUNSTLER: Created by nothing other than what you have done to this man.

MR. HOFFMAN: You come down here and watch this, Judge.

MR. FORAN: May the record show that the outbursts are the defendant Rubin.

MR. SEALE: You fascist dogs, you rotten low life son of a bitch. I am glad I said it about Washington used to have slaves, the first President - -

MR. DELLINGER: Somebody go to protect him.

MR. FORAN: Your Honor, may the record show that that is Mr. Dellinger saying, 'Someone go to protect him,' and the other comment is by Mr. Rubin.

MR. RUBIN: And my statement, too.

THE COURT: Everything you say will be taken down." Official Transcript, Page 4,815-16. **4 months**

Specification 6: On October 30 when the Court recessed for the lunch hour, the defendant Rubin once more refused to rise in the traditional manner. Official Transcript, Page 4,849-50. **1 day**

Specification 7: At the beginning of the afternoon session on October 30, the defendant Rubin once more refused to rise in the customary manner. Official Transcript, Page 4,853. **1 day**

Specification 8: On January 15, during the testimony of the witness Weiss, the defendant Rubin inserted several comments into the proceedings after the Court sustained objection to several defense exhibits. They follow:

"THE COURT: They laugh at that.

MR. RUBIN: We are standing.

THE COURT: They laugh at that. And talk about racism. I see no proof of racism in the many months we have been here.

Bring in the jury.

MR. RUBIN: Bobby Seale gagged and chained - -" Official Transcript, the page is missing there; it will have to be found. **1 month**

Specification 9: On January 23, the marshals determined that several spectators had been rowdy and had to be removed from the courtroom. One of those spectators was Jerry Rubin's wife. As she was being removed, Mr. Rubin protested loudly and violently. The incident is reported as follows:

"THE COURT: Since you refer to Bobby Seale, your client, I recall - -

MR. KUNSTLER: Not my client, your Honor.

THE COURT: - - I recall being called various kinds of pigs by that man.

MR. RUBIN: Bill, they are taking out my wife.

MR. KUNSTLER: Well, your Honor would not let him defend himself. Everyone knows that now.

(Cries of 'Hey, stop it.')

MR. KUNSTLER: Your Honor, must we always have this, the force and power of the Government?

MR. FORAN: Your Honor - -

MR. RUBIN: They are dragging out my wife - - will you please - -

THE COURT: We must have order in the courtroom." Official Transcript, Page 17,374.

Shortly thereafter, he raised another protest on the same issue.

"THE COURT: I will ask you to sit down, and I ask you again, sir—I order you to sit down.
MR. RUBIN: Am I entitled to a public trial?
THE COURT: No—you have a public trial.
MR. RUBIN: Does the public trial include my wife being in the courtroom? Am I entitled to a public trial?
THE COURT: I don't talk to defendants who have a lawyer.
MR. RUBIN: You didn't listen to my lawyer, so I have to speak. Am I entitled to a public trial?
THE COURT: Mr. Marshal, will you ask that man to sit down.
MARSHAL JOHNSON: Will you sit down, Mr. Rubin." Official Transcript, Page 17,385-86.

6 months

Specification 10: On February 3, the Government called as a rebuttal witness, James Murray. When that witness was excused, as he was walking out of the courtroom, the defendants at their table mocked him by saying, 'Thanks a lot. Thanks a lot.' And Mr. Rubin got up and mockingly offered to shake the man's hand. The incident is reported as follows:

"THE COURT: Call your next witness.
THE DEFENSE TABLE: Thanks a lot. Thanks a lot.
MR. SCHULTZ: Your Honor - -
MR. FORAN: Look at that - -
MR. SCHULTZ: These men who say they have such compassion and love for human beings are trying to humiliate a man, a poor man, a man who is frightened enough to be in this courtroom, who has - -
THE COURT: I have personally noted that the defendant Rubin stood up as the witness was walking out with dignity and tendered his hand.
MR. RUBIN: I wanted to shake his hand.

MR. KUNSTLER: Your Honor, we wanted to thank him. We thought that testimony was helpful." Official Transcript, Pages 19,443-44. **2 months**

Specification 11: On February 4, after the Court had determined that it must terminate the bail of the defendant Dellinger, Mr. Rubin made the following comments:

"MR. RUBIN: Everything in this court is - -"

Miss Reporter, using what has been described as a barnyard term, sometimes familiarly known as b-s, but the full two words are spelled out in the transcript, which you will consult (bull shit).

"MR. RUBIN: You are not going to separate us. Take us, too. Take us all. Show us what a big man you are. Take us all.

MR. RUBIN: Keep your hands off her. You see them taking away my wife?" Official Transcript, Page 19,778-79.

After the Court had recessed that case and ordered the courtroom cleared, Mr. Rubin approached the lectern, pointed his finger directly at the Court and said, "You are a fascist, Hoffman - -" Official Transcript, Page 19,781.

6 months

Specification 12: On February 5, after the Court refused to vacate its order revoking defendant Dellinger's bail, Mr. Rubin engaged in several loud outbursts in the courtroom which are reported as follows:

"MR. RUBIN: You haven't been patient at all. You interrupted my attorney right in the middle of his argument. He was right in the middle of his argument and you interrupted him. You are not being very patient at all. That is not patience.

THE COURT: Ask that man to sit down. Note who he is. That is Mr. Rubin.

MR. RUBIN: Jerry Rubin. Can he finish his argument? Can he finish his argument?

THE COURT: I will ask you to remain quiet, sir.

MR. RUBIN: I will ask you to remain quiet when our attorney [who] represents us is making his arguments." Official Transcript, Pages 19,759-96.

MR. RUBIN: Gestapo.

MR. HOFFMAN: Show him your .45. Show him a .45. He ain't never seen a gun.

MR. RUBIN: This is justice? Huh? Lawyers can't even make an argument? You're a disgrace.

THE CLERK: That is all.

THE COURT: Bring in the jury, Mr. Marshal.

MR. RUBIN: You are the laughing stock of the world, Julius Hoffman; the laughing stock of the world.

MR. HOFFMAN: Mies van der Rohe was a Kraut, too.

MR. RUBIN: Every kid in the world hates you, knows you, what you represent.

MARSHAL DOBOWSKI: Be quiet, Mr. Rubin.

MR. RUBIN: You are synonymous with the name of Adolf Hitler. Julius Hoffman equals Adolf Hitler today." Official Transcript, Pages 19,802-03.

A few minutes later, after the witness lawyer had taken the stand and the jury had re-entered the room, Mr. Rubin again engaged in the following outburst:

"THE COURT: Mr. Marshal, will you tell the defendant Hoffman to remain quiet.

MR. HOFFMAN: Schtunk.

MR. RUBIN: You are a tyrant; you know that.

THE COURT: Mr. Marshal, will you ask Mr. Rubin to remain quiet.

MR. RUBIN: Black robes of death.

MARSHAL DOBOWSKI: Mr. Rubin, I am asking you to be quiet again.

MR. RUBIN: Why don't you ask him so the lawyer can argue.

MARSHAL DOBOWSKI: Be quiet.

MR. RUBIN: You're in a very funny role, Ron. You're in a very funny role. If he ordered you to kill me, would you do it?

MARSHAL DOBOWSKI: Be quiet.

MR. RUBIN: You tell him to keep quiet so my lawyers can speak." Official Transcript, Pages 19,814-15.

MR. KUNSTLER: May we have a time when your Honor would sign this order?

THE COURT: I will do it as soon as I can, sir.

MR. RUBIN: Tyrant.

THE COURT: Mr. Marshal, please have that man refrain from using those epithets.

MR. RUBIN: It is just descriptive. Just describing what I see." Official Transcript, Pages 18,818-19.

At the close of that morning session on February 5, the defendant Rubin once more exclaimed in a loud voice:

"MR. RUBIN: Tyrant." Official Transcript, Page 19,877. **6 months**

Specification 13: On February 6, the defendant Rubin entered the courtroom wearing judicial robes. This conduct was an attempt to hold the Court up to ridicule. The incident is reported as follows:

"THE COURT: May the record show defendants Hoffman and Rubin came in at 1:28 - -"

There is a correction there, Miss Reporter. It should be 10:28.

"THE COURT: - - with their - -

MR. RUBIN: The marshal just came and asked us to come in. We came in as soon as we were asked.

THE COURT: And also attired in what might be called collegiate robes.

MR. RUBIN: Judge's robes, sir.

A DEFENDANT: Death robes.

THE COURT: Some might even consider them judicial robes.

MR. RUBIN: Judicial robes." Official Transcript, Page 19,888. **7 days**

Specification 14: On February 6, as the witness Irv Bock was leaving the stand and passing the defense table, the defendant Rubin commented to him, in a voice loud enough to be heard by the jurors and the Court:

"MR. RUBIN: Tough luck, Irv." Official Transcript, Page 20,019. **7 days**

Specification 15: On February 7, while the Court was hearing argument on a motion for a continuance at the close of the Government's rebuttal case, the defendant Rubin interjected the following comment:

"MR. RUBIN: Refuse to rest." Official Transcript, Page 20,270. **3 days**

I will hear Mr. Rubin if he desires to be heard.

MR. ————: Your Honor, before you hear Mr. Rubin, I want to - -

THE COURT: I will not hear counsel.

MR. KUNSTLER: No, we have to make - - I have to just, without repeating it, say that for the record we make the same argument that I have made and that Mr. Weinglass has made - -

THE COURT: This is conduct—contemptuous conduct, committed in the presence of the Court.

MR. KUNSTLER: Yes, I know, but our claim is you don't have the power - -

THE COURT: I will let your statement remain. The direct contempt seen and heard by the Court in its actual presence, during this—the trial of this case. In such circumstances, I am not obligated here to hear counsel, but I did yesterday, and, if you will want to make your —make a motion on jurisdictional grounds, I will consider that you made it on the same ground that you did yesterday.

MR. KUNSTLER: I make it on the same ground as I did yesterday.

THE COURT: I will hear Mr. Rubin, if he desires to be heard, but only if he is respectful to the Court. I say to you, Mr. Rubin, as long as you are respectful and confine your observations and remarks to the issues here, which are the alleged contempts committed by you in the presence of the Court.

MR. RUBIN: I want to discuss the contempts and the motivation behind them, which would affect your punishment and I want to start with the references that I have made on a number of occasions to Gestapo, fascism and Hitler, and I want to explain what motivated me to say that.

Everything that happened in Nazi Germany was legal. It happened in courtrooms, just like this. It was done by judges, judges who wore robes and judges who quoted the law and judges who said, "This is the law, respect it."

We saw Nazi Germany immoral, and I think that this is the closest thing that I personally experienced to what happened in Nazi Germany, and it was the closest thing in my experience to say to you, to communicate to you, that just quoting the law is no answer, because the law in the courtroom gagged and chained Bobby Seale and I refuse to stand up and say, "Heil Hitler" when a black man was gagged and chained and I think that any human being sitting in that courtroom refused to stand up and that's why I refused to stand up, because I came to this trial, I wanted to be indicted.

I issued a statement I was indicted upon the Academy Award protest. I was ready for a trial with lawyers, a full defense. The moment you walked in, I don't know what day it was, for the arraignment, we got from you instantly the message we were going to jail, and I think it's interesting that while the jury is out, before it reaches a verdict, the 10 of us are going to jail. Who has respect for the law?

THE COURT: Speak to the --

MR. RUBIN: I am speaking to the specification.

THE COURT: -- matters I have referred to or I will have to ask you to sit down.

MR. RUBIN: Okay, I am trying.

THE COURT: No, you are not succeeding.

MR. RUBIN: You tell me what I --

THE COURT: You are not succeeding. And I will not suffer any further additional insults from you.

MR. RUBIN: Let me try again.

THE COURT: I will let you speak in mitigation, if you have anything in mitigation.

MR. RUBIN: I am --

THE COURT: But I shall not let you make untruthful statements such as the moment I walked in, on the first day of trial --

MR. RUBIN: I was saying that was the impression that we got.

THE COURT: There is no proof of that in the record. It is not true and I will not permit such a statement to be made. I strike the remark from the record. Don't make such a statement again or anything like that, or I will ask you to sit down, sir.

MR. RUBIN: Okay.

THE COURT: By "Okay," you promise me that you

will confine your remarks?

MR. RUBIN: Yes, sir. O.K.

THE COURT: By O.K. you mean you promise me that you will confine your remarks?

MR. RUBIN: It is very hard for me to confine my remarks to exactly the specifications you adapted in advance.

THE COURT: You speak only in mitigation.

MR. RUBIN: But you correct me if I make a misstatement.

THE COURT: I have some misgivings as to whether you even have the right --

MR. RUBIN: You can punish me for these words, but let me say my opinion.

THE COURT: I won't argue with you.

MR. RUBIN: O.K. Can I have a second start?

THE COURT: Go. ahead. Take your second start.

MR. RUBIN: Now I have -- I don't know, I think you quoted that I said, "Julius Hoffman equals Adolf Hitler." I said that because I think what we are experiencing in this courtroom is the tyranny of the state, the tyranny of the law, and you have said to us, "Respect or else," and you haven't given moral arguments, and, as a matter of fact, you have shown more disrespect toward us than we have toward you.

What has been our disrespect toward you?

THE COURT: Now, you are not -- my what you call disrespect for you isn't an issue.

MR. RUBIN: You have interrupted us every time. You have interrupted us every time we speak.

THE COURT: I will not permit you --

MR. RUBIN: You have accused us of laughing at you.

THE COURT: I have endured just about enough.

MR. RUBIN: You are paranoiac sending us off to jail.

THE COURT: I will ask you to sit down.

MR. RUBIN: I want to talk about punishment. I want to talk about punishment.

THE COURT: I will ask you to sit down -- If you want to talk about punishment, I will hear you on that.

MR. RUBIN: O.K.; O.K. What is the purpose of punishing the ten of us?

THE COURT: Not "the ten of us."

MR. RUBIN: By punishing the ten of us --
THE COURT: No.
MR. RUBIN: -- we're all one and one for all, just ten. That's because --
THE COURT: No --
MR. RUBIN: -- because we identify with each other. By punishing the ten of us --
THE COURT: -- we are considering your contempt only.
MR. RUBIN: By punishing us, you are going to have ten million in two weeks. Deterrent? Putting us in jail is just going to produce more trials like this. You have done more to destroy the judicial system. That's what punishment is going to be; that's what punishment is going to be. Revenge never got you anywhere. By having to punish us, you have shown the world that this judicial system has lost the respect of the youth, and the youth will free us. We're going to go to jail with smiles on our faces because we know that in jail, there are millions of kids, young kids out there who identify with us, and are going to fight to free us, and that's the revolution. And your jailing us is a vindictive, revengeful act.

Obscenity. I am accused of obscenity. What is obscenity? To me, the war in Vietnam is an obscenity. Racism is an obscenity.
THE COURT: I will tell you, sir --
MR. RUBIN: My gosh, for you, obscenity is words connected to the body, to the body. That is obscenity. A sexual act becomes obscenity in your mind, and we get punished for that.
THE COURT: Don't speak for what is in my mind. You may speak --
MR. RUBIN: I am speaking for what I am going to jail for. I am speaking for what I am going to jail for.
THE COURT: You may speak in mitigation of your punishment.
MR. RUBIN: By the way, there are a lot of inaccuracies in here, a lot of things that I didn't say and that someone else said, but I'm not going to correct them because, I repeat, you're not going to divide us here at this defense table as you tried to do when you gagged and chained Bobby Seale and when you put Dave Dellinger in jail on his bail. We're going together.

There were 25,000 people in the Stadium in Los Angeles last night, and there are going to be meetings across the country and demonstrations across the country. And you have destroyed the judicial system. You have done more harm to this country than any other single person alive today.

You should be ashamed of yourself.

THE COURT: You may sit down.

MR. RUBIN: I am happy to.

THE COURT: In conformity with Rule 42(a) of the Federal Rules of Criminal Procedure in Title 18 of the United States Code, Section 401, I certify that I saw and heard the conduct which I have just described here in open court this morning in the case United States of America vs. David Dellinger, 69 CR 180, which commenced on September 24th, 1969, and has continued for about four and a half months.

MR. RUBIN: And tomorrow and the next day, until I am dead.

THE COURT: Yes, that may be recorded, that the defendant Rubin said "And tomorrow."

MR. RUBIN: Until I am dead.

THE COURT: I find the acts, statements and conduct of the defendant Jerry C. Rubin constitute a separate—each constituted a separate contempt of this Court and each constituted a deliberate and wilful attack upon the administration of justice, in an attempt to sabotage the functioning of the federal judicial system; that this misconduct was of so grave a character as to continually disrupt the orderly administration of justice. Accordingly, I notice that it is difficult, that a reading of this record cannot and does not reflect the true intensity and extent of the disruptions which in some instances were accompanied by physical violence, which occurred in the presence of the Court. Accordingly, I adjudge the defendant Jerry C. Rubin guilty of several criminal contempts which I have described, and I might say that in citing these specific acts and statements of the defendant Rubin this morning as contemptuous, I have selected the most flagrant.

On Specification 1, the defendant Rubin will be committed to the custody of the Attorney General or his authorized representative for imprisonment for a period of 1 day; Specification 2, 1 day; Specification 3, 1 day; Specification 4, 1 day; Specification 5, 4 months; Specification 6, 1 day; Specification 7, 1 day; Specification 8, 1 month; Specification 9, 6 months; Specification 10, 2 months; Specification 11, 6 months; Specification 12, 6 months. The sentence is to run accumulatively and consecutively.

I direct the United States Attorney to prepare the appropriate documents.

MR. SCHULTZ: You haven't covered the remaining counts. I think there were more counts than 12.

That's the total sentence we should cover in the order.

THE COURT: You mean the specifications --

MR. SCHULTZ: There were 15 specifications.

THE COURT: 15.

MR. SCHULTZ: Do you want to leave the remaining specifications out?

THE COURT: On Specification -- what was the last one I read?

THE CLERK: 12.

THE COURT: Yes, you are quite right. There is a blank space here.

Specification 12, 6 months; Specification 13, 7 days; Specification 14, 7 days; Specification 15, 3 days.

Those cover all of the specifications and I direct the United States Attorney to prepare the necessary documents reflecting the views of the Court and I direct the marshal to take the defendant Rubin into custody.

MR. KUNSTLER: For the record, I would like to move for bail pending appeal for Mr. Rubin.

THE COURT: Bail is not indicated in this case. It would be frivolous in view of what appears on the record itself, Mr. Kunstler.

MR. RUBIN: Sadist.

THE COURT: I deny the motion.

MR. RUBIN: Sadist.

WEINER

THE COURT: We come now to the consideration of the conduct of Defendant Lee Weiner.

Specification 1: On October 28 at the end of the session, the defendant Weiner refused to stand in the traditional manner when directed to do so by the marshal. Official Transcript, Page 4,618-19. **1 day**

Specification 2: On October 29 when the Court called a recess, the defendant Weiner once more refused to rise in the traditional manner. Official Transcript, Page 4,728-29. **1 day**

Specification 3: On October 29 when the Court was compelled to call a recess because of the conduct of the defendant Seale, the defendant Weiner once more refused to rise in the customary manner when the Court left the bench. Page 4,763 of the transcript. **1 day**

Specification 4: On October 30 at the beginning of the court session, the defendant Weiner refused to rise in the customary manner when the Judge entered the courtroom. Page 4,801. **1 day**

Specification 5: On December 1, while the witness Rochford was on the stand, the defendant Weiner made the following comment in a voice loud enough to be heard by the Court and others present, including the jurors:

> "DEFENDANT WEINER: Bill, the executioner is mumbling and I can't hear him.
>
> "MR. KUNSTLER: Your Honor, is it possible to tell the witness to keep his voice up?
>
> "THE COURT: I think it is possible. I have demonstrated that because I have asked him two or three times already.

"MR. FORAN: May the record show the comment? Did you get that comment?
"DEFENDANT DELLINGER: He was speaking to his lawyer.
"MR. FORAN: The comment was: 'The executioner is mumbling and I can't hear him.' I would like the record to show that.
"MR. KUNSTLER: Your Honor, it is just like a school marm that has to every time point out - -
"THE COURT: Yes, I heard it. I heard that. It is in the record." Page 8,610. **1 month**

Specification 6: On January 14, during the redirect examination of the witness Edmundson, the defendant Dellinger rose and made a speech. After that speech, the Defendant Weiner sat at the table and openly applauded him. The following colloquy occurred:

"THE COURT: Will you let the record show - - I don't know, I get twisted between the defendants - - the one in the middle.
"MR. WEINER: Weiner.
"A DEFENDANT: Davis.
"MR. WEINER: Weiner.
"THE COURT: Mr. Weiner applauded after that speech." Page 15,591 of the transcript. **14 days**

Specification 7: On January 28, in front of the jury, the defendant Weiner engaged in the following exchange:

"MR. SCHULTZ: I wish Davis, who was such a gentle boy on the stand the last couple of days, smiling at the jury and pretending he was just a little boy next door, would stop whispering and talking to me while I am talking.
"MR. DAVIS: You are a disgrace, sir. I say you are a disgrace. I really say you are a disgrace.
"VOICES: Yes. Yes.
"MR. SCHULTZ: I think he has a split personality, like a schizophrenic.
"MR. WEINER: Now he is a psychological student.
"MR. SCHULTZ: So, your Honor, I would ask that you do follow proper procedure considering the representation - -
"THE COURT: Will you excuse me, please.

Mr. Marshal, if you can't do it alone, have another marshal assist you, and stand at that table there so that I can listen to the United States Attorney make his presentation as I expect to try to listen to counsel for the defense when I call on them to reply. This thing has been going on all through this trial, but very little can be done about it at the moment." Pages 18,397-98. **1 month**

THE COURT: Mr. Weiner -- Mr. Weinglass, within the limitation suggested to Mr. Kunstler, I will let you address the Court. While I did indulge the lawyers yesterday, there is no precedent in law in a proceeding of this kind.

MR. WEINGLASS: That is precisely why we feel compelled --

THE COURT: In making your argument, I will let you protect your record or Mr. Weiner's record, in respect to this proceeding which is separate and apart from the case that has been tried.

MR. WEINGLASS: Yes. I will adopt Mr. Kunstler's original argument, an argument which I repeated several times yesterday.

I furthermore would like to point out to the Court that the total length of time that it took the Court to read the disruptions attributable to Mr. Weiner, over a 20-week period of time, was six minutes. And, again, if we concede that Mr. Weiner made all these statements, your Honor will recall in not a single instance was the jury required to leave the room, were the proceedings interrupted any longer than it took the time for the words to be uttered, so there is a man before you, who stands before you with a six-minute disruption of a 20-week trial. I think in light of that fact, the punishment, whatever it is, should be given accordingly.

As a matter of fact, I used to have some questions or some concern in my heart, my gut, about things and now, now, I feel very much more confident that my three-year-old child will make the revolution that we are only slowly groping for. Thank you for that.

THE COURT: Mr. Weiner, if you will confine your remarks to the thoughts you have in respect to mitigation of punishment, I will hear you, sir.

MR. WEINER: Sure, sure.

THE COURT: I don't think that you can -- at least I got the impression that you were a university teacher, and I don't think that you would be insulting to the court. I will hear you, sir.
MR. WEINER: I doubt very seriously whether you consider my university teaching other than insulting.

I will say, let me just say that I have sat here quietly for the most part, especially at the start, as you have really abused and finally buried --
THE COURT: I didn't hear that.
MR. WEINER: I think I stand here as I have seen you abuse and finally bury any left-over notions, childlike notions, that the courts of America are a place that some form of social justice is ultimately somehow handled. Now we know, I think, how childlike those notions were. I don't have any --
THE COURT: You will have to address yourself --
MR. WEINER: I will; I will.
THE COURT: -- to your own proceeding here which is one that involves you --
MR. WEINER: I intend to.
THE COURT: -- and you alone.
MR. WEINER: I intend to. You caught me not standing four times and take that as a measure of my disrespect for the Court.

While I appreciate the latest attempt to mitigate a particular kind of sentence, I suppose I am interested in mitigating the sentence, I have my self-interest, I would say that throughout this trial, I have sat in a quiet rage as I have seen over and over again the best men of our country, most of my brother defendants, but this has to do with the witnesses as well, the best men and women belittled and attacked in small ways, and sometimes in very great ways, such as Bobby.

If I didn't stand four times and that constitutes a contempt of court, I can only say to you that I feel that contempt of court very deeply, very strongly in my heart.

I think the judicial system is a fairly reasonable one—twelve jurors, the evidence—that is kind of good; that is kind of good.
THE COURT: The judicial system is what?
MR. WEINER: I think the judicial system as an idea,

an abstract idea, is a fairly reasonable one, and so I have a great deal of sympathy, and, I guess, pity for Lennie and Bill who have worked so hard to gain some expertise in a system which should, if it functioned adequately, provide some opportunity for some kind of an abstract notion of justice to come at least close to, but I think that here, you, not necessarily because you are anything necessarily evil, but simply because you are what you are, who you are - - you are older than us - -

THE COURT: I didn't hear that last. You are talking about me. I want to hear that.

MR. WEINER: I say you are older than us. I say that you are a judge in an institutional form, the courtroom, which supports all your notions of omnipotence, all of your notions of being able to abstractly punish the grief that all of us willingly will bear in jail. It is an abstract reason, one that doesn't touch you. It is all right. I neither forgive you, nor do I necessarily personally condemn you for being what you are, just as I don't personally condemn Tom or Dicky. They are technicians; they do their job for a fascist state.

I think when I talked to Bill when the policeman was on the stand, when I said, "Bill, the executioner is mumbling," I'd say that that represents another abstract notion of what this courtroom is about. Just as you see us as defendant, we see ourselves as revolutionaries. You see us on trial in a criminal trial. We see ourselves under the gun of a political trial being used as a weapon in the hands of the government in an ongoing political war against dissent and youth in this country. There are different ways of looking at it. I don't consider calling a policeman an executioner anything other than a relatively direct expression of how I see the world.

Applauding Dave's speech - - Dave is probably one of the most moral and brave men in America. I don't necessarily - -

THE COURT: I heard that yesterday, but that isn't an issue here.

MR. WEINER: Yes. Well, the problem is I tried to put my applause - - I am trying to put my applause - -

THE COURT: I must admonish you, sir - -

MR. WEINER: Yes.

THE COURT: - - I am supposed to be especially tolerant because years ago when I was a much younger man, I was a member of the faculty of the school that you - - I don't know whether you still are; at least it has been suggested here during this trial that you are or were a teacher there.

MR. WEINER: I even understand that there is a plaque naming an auditorium after you at the Law School. At latest report, by the way - -

THE COURT: You are nice to tell the assembled spectators here - -

MR. WEINER: I tell them actually for an evil reason.

THE COURT: - - that there is a Hoffman Hall on Northwestern University's campus.

MR. WEINER: I tell them actually because I am suggesting it is evil.

THE COURT: Perhaps those who think ill of me because of some of the things that have been said might have a little compassion.

MR. WEINER: I am pleased to report to you that the plaque has been ripped off the wall.

THE COURT: The plaque?

MR. WEINER: The plaque has been ripped off the wall in the auditorium. Apparently while the Board of Trustees feel affection for you, the student body does not.

THE COURT: Did they take the sign off the door?

MR. WEINER: They have done their best. They have done their best.

THE COURT: I haven't been there.

MR. WEINER: I wouldn't suggest immediately appearing at the Law School after you get through with this trial. You might be mobbed, not necessarily as a tourist of our law building.

THE COURT: I appreciate your warning, but I wish you would talk about your contempt case here.

MR. WEINER: I guess I would say that I think the spirit of rebellion that you are concerned with and for which you punish us for engaging in has, if anything, been encouraged, if anything, has been brought closer by your actions.

I think that the revolution that we all work for, and our brothers and our sisters, and I am happy to say my

child, will work for --
THE COURT: You, as a person concerned with the teaching profession, ought to clearly understand that what I am permitting you to do is to speak in mitigation.

Whether you have been rightfully charged or wrongfully charged depends upon the verdict of the jury and the law of the case. How you behave during a trial is something else again. A man can be charged, and an innocent man, this has happened, can be charged with a crime of murder and, yet, he must sit in court with his lawyer and let a trial be conducted according to the rules until those rules are changed. No individual can himself change the rules in the middle --
MR. WEINER: Let me say --
THE COURT: -- in the middle of a trial, and, in the process, insult the judge and abuse the judge.
MR. WEINER: Fine.
THE COURT: I am telling you something that you do know. You must know. I don't think the University would have employed you to teach if you hadn't known at least that much.
MR. WEINER: There is no question about it. I am smart. I am smart. There is no question about it.
THE COURT: If you have anything to say --
MR. WEINER: About punishment.
THE COURT: -- in mitigation of your sentence --
MR. WEINER: Sure, I do. Sure, I do. I do.
THE COURT: I will hear that.
MR. WEINER: I think --
THE COURT: I will hear that.
MR. WEINER: I think I agree with you. You see, for now, it is your court. For now, they are your prisoners. It is your government.
THE COURT: It is a court, sir, one court in the federal system. I happen to have been appointed to preside as one of eleven judges here in this district. That is all. Just one judge.
MR. WEINER: I have known that.
THE COURT: This is a case assigned to me on the turn of the wheel.
MR. WEINER: I would say the ten of us --
THE COURT: I have done the best I can.

MR. WEINER: I am sure. I am sure. I am absolutely positive of that.

THE COURT: My best hasn't accorded with what you perceive and some of your co-defendants perceive to be the best kind of judicial conduct.

MR. WEINER: I think it has been terrific.

THE COURT: One thing I have learned in this work, that a judge can't always please everybody.

MR. WEINER: You have pleased me.

THE COURT: If a judge starts out to please everybody, he will end up being a pretty bad judge.

MR. WEINER: Let me just say one last thing, then. I think you have pleased me.

I think we ten, and I mean my brothers and sisters here in the audience, and downstairs, and across the country, are only slowly groping toward a revolution. I think that you in your own inimitable style have made real a world, and people must struggle in making their political revolution against a real world, not a fantasy world. You have helped educate people younger than ourselves as to what the real world is.

THE COURT: In conformity with the Rule 42(a) of the Federal Rules of Criminal Procedure, Titile 18, United States Code, Section 401, I hereby certify that I saw and heard the conduct set forth in my observations of this morning, which conduct took place in the actual presence of the Court during the trial, in the case entitled United States of America vs. David Dellinger and others, 69 CR 180, which commenced on September 24, 1969 and has continued for about four and a half months.

I find that the acts, statements and conduct of the defendant, Mr. Weiner, Lee Weiner, each constitute a separate contempt of this Court, each constituted a deliberate and wilful attack upon the administration of justice in an attempt to sabotage the functioning of the federal judicial system, that finding is supported by the observations of the defendant just made in open court, that this misconduct was of so great a character as to continually disrupt the orderly administration of justice.

Mr. Clerk, with respect to Specification 1, the defendant Weiner will be committed to the custody of the United States Attorney or his authorized representative for a period, for imprisonment, a period of 1 day; with respect to Specification 2, 1 day; with respect to Specification 3, 1 day; with respect to Specification 4, 1 day; with respect to Specification 5, 1 month; with respect to Specification 6, 14 days; with respect to Specification 7, 1 month; these sentences to be cumulative and consecutive and the defendant is ordered into the custody of the United States Marshal for the Northern District of

FROINES

We come now to the consideration of the matters involving the defendant John Froines.

Specification 1: The record reveals that on August 28 the defendant Froines laughed openly and subsequently commented on his laughter. The - -

MR. KUNSTLER: Your Honor, I think you are mistaken. August 28, we weren't even here.

THE COURT: I said August; I meant October.

MR. KUNSTLER: Right.

THE COURT: I am mistaken. I thank you for correcting me.

On October 28, the record does indicate October 28, the defendant Froines laughed only and subsequently commented on his laughter. The United States Attorney suggested that that remark be made a part of the record. Mr. Kunstler, the attorney, indicated there was no objection to its being made a part of the record. The interchange appears as follows:

> "THE COURT: Your hearing - -
>
> "MR. FORAN: Your Honor, may the record show that the defendant Froines just made a comment, saying, 'We laughed - - we laughed because it was a stupid answer.' I would like to put that in the record also.
>
> "MR. KUNSTLER: We have no objection to that going into the record, your Honor.
>
> "THE COURT: It stands on the record then, and I will sustain the objection to the last question." Page 4,544 of the transcript of record. **1 month**

Specification 2: At the close of the session on October 28, the defendant Froines refused to rise in the traditional manner, despite being instructed to do so by the United States Marshal. Page 4,618-19. **1 day**

Specification 3: When the Court was required to call a recess on October 29 because of the conduct of Mr. Seale, the defendant Froines refused to rise in the traditional manner when the Court left the bench. Page 4,763 of the transcript of record. **1 day**

Specification 4: At the beginning of the session on October 30 when the Court entered the room, the defendant Froines once more refused to rise in the traditional manner. Page 4,801 of the transcript of record. **1 day**

Specification 5: On December 17 while the lawyers were engaged in an argument, Mr. Froines made an interjection. The following reflects the incident:

> "MR. SCHULTZ: If the Court please, there is further evidence not only that such objects existed but we tie them into the defendants themselves because Mr. Frapolly testified that on Tuesday night in Lincoln Park at 10:30 while sitting with the ministers --
> "MR. KUNSTLER: If he is going to recapitulate the testimony, it is totally improper.
> "MR. SCHULTZ: I am answering Mr. Kunstler, if the Court please. I am answering Mr. Kunstler that the defendant John Froines was sitting with a group where they were discussing nails and putting objects --
> "MR. FROINES: That is a lie. That was not the testimony." Page 11,549. **1 month**

Specification 6: On December 30 Mr. Dellinger was engaged in a colloquy with the Court. In the course of that discussion Mr. Froines interjected a comment. That is recorded as follows:

> "MR. DELLINGER: Decorum is more important than justice, I suppose.
> "THE COURT: I have never sat in a trial, over the many years, where a defendant has spoken upon his own when --
> "MR. FROINES: Perhaps you can give him four years like you gave Bobby Seale.
> "MR. DELLINGER: We just walk politely into jail.
> "MR. SCHULTZ: Mr. Froines is the one who just

made that comment about Bobby Seale. I am sure the Court saw that." Page 12,915. **1 month**

Specification 7: On February 2, the Court ruled that the defendants had rested their case in chief in that they were not prepared to put another witness on the stand, and they made representations concerning their intentions to rest. The Court further ordered the defendants to make no reference before the jury of the fact that they had wanted Dr. Ralph Abernathy to testify. Page 19,140.

Subsequently that morning before the jury, during the direct examination of the witness Lynskey, Mr. Froines made the following comment from the defense table:

"MR. FORAN: Your Honor, the interruption in the midst of the questioning of a witness in the presence of the jury is unheard of, your Honor. I wish he would - -

"MR. FROINES: So is not putting on a witness." Page 19,156. **14 days**

Specification 8: On February 2, the Court objected to Mr. Kunstler's demonstration of affection for Dr. Abernathy in front of the jury. The following colloquy took place between the Court and Mr. Kunstler in which Mr. Froines interjected a comment:

"THE COURT: I have never seen that in a courtroom.

"MR. KUNSTLER: But you have never seen us before, your Honor, and the movement - -

"THE COURT: That's right.

"MR. KUNSTLER: - - and the movement has a physically touching quality to it which is sort of irrpressible sometimes.

"THE COURT: There are certain kinds of conduct one engages in in a courtroom and in other places.

"MR. KUNSTLER: Well, there is, because there are different life styles in this courtroom.

"MR. FROINES: We will change that." Page 19,194 of the transcript. **14 days**

Specification 9: On February 2, when the witness Murray left the stand, the defendants mockingly said, 'Thanks a lot. Thanks a lot,' and the defendant Rubin stood and mockingly offered to shake hands with the witness. Mr. Froines interjected the following remarks, along with others:

"MR. KUNSTLER: Your Honor, we wanted to thank him. We thought that testimony was helpful.
"MR. FROINES: I beg your pardon. That man wants to put us away for ten years by lying and we think this proves it and we have a right - -
"THE COURT: Make a note that that man is Mr. Froines.
"A VOICE: Froines.
"MR. FROINES: Disgusting." Official Transcript, Page 19,444. **2 months**

Specification 10: On April 5, a loud conference was taking place at the defense table. The Court instructed the marshal to quiet the conference down and - -
MR. KUNSTLER: Excuse me, your Honor. I think you said "April."
THE COURT: Did I say "April" again? I am sorry.
MR. KUNSTLER: You said that on two occasions.
THE COURT: Thank you for the correction.
MR. KUNSTLER: In Specification 8, you also have April. You meant February, I am sure.
THE COURT: I will have to see whether there is an error in the notes here.

You are quite right. Miss Reporter, change the month in Specification 8 from April to February, and also Specification 9. I continue and then continue on with what I have said in connection with Specification 9.

On Specification 10, on February 5, a loud conference was taking place at the defense table. The Court instructed the marshal to quiet the conference down and Mr. Froines interjected a comment:

"MR. FORAN: Your Honor, it is very difficult to present a witness who has got a soft voice when there is agitation at the defense table, whispering and motion over there. It is extremely difficult for the jury to hear what is going on. I wish we could have the defense table sit quiet.
"THE COURT: The marshal will try to maintain

quiet at the table while examination of the witness is going on.

"MR. FROINES: I am sorry, there was no agitation. They were simply discussing the revocation of David Dellinger's bond." Official transcript, Page 19,847

14 days

In the same manner as heretofore this morning, I will hear counsel for Mr. Froines.

MR. KUNSTLER: Your Honor, just a nune pro tunc with reference to Mr. Weiner. We want to move for bail pending appeal for him. We have got to do that.

THE COURT: That will be denied for the reasons previously indicated. Such an appeal, in the opinion of the Court, in view of the record here, would be frivolous.

MR. KUNSTLER: As with all the others, your Honor, we move to vacate any findings of contempt on the ground that your Honor lacks jurisdiction to impose summary contempt at the close of the case and for all the other reasons advanced by us previously.

THE COURT: I deny the motion.

Mr. Froines, you - -

MR. KUNSTLER: I have one more point, your Honor, with reference to the incident of February 5 when there was a conference at the defense table. At that time, Mr. Froines was consulting with Stuart Ball. We meant to put this on the record then. Stuart Ball was at the defense table and they were discussing legal aspects of Mr. Dellinger's bond revocation. I recall that myself, and I know that both Mr. Weinglass and I intended to put it on the record.

THE COURT: So far as I know, the record does not reflect that.

MR. KUNSTLER: No, it does not, but I am just stating it.

THE COURT: For whatever importance it has, it does not reflect that.

MR. KUNSTLER: I am stating that as my own personal remembrance of the situation.

THE COURT: Did you wish to say something?

MR. ————: With regard to that conference Mr. Kunstler brought up, your Honor did not state in the reading of the citation that prior to that, when Mr. Dellinger's bond had been revoked, there had been a colloquy in court where the defendants and defendants' counsel, I believe, was directed - - all were directed not to mention the revocation of the bond in the presence of the jury. Your Honor did not include that. I wasn't going to mention it, but since Mr. Kunstler is explaining it away, I thought that it would be appropriate to call that to your Honor - -

THE COURT: Well, I will let - - I can't insert in the record something that does not appear, but I will let Mr. Kunstler's observations about the attendance of Mr. Ball remain of record for whatever it is worth.

I will next consider the conduct of the lawyers in this case - - oh, I beg your pardon. We have - - I almost forgot to take care of Mr. Froines. Mr. Kunstler has finished. Mr. Froines, I give you the same opportunity I accorded all of the others to speak in mitigation of punishment here, but without saying offensive things to the Court.

MR. FROINES: It's part of being a media unknown that even the Judge finally forgets you're here.

THE COURT: I didn't hear that.

MR. FROINES: It's perhaps an in joke, your Honor.

I have just as another side and in no way disrespectful of the Court, Mr. Schultz is the kind of man I met years ago in the fourth grade who always used to tell the teacher when you were talking to your friends. He is basically a tattle-tale. I think the - -

THE COURT: You are talking down into the tables and I want to hear what you are saying, if you will stand up - -

MR. FROINES: You see, it's very difficult for me to speak because I am supposed to speak about the punishment, or in mitigation of punishment.

THE COURT: That's the rules. There is no provision in the rules to let a man philosophize.

MR. FROINES: I appreciate that. It's just that - -

THE COURT: In these circumstances. We are considering only the contempt, you know. This proceeding is quite apart from the trial of the main case.

MR. FROINES: I appreciate that, your Honor.

What I feel is that for me in some respects to speak about the punishment is to dignify it in some way, to dignify this punishment that we are all going to receive. So I feel very tied up in terms of talking about it but I think that some way people should say things. I think things finally have to be said.

THE COURT: I agree, but at an appropriate time. This isn't the time to talk about anything except matters that affect the allegedly contemptuous [acts] of yourself and others.
MR. FROINES: Well, I am the last defendant - -
THE COURT: That's right.
MR. FROINES: - - to be sentenced, although it is quite clear that there are two other defendants at this table besides myself, as there are millions of defendants throughout this country and throughout the world in this particular courtroom who still have to be charged.

I think that as Tom said yesterday, you nor anybody like you can ever sentence and punish all those people that you finally and all that is represented will, in fact, finally be vilified by history; that, when history is written, the men who have sat at this table, men there in the spectators' section who stood all night to come to this courtroom, our people here, that's the heroes. That is what this trial is about.

But what is going to happen in this country and across this world, Vietnam in the living room - -
THE COURT: Crowd out of your mind, sir, that I have ever had a desire to be a hero. A judge who sets out to be a hero and all things to all people will end up being a mighty incompetent judge.
MR. FROINES: Well, I am not - -
THE COURT: You are - - your lawyers made various motions in this court preliminary to trial. They were what we call - - you are not legally trained, are you? You are a chemist by profession.

I say to you that we describe those motions as pretrial motions and they were very well prepared, prepared, I think it was said here, by a professor of law at Northwestern University, a friend of mine. I think that was said in open court. Those weren't the exact words. We studied those motions and the briefs filed, memorandum filed in support of them as we studied the memoranda and the briefs filed by the Government. That was your right to make those motions, given you under the federal system of justice which prevails. You sought among other things, you and your associates, to have the law involved here declared unconstitutional.

MR. FROINES: I am so - - I don't understand that this is relative.
THE COURT: I don't see how any can complain of a system of law that permits a person to take a position opposed to that of the Government, argue it in writing, and have a trial judge decide a case, and then go on to, later, if it becomes necessary, to another court. I just fail - - this thought has been expressed so often, and I am unable to understand it.

I am not biased in favor of the law. I am alive to the fact that there are incompetent teachers of chemistry and incompetent teachers of law and incompetent judges. That is the nature of a democracy. We are going to get - - we have some reporters who are objective in - - who write accurate stories, sometimes even though they are accurate they are entertaining. Some sacrifice accuracy for pure entertainment, or other reasons. But every man in his own profession can't be perfect, but you and your co-defendants have availed yourself of the benefits of the American, United States judicial system.
MR. FROINES: You have that a little backward because we didn't ask actually to come here.
THE COURT: What do you say?
MR. FROINES: We didn't ask to come here. I would prefer to stay where I was.
THE COURT: If the law enforcement agencies of the Government were to wait for all alleged lawbreakers to invite themselves here, I am afraid that most of the courthouses in the land could be burned down. There would be a lot of people - -
MR. FROINES: You have got a thought there.
THE COURT: - - and you can see the thinking. You could hear the noise back there after I expressed that thought. And I meant it, and I wasn't being facetious, but, of course, you weren't invited to come here. The constituted authorities thought you had - - and your co-defendants had violated the law. We try many cases here. I have tried as many as any other judge during my tenure in this district, perhaps in any district. Sometimes we are held to be right, sometimes wrong, but that is the American way. I know of no better way and I am not being chauvinistic when I say that. I believe it sincerely, not because I happen to have chosen

the law as my profession. I haven't been able to find in my reading any better way of determining issues. Certainly we can't let seven or eight defendants at a defense table try their own cases. Now, maybe it will come to that. If it is —and I am living—I will try to become reconciled to it. I will have to because I will be out of a job. It will all be decided at that table.

MR. FROINES: We're working on that one.

THE COURT: What did you say?

MR. FROINES: We're working on that.

THE COURT: I suspect you are, from what I hear.

MR. FROINES: I have a little more - - I would rather go - - I appreciate the chance to have an interchange about the basic facts of American life, but I would like to go to my friends.

THE COURT: To your friends?

MR. FROINES: Yes, I would. As much as I appreciate the opportunity to listen to you, I also thought it was me who was to do the talking.

THE COURT: No, you talk about yourself, you are right. I was only trying to reply to your observation about the American judicial system or system of law, that's all.

MR. FROINES: I come, as you know perhaps, from the state of Oregon and - -

THE COURT: I have read that.

MR. FROINES: In the Oregon Constitution there is an article which I think describes some of which we do and that is entitled "Natural Rights Inherent in the People." It says that we declare all men, when they form a social compact, are equal in right, that all power is inherent in the people, and all free governments are founded on their authority and instituted for their peace, safety and happiness and they have at all times a right to alter, reform or abolish the government in a manner as they may think proper. And I think that's what we did, that's what - -

THE COURT: I would agree with that statement in its entirety but I would want to be sure that the words "in a manner they think proper" means a manner that runs counter to the provisions of the law. We have in this state —I don't know whether you read the Chicago papers, I certainly know you—I feel that you must read certain of the articles in the Chicago papers, because you have been very widely publicized. We have going on here now in the state of Illinois a Constitutional Convention, trying to improve the provisions of the present Constitution, but to say that the people may change laws or do things in a manner they think proper doesn't mean they may do it in the wrong way or illegal way. I am sure you appreciate that.

MR. FROINES: Well, I was - - after attempting to read that with some emphasis on the power resides in the people and people have a right to abolish the government in such manner as they deem fit, I want to read it with the kind of emphasis that you read our indictment, because I want you to understand my emphasis, as you force the jury to understand your emphasis. So maybe I should stop at that point.

THE COURT: I don't force the jury to do anything.

In conformity with Rule 42(a) of the Federal Rules of Criminal Procedure, Title 18, United States Code, Section 401, I certify that I saw and heard the conduct which - - of the defendant Froines, in the case of the United States of America vs. David Dellinger and others, 69 CR 180, which I have described here a short time ago. I find that the acts, statements and conduct of the defendant Froines, as I described those acts, statements and conduct, each constitutes a separate contempt of this Court, that each constitutes a deliberate and wilful attack upon the administration of justice in an attempt to sabotage the functioning of the federal judicial system, the result of which was to disrupt the orderly administration of justice.

Mr. Clerk, there will be an order committing - - with respect to Specification 1, there will be an order committing the defendant Froines to the Attorney General of the United States or his authorized representative for imprisonment for a period of 1 month; with respect to Specification 2, 1 day; with respect to Specification 3, 1 day; with respect to Specification 4, 1 day; with respect to Specification 5, 1 month; with respect to Specification 6, 1 month; with respect to Specification 7, 14 days; with respect to Specification 8, 14 days; with respect to Specification 9, 2 months; with respect to Specification 10, 14 days.

I think that is all there are. The sentence is to run cumulative and consecutive and I commit the defendant Froines to the custody of the United States Marshal for

the Northern District of Illinois.
MR. KUNSTLER: Your Honor, as for all the rest, I would like to move for bail pending appeal.
THE COURT: As I have done in all the others, I deny bail for the same reasons.
VOICES: Right on; Right on, John.
MR. FROINES: Thank you.
THE COURT: The Court will be in recess for a very brief period, Mr. Marshal.

(There was a brief recess, after which the following further proceedings were had in open court:)

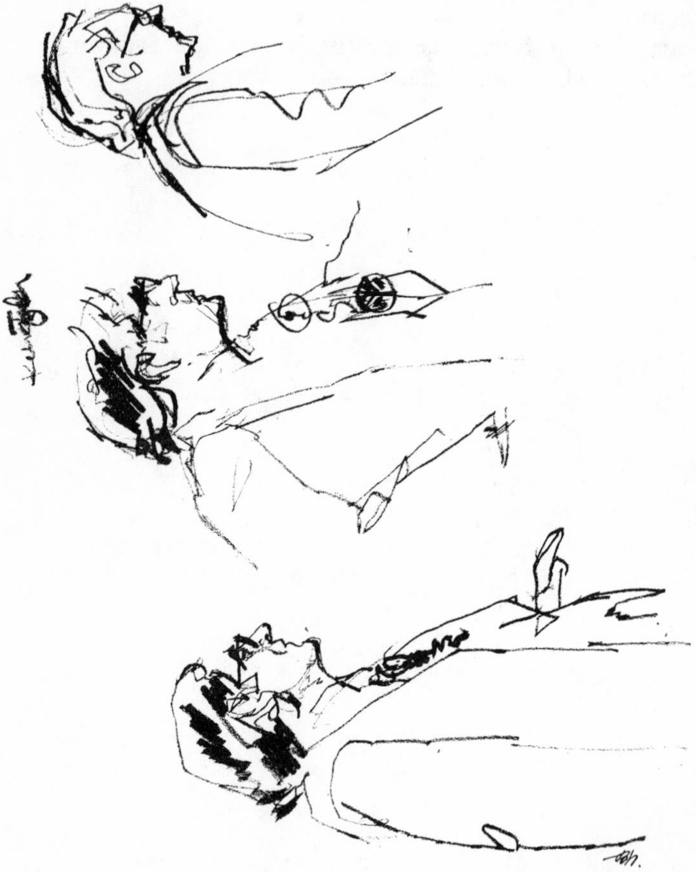

KUNSTLER

THE COURT: We come now -- will you call this case, please.
THE CLERK: 69 CR 180, United States of America vs. David Dellinger, et al.
THE COURT: This matter now involves the conduct of Mr. William Kunstler, counsel for some of the defendants here, who has participated in this trial from the very beginning.

I have said here frequently that the Court has never had occasion to hold a lawyer in contempt, and only on one occasion did the Court hold someone who is not a lawyer in contempt. That that sentence in that case was concurrent with the sentence in the main case.

I recognize the obligation of a lawyer to defend a client with vigor, and secure for his client the full benefits under the law. Nevertheless, if he crosses the bounds of legal propriety, the Court must deal appropriately with that conduct.

Mr. Kunstler's conduct in this case, which I shall review in detail, has created a record replete with direct violations of the orders of the Court, and I could characterize them now, but I think I shall proceed with the recitations of the specifications in conformity with Rule 42(a) of the Federal Rules of Criminal Procedure, Title 18, United States Code, Section 41.

I am certifying that I saw and heard the conduct which I am about to describe, which occurred in the actual presence of the Court, during the trial in the case entitled United States of America vs. David Dellinger and others, 69 CR 180, and which commenced on September 24, 1969 and continued for about four and a half months.

I go on to recite these specifications:

Specification 1: On October 9, the Court made an evidentiary ruling and ordered, with reference to Defendants'

Exhibit D-23, that Mr. Kunstler on cross-examination of the witness Pierson could only have the document identified but was not privileged to go into the substance of the document, until and when the document had been admitted into evidence. After this order was entered, Mr. Kunstler repeatedly, before the jury, asked questions designed to delve into the substance of the document. He ignored the Court's admonitions and proceeded as is recorded, as follows:

> "Question: I show you D-23 for identification and ask you whether this is not the story which Mr. Judge wrote.
>
> "MR. SCHULTZ: Well, I object to the question, your Honor. If the witness knows what Mr. Judge wrote, that is one thing, but if he can --
>
> "THE COURT: All you may do at this time, Mr. Kunstler, under the law, is to have this document identified by the witness. You may not go into its substance.
>
> "BY MR. KUNSTLER:
>
> "Q All right. I will ask you, is that the story which you saw appear in the Chicago Tribune on August 31, 1968?
>
> "A. Yes, sir, I believe it is.
>
> "Q Now, in the interview did you tell Mr. Judge that the diary of Jerry Rubin had been given to you on Monday, August 25, instead of August 27?
>
> "A No, sir, I did not.
>
> "Q Would you look on Page 2 of that story? Does that story indicate that the diary was given on August 25?
>
> "THE COURT: I don't think you understand me.
>
> "MR. SCHULTZ: Objection.
>
> "THE COURT: I had always thought I talked so clearly. I said you may not question the witness about the substance or contents of the document until it is in evidence. This exhibit is not in evidence. It has been, in a way, identified as Defendants' Exhibit 23 for identification. I sustain the objection to the question.
>
> "BY MR. KUNSTLER:
>
> "Q I will ask you just to look, then, at the portion

which refers to the incident which you have described in the book being given to you by Mr. Rubin. Do you see that in there? I have marked it, it should be easy to find.

"A I see a marking here and reference made to a diary.

"Q Is that statement there correct or incorrect?

"MR. SCHULTZ: Objection.

"THE COURT: I sustain the objection and I must admonish you, Mr. Kunstler, you are disregarding the Court's direction.

"MR. KUNSTLER: Your Honor, I would like the jury excused so we may discuss and argue this question.

"THE COURT: I shall not discuss -- dismiss the jury at this time, sir.

"MR. KUNSTLER: Well, then, I would like to argue it, your Honor.

"THE COURT: I don't want to argue that one. I won't permit you to argue it.

"MR. SCHULTZ: Your Honor, if I may explain, the proper way is to ask the witness a question, a question which is in substance what Mr. Kunstler thinks he told somebody else, and if the witness denies the truth of that question, then he can impeach him by saying, 'Didn't you say the following to such and such a person?' and then if he denies it, that person will testify.

"THE COURT: Oh, I have been trying to point out what the proper procedure is, but that is not the way that counsel has been doing it. All I can do is rule on objections if they are made and I shall continue to do so.

"BY MR. KUNSTLER:

"Q Did you tell Mr. Judge in your interview that a diary had been taken from Jerry Rubin or given by Jerry Rubin to you on August 25, a Monday evening, 1968? Did you tell him that?

"A No, sir, I did not.

"Q I will ask you whether this statement which appears in the article was what you told Mr. Judge or not --

"MR. SCHULTZ: Objection.

"THE COURT: I sustain the objection and now I will excuse the jury.

"Ladies and gentlemen of the jury, you are excused. Before you return to the jury room, I must, of course, order you not to talk with anybody about this case, not to let anybody speak with you about it, and do not discuss the case among yourselves.

"I order you not to read the newspaper or any other journals, not to look at radio or television, or listen to television. I direct you that if anybody attempts to communicate with you in any manner about this case, you notify the United States Marshal who will, in turn, lay the matter before me. You are excused for a few minutes.

"I excused the jury, Mr. Kunstler, to say on the record that your persistent disregard of the Court's directions in asking questions, objections to which have been repeatedly sustained, I regard as unprofessional conduct, and I want that statement on the record.

"MR. KUNSTLER: Your Honor, may we argue this point now? I brought the law in, I think I have a right - - you called me unprofessional and I have a right to say what I think my authority is.

"THE COURT: When I tell you that you may not inquire about a document that is not in evidence, which is elementary, I don't want you to persist in asking about it.

"MR. KUNSTLER: Your Honor, I want to do what is right and I have brought in Judge Holtzoff - -

"THE COURT: You are not doing what is right. I don't want to argue it. It is elementary. I have taken the trouble to give you the citations early in this trial and I will give them to you again. I have them right here.

"MR. KUNSTLER: I have got McCormick on evidence, I have got Judge Holtzoff, Learned Hand - -

"THE COURT: We have the United States Supreme Court up here.

"MR. KUNSTLER: I have the Supreme Court as well, your Honor.

"THE COURT: I don't want you to do it and that is the reason why I excused the jury. Mr. Marshal, you may now bring in the jury." Official Transcript, Pages 1,644-50. **1 month**

Specification 2: On October 15, following the incident of the Vietnam Moratorium demonstration alluded to in the citations of contempt by the defendant Dellinger, the following colloquy took place with Mr. Kunstler:

"MR. KUNSTLER: Are you turning down my request after this disgraceful episode. You are not going to say anything?

"THE COURT: I not only turn it down, I ignore it.

"MR. KUNSTLER: That speaks louder than words, too, your Honor.

"THE COURT: And let that appear of record, the last words of Mr. Kunstler, and, Miss Reporter, be very careful to have them on the record." Official Transcript, Page 2,435. **14 days**

Specification 3: On October 30, as the Court was attempting to maintain order by restraining the defendant Bobby Seale, Mr. Kunstler not only made no attempt to aid the Court in maintaining order, but engaged in the following colloquy as well:

"MR. KUNSTLER: Your Honor, are we going to stop this medieval torture that is going on in this courtroom? I think this is a disgrace.

"MR. RUBIN: This guy is putting his elbow in Bobby's mouth and it wasn't necessary at all.

"MR. KUNSTLER: This is no longer a court of order, your Honor; this is a medieval torture chamber. It is a disgrace. They are assaulting the other defendants also.

"MR. RUBIN: Don't - -"

And I don't use this kind of language here if I can help it, but, Miss Reporter, I refer you to the notes here, if you are not able to get this, from the way I give it to you.

"MR. RUBIN: Don't hit me in the b-a-l-l-s, m-f."

As has been used during this trial on numerous occasions.

"MR. SEALE: This m-f is tight and it is stopping my blood.

"MR. KUNSTLER: Your Honor, this is an unholy disgrace to the law that is going on in this courtroom and I as an American lawyer feel a disgrace.

"MR. FORAN: Created by Mr. Kunstler.

"MR. KUNSTLER: Created by nothing other than what you have done to this man.

"MR. HOFFMAN: . . . -- being a defendant -- . . . You come down here and watch it, Judge.

"MR. FORAN: May the record show that the outbursts are the defendant Rubin.

"MR. SEALE: You fascist dogs, you rotten, low-life son of a b. --"

The word is spelled out.

"MR. SEALE: -- I am glad I said it about Washington used to have slaves, the first President.

"MR. DELLINGER: Somebody go to protect him.

"MR. FORAN: Your Honor, may the record show that it is Mr. Dellinger saying 'Someone go to protect him' and the other comment is by Mr. Rubin.

"MR. RUBIN: And my statement, too.

"THE COURT: Everything you say will be taken down.

"MR. KUNSTLER: Your Honor, we would like the names of the marshals. We are going to ask for a judicial investigation of the entire condition and the entire treatment of Bobby Seale.

"THE COURT: You ask for anything that you want. When you begin to keep your word around here that you gave the Court, perhaps things can be done.

"MR. KUNSTLER: If we are going to talk about words, I am prepared to give you back your word about Mr. Ball yesterday and what he said you said to him. We have the transcript now.

"THE COURT: Don't point at me, sir, in that manner.

"MR. KUNSTLER: If we are going to talk about words, I'd like to exchange some.

"THE COURT: Don't point at me in that manner.

"MR. KUNSTLER: I just feel utterly ashamed to be an American lawyer at this time.

"THE COURT: You should be ashamed of your conduct in this case, sir.

"MR. KUNSTLER: What conduct, when a client is treated in this manner.

"THE COURT: We will take a brief recess.

"MR. KUNSTLER: Can we have somebody with Mr. Seale? We don't trust - -" Official Transcript, Pages 4,815-17.

3 months

Specification 4: Mr. Kunstler continually defied the Court's orders to sit down when the Court had determined that the argument was completed. One such occasion occurred on October 30 and is set forth in the following colloquy:

"MR. WEINGLASS: Mr. Kunstler is his attorney.

"MR. SCHULTZ: Mr. Kunstler is his attorney and Mr. Weinglass who just spoke have both encouraged Mr. Seale to proceed in violation of the Court's order when he has an appellate process of review.

"MR. KUNSTLER: Your Honor, just to compare hearsay with the right of a black man to defend himself - -

"THE COURT: I will not hear you any longer.

"MR. KUNSTLER: - - after three hundred years of slavery - -

"THE COURT: I will hear you no longer.

"MR. KUNSTLER: But, your Honor, he said - - he is comparing it to hearsay. This is a sovereign right which is a right black men fought and died for.

"THE COURT: Will you ask that man to sit down, Mr. Marshal.

"MR. KUNSTLER: I may no longer continue in answer to Mr. Schultz?

"THE COURT: No, no. We will go on forever.

"MR. KUNSTLER: Not forever, your Honor, just long enough to make a point." Official Transcript, Pages 4,842-43.

14 months, or **14 days**, I beg your pardon.

Specification 5: On December 9 the Court refused to permit Mr. Kunstler to leave the room during the proceedings. His absence would have left three of the remaining seven defendants unrepresented. The following argument and insults are reported in the record:

"THE COURT: You will remain.
"MR. KUNSTLER: We don't have --
"THE COURT: You will remain here at this trial, sir.
"MR. KUNSTLER: All right. Then, your Honor is interfering with the defense of this case.
"THE COURT: All right. Your motion is denied.
"MR. KUNSTLER: All right.

"Then, your Honor, I am going to have the witness come to the counsel table and sit with the attorneys.
"THE COURT: You are not going to have witnesses at the counsel table.
"MR. KUNSTLER: Your Honor, how can you be so inhumane as to not permit the lawyers to sit with the witnesses? I just don't understand it. It is with the consent of the defendants.
"THE COURT: That is a very serious word to apply to a judge, and I make a special ruling --" Official Transcript, Page 9,887. **14 days**

Specification 6: On December 12, during the direct examination of the witness Ginsberg, the Court determined that a recess was appropriate. Mr. Kunstler opposed that recess in a shouting and disrespectful manner as is set out in the following selection from the record:

"MR. FORAN: I think at least several minutes, your Honor, ten, fifteen minutes.
"THE COURT: Are you suggesting we recess?
"MR. FORAN: I would think possibly yes, your Honor, because I would just get back up here and get started.
"THE COURT: You mean recess until the afternoon?
"MR. FORAN: After lunch.
"THE COURT: All right. We will go until 2:00 o'clock.
"MR. WEINGLASS: Your Honor --
"MR. KUNSTLER: Your Honor, we have witnesses who are leaving the country this afternoon who are presently here. I don't think there should be any delay in the cross-examination.
"MR. FORAN: Your Honor, after each --
"MR. WEINGLASS: Wait --

"MR. KUNSTLER: Mr. Foran, may I finish my statement?

"MR. FORAN: Excuse me, Mr. Kunstler.

"MR. KUNSTLER: We have two witnesses in the witness room now waiting around here for two days. One is leaving the country tomorrow morning and must testify or we lose him forever, and the other has to return to the West Coast.

"THE COURT: I have granted the request of the defendant - -

"MR. KUNSTLER: We asked for five minutes two days ago in front of this jury and you refused to give it to us.

"MR. FORAN: Your Honor, on every - -

"THE COURT: You will have to cease that disrespectful tone.

"MR. KUNSTLER: That is not disrespectful; that is an angry tone, your Honor.

"THE COURT: Yes, it is. Yes, it is. I will grant the motion of the Government.

"MR. KUNSTLER: You refused us five minutes the other day.

"MR. FORAN: Your Honor, on every - -

"THE COURT: You are going to have to learn - -

"MR. KUNSTLER: I am trying to learn.

"THE COURT: I have given up trying to point it out to you.

"MR. KUNSTLER: Why the different treatment?

"THE COURT: I will not sit here and have you assume a disrespectful tone to the Court.

"MR. KUNSTLER: This is not disrespect.

"THE COURT: Yes, it is.

"MR. KUNSTLER: I am asking you to explain to the defense which claims it is getting different treatment, why a simple request of five minutes was not granted.

"MR. FORAN: Your Honor, may I comment that after the direct examination of every single Government witness in this case, the defense had a recess to prepare their cross-examination. That was after 54 witnesses. Every one had a recess.

"MR. KUNSTLER: Your Honor, this is the grossest statement I have ever heard in a courtroom. This jury doesn't know that after every Government witness—we might as well tell them—there is a series of documents that are given to the defense and the defense must read, and that is the only reason the request was granted. They have no documents - -

"MR. FORAN: That is right, your Honor. That is - -

"MR. KUNSTLER: They must go on.

"MR. FORAN: We don't - - it is a two-way street - - it is a one-way street.

"MR. KUNSTLER: They have no documents to read.

"MR. FORAN: Your Honor - -

"MR. KUNSTLER: It is a one-way street, your Honor. That is what we are on.

"MR. FORAN: From the Government to the defense, your Honor.

"THE COURT: Now, sir - -

"MR. KUNSTLER: We are on a one-way street, your Honor. Five minutes we requested from you.

"THE COURT: Mr. Kunstler - -

"MR. KUNSTLER: Your Honor, what else can I think?

"THE COURT: I have admonished you time and again to be respectful to the Court. I have been respectful to you.

"MR. KUNSTLER: Your Honor, this is not disrespect for anybody but - -

"THE COURT: You are shouting at the Court.

"MR. KUNSTLER: Oh, your Honor - -

"THE COURT: Shouting at the Court, the way you do - -

"MR. KUNSTLER: Everyone has shouted from time to time, including your Honor. This is not a situation - -

"THE COURT: Make a note of that, please. I have never - -

"MR. KUNSTLER: Voices have been raised - -

"THE COURT: I never shouted at you during this trial.

"MR. KUNSTLER: Your Honor, your voice has been raised.
"THE COURT: You have been disrespectful.
"MR KUNSTLER: It is not disrespectful, your Honor.
"THE COURT: And sometimes worse than that.
"THE WITNESS: O-o-m-m-m-m.
"THE COURT: Will you step off the witness stand, please, and I direct you not to talk with anybody about this case or let anybody speak with you about it until you resume the stand at 2:00 o'clock, at which time you are directed to return for further examination.
"MR. KUNSTLER: He was trying to calm us both down, your Honor.
"THE COURT: Oh, no. I needed no calming down.
"MR. KUNSTLER: Your Honor has --
"THE COURT: I am pointing out to a lawyer that we will not tolerate disrespect in this court.
"MR. KUNSTLER: Your Honor, how --
"THE COURT: That will be all.
"MR. KUNSTLER: What about our witnesses who have to leave the country? You are depriving us of these witnesses.
"THE COURT: We will recess, Mr. Marshal, until 2:00 o'clock.
"MR. KUNSTLER: Oh, that is unfair." Official Transcript, Pages 10,783-788. **3 months**

Specification 7: On December 23, Mr. Kunstler indicated that he had some information concerning a possible challenge by the Government to one of the jurors. Mr. Schultz raised an objection indicating that this matter should be discussed outside the presence of the jury. The Court then excused the jury. As the jury was walking out Mr. Kunstler repeated those charges in a loud voice so that the jury could hear him as they were exiting. This incident is set out in the record as appearing in the following summary:

"MR. WEINGLASS: Your Honor, the defendants and Mr. Kunstler will be in the courtroom momentarily.

"THE COURT: Will you please call your next witness.
"MR. KUNSTLER: Your Honor, before calling next witness the defense has an inquiry to make.
"Your Honor will recall that I asked certain questions about the half-hour delay - -
"MR. SCHULTZ: If the Court please, I think that the matter that Mr. Kunstler made inquiry about out of the presence of the jury, if he wants to make inquiry now, we should have it with the Court solely.
"MR. KUNSTLER: Your Honor, I am not going into that but I want to indicate this, that we are prepared to call another witness but since this witness is a defendant, we have an inquiry to make. We have heard from people outside the courtroom here, reporters and others - -
"MR. SCHULTZ: Your Honor - -
"MR. KUNSTLER: - - that the Government is planning to launch an attack on the jury.
"MR. SCHULTZ: I don't [know] what it is Mr. Kunstler is going into, but I do know that it is improper for him to say what it is in the presence of the jury.
"THE COURT: I will excuse you.
"MR. KUNSTLER: Your Honor, it is an attack on the jury, and that is why I am mentioning it with the jury here.
"MR. SCHULTZ: Mr. Kunstler has just heard the Court's ruling and he knows that the Court has ordered the jury excused for the purpose of this argument, but that doesn't stop him. He wants to continue. We are bound by Court - -
"THE COURT: Now I will hear you.
"(The following proceedings were had in open court, out of the presence and hearing of the jury.)"
Official Transcript, Pages 12,391-92. **3 months**

Specification 8: On January 6 the defendants called Mayor Richard J. Daley of Chicago to the stand as their witness. In a colloquy prior to the witness taking the stand Mr. Kunstler clearly indicated his understanding of the limitations on interrogating one's own witness. Furthermore, the Court ordered that any motions to declare the witness Daley a "hostile witness" be made outside the presence of the jury. In the course of the direct examination of this witness which runs from Page 13,900 to 14,024 of the official transcript, Mr. Kunstler asked no less than 83 questions which were objectionable, mostly leading and suggestive. Furthermore, he directly violated the Court's order by moving to have the witness Daley declared a "hostile witness" in the presence of the jury. Official Transcript, Page 13,944.

After this motion was denied, Mr. Kunstler continued asking leading and suggestive questions which he knew to be improper. His conduct was repeated so many times that it must be considered contemptuous. **6 months**

Specification 9: On January 12 Mr. Kunstler refused to be seated and discontinue his argument despite admonitions and directions to do so by the Court. This incident is reported thusly in the transcript:

> "THE COURT: -- forbidding the defendants from going out at their pleasure ostensibly to what has been referred to not infrequently by counsel as the bathroom. I have never sat in a case where lawyers mention that word as often. I wonder if you, Mr. Marshal, can keep that man quiet while I am speaking. I am trying to decide his lawyer's motion. Please go to him and tell him to keep quiet.
> "THE MARSHAL: Mr. Dellinger --
> "THE COURT: Let the record show that after I requested the marshal to keep Mr. Dellinger quiet he laughed right out again, out loud. The record may so indicate.
> "MR. DELLINGER: And he is laughing now, too.
> "THE MARSHAL: And the defendant Hayden, your Honor.
> "THE COURT: Mr. Hayden also.
> "MR. KUNSTLER: Oh, your Honor, there is a certain amount of humor when talking about a bathroom --
> "THE COURT: Oh, I know that is your favorite reply.

"MR. HOFFMAN: I laughed, too.
"MR. KUNSTLER: But people can't help it sometimes, your Honor. You have laughed yourself.
"THE COURT: I really have come to believe you can't help yourself. I have come to believe it.
"MR. KUNSTLER: But that is true. A whole courtroom full of people laugh when I say something and when you say something.
"THE COURT: What I am saying is not very funny.
"MR. KUNSTLER: I know, but you are so ultrasensitive to laughter.
"THE COURT: Will you sit down and not interrupt the Court when a decision is being made?

"All I ask from you, sir, is simple manners. I don't reach the question of law.
"MR. KUNSTLER: A laugh is not bad manners. Really.
"THE COURT: I have never been in a case where I have seen such bad manners.
"MR. KUNSTLER: I know, but your Honor, when you make a joke and the courtroom laughs, nobody is thrown out.
"THE COURT: Just sit down. I have not made any jokes.
"MR. KUNSTLER: I know, but you do from time to time.
"THE COURT: I ask you to sit down during the rendering of this decision, sir.

"Let the record show that the defendants—rather the defendants' counsel, Mr. Kunstler, on two occasions here refused to sit down when the Court directed him to sit down.
"MR. KUNSTLER: Oh, that's not fair, your Honor.
"MR. WEINGLASS: He sat down on both occasions, your Honor. I must object to that.
"MR. KUNSTLER: I sat down on both occasions.
"THE COURT: I mean right now, in this decision.
"MR. KUNSTLER: I sat down.
"THE COURT: You did finally after I urged you.
"MR. WEINGLASS: Your Honor, that is not a fair characterization.
"THE COURT: Will you sit down.

"MR. WEINGLASS: Mr. Kunstler did sit down both times.

"THE COURT: I didn't ask you to stand. I am giving a decision, sir.

"MR. WEINGLASS: I think it should be on the record --

"THE COURT: I am giving a decision, and if you don't sit down -- he has sat down now.

"Mr. Marshal see that Mr. Weinglass remains in his chair while the Court is rendering a decision on this motion made by Mr. Weinglass. Official Transcript, Pages 14,824-27. **21 days**

Specification 10: On January 13 Mr. Kunstler again argued and refused to desist when the Court ordered him to do so:

"MR. KUNSTLER: Your Honor, I move to strike your Honor's last remarks from the record.

"THE COURT: I deny your motion.

"MR. KUNSTLER: I think they are derogatory.

"THE COURT: I deny the motion.

"MR. KUNSTLER: And prejudice these defendants in front of the jury.

"THE COURT: Did you hear me, sir.

"MR. KUNSTLER: I am ready to argue it.

"THE COURT: I am not ready to hear you. It is so clearly ill founded.

"MR. KUNSTLER: It is not. I read to your Honor yesterday a decision of another court, a Federal Court.

"THE COURT: I denied your motion.

"MR. KUNSTLER: The derogatory comments to counsel --

"THE COURT: Mr. Marshal, will you have that man sit down.

"MR. WEINGLASS: Mr. Kunstler.

"MR. KUNSTLER: I just want the record to show I am sitting down because I don't want to have a marshal come and throw me into my seat, but I am sitting down under protest." Official Transcript, Pages 15,309-310. **14 days**

Specification 11: On January 4, Mr. Kunstler engaged in

the following colloquy, twice more refusing to sit down, the Court ordered him to do so, and continuing his argument until the marshal approached him. The incident is set forth in the following excerpt from the record:

"THE MARSHAL: Mr. Dellinger, also, will you refrain from laughing.

"MR. DELLINGER: That is a lie. And it wasn't Mr. Rubin. We laugh enough and you can catch us when we do but you just happened to get that one wrong.

"MR. KUNSTLER: Your Honor, I don't think the record should constantly have these references to chuckles - -

"THE COURT: I think the record should show that and I see that the record does. I don't share your view.

"MR. KUNSTLER: The Court has made a sally before and the room laughed and you didn't say put that on the record.

"THE COURT: I will not sit here—and you must know it by now, certainly—and have defendants laugh at my rulings, sir. And I will not hear you on that.

"MR. KUNSTLER: You don't mind if they laugh at me or if they laugh at someone else.

"THE COURT: I will ask you to sit down.

"MR. KUNSTLER: I don't think your Honor's ultrasensitivity should make a difference in rulings in this court.

"THE COURT: It isn't ultrasensitivity. It is a proper understanding of the conduct of a trial in the Federal District Court.

"MR. KUNSTLER: When you interpret it as a laugh at you - -

"THE COURT: Some people here don't seem to know about it.

"MR. KUNSTLER: No, but, your Honor, when you try to interpret a laugh as meaning you are the butt of a joke, then you react - -

"THE COURT: I will ask you to sit down. Did you hear me?

"MR. KUNSTLER: I just don't want to get thrown

in my chair by the marshal, so I will have to sit down, but I just don't think it is fair to do that.
"MR. HOFFMAN: I laughed anyway.
"THE COURT: Will you be quiet, Mr. - -
"MR. HOFFMAN: I laughed. It wasn't Jerry. It was me.
"THE COURT: Did you get that, Miss Reporter?
"MR. HOFFMAN: - - at that ruling. I laughed. He didn't.
"THE COURT: That was Mr. Dellinger.
"MR. KUNSTLER: That was not Mr. Dellinger."
Official Transcript, Page 15,585-87. **7 days**

Specification 12: On January 16, in his direct examination of the witness Goodwin, Mr. Kunstler blatantly ignored the directions of the Court on evidentiary rulings. After a question was held to be objectionable, rather than move to the next question, he deliberately asked it again. He also made highly improper statements in front of the jury. The incident is reflected in the following excerpt from the transcript:

"BY MR. KUNSTLER:

"Q. Mr. Goodwin, I call your attention to approximately three weeks before the opening of the Democratic National Convention. At that time you were campaign director, were you not, for Eugene McCarthy?

"A. That is correct.

"Q. At that time did you make any recommendations to Senator McCarthy?

"MR. FORAN: Objection.
"THE COURT: I sustain the objection.
"BY MR. KUNSTLER:

"Q. Did you have a conversation at that time with Senator McCarthy about whether he should or should not urge his supporters to come to Chicago?

"A. Yes.

"MR. FORAN: Objection, your Honor, as immaterial and irrelevant. Neither Senator McCarthy nor Mr. Goodwin are in this charge.
"MR. KUNSTLER: No, your Honor, but what is at issue is the atmosphere in the city of Chicago

created by Mayor Daley.
"THE COURT: I have ruled - -
"MR. FORAN: I object to Mr. Kunstler constantly attempting to testify.
"THE COURT: I have ruled. Ask another question.
"MR. KUNSTLER: If Mayor Daley was preventing anybody from - -
"MR. FORAN: I object to that.
"THE COURT: Will you ask another question, please? Mayor Daley is not in this one. He has come and gone.
"MR. KUNSTLER: Yes, your Honor, but he is in this case. He is the chief and only defendant here.
"MR. FORAN: I object to that comment and ask that it be stricken and that the jury be directed - - I ask that it be stricken from the jury's hearing and also that your Honor admonish counsel.
"THE COURT: I do so and I direct the jury to disregard it and anything like that, Mr. Kunstler.
"MR. KUNSTLER: But that is part of our defense, your Honor. We are trying to show who - - if you had a simple robbery case, you could show who the true robber was.
"THE COURT: Don't make another statement like that.
"BY MR. KUNSTLER:
"Q. Did there come a time when Senator McCarthy did tell his supporters not to come to Chicago?
"A. Yes.
"MR. FORAN: I object to that form of the question and ask that the jury be directed to disregard the statement of counsel.
"THE COURT: Yes. I sustain the objection. I do strike it and direct the jury to disregard it." Official Transcript, Pages 16,129-31. **14 days**

Specification 13: On January 20, after a colloquy between the Court and Mr. Weinglass, Mr. Kunstler rose to join the argument. He again resisted the admonitions of the Court to desist. The event is set forth in the transcript as follows:

"MR. SCHULTZ: Your Honor, I ask that that statement be stricken from this record and Mr. Weinglass admonished to conduct himself in a professional manner in this courtroom.

"MR. KUNSTLER: Your Honor, that was highly professional. Mr. Schultz opened the door - -

"MR. SCHULTZ: And the same goes for Mr. Kunstler.

"MR. KUNSTLER: - - for that document to be offered.

"THE COURT: Mr. Weinglass is taking care of this witness.

"MR. KUNSTLER: I am not going to stand by and have him—a colleague of mine—called anything like that.

"THE COURT: Sit down.

"MR. KUNSTLER: I am not going to sit down unless I am directed - -

"THE COURT: I direct you to sit down.

"MR. KUNSTLER: Am I to be thrown in the chair by the marshal if I don't sit down?

"THE COURT: I haven't asked the marshal to throw anybody in the chair. I have asked the marshal on occasion, sir, to direct you to sit down, and you have always followed his word.

"MR. KUNSTLER: I have followed. I am just indicating, your Honor, I don't think that kind of conduct should be permitted.

"THE COURT: I will permit only one defense counsel to participate in the examination of this witness.

"MR. KUNSTLER: I am not participating in the examination. I am only defending Mr. Weinglass." Official Transcript, Pages 16,663-64. **14 days**

Specification 14: On January 22 the Court was again engaged in a colloquy with Mr. Weinglass when Mr. Kunstler rose to interject himself into the argument. Again Mr. Kunstler refused to desist when the Court told him to sit down. The incident is reflected in the record thusly:

"THE COURT: I direct the jury to disregard the last statement.

"MR. FORAN: That is the law.
"MR. KUNSTLER: Your Honor - -
"THE COURT: I will not hear from you.
"MR. KUNSTLER: - - he said that I said something that is improper. It is not improper. I have heard this in court after court.
"THE COURT: I will not hear from you while your associate is examining this witness.
"MR. KUNSTLER: It has nothing to do with this witness.
"MR. FORAN: The reference was to Mr. Weinglass.
"MR. KUNSTLER: He said I said something that was improper. It was not improper.
"THE COURT: I ask you to sit down. Sir, you may continue your examination.
"Mr. Marshal, have that man sit down." Official Transcript, Pages 17,088-89. **1 month**

Specification 15: On January 22, after a ruling by the Court, there were loud groans from the defense table. Instead of attempting to aid the Court in keeping order, Mr. Kunstler indicated that he encouraged and approved of such behavior by the defendants. The incident is reported in the record as follows:

"(Groans)
"THE COURT: Mr. Marshal, I wish you'd take care of that.
"MR. KUNSTLER: Your Honor, those groans are highly appropriate. I get no help from you, so a groan of a client once in a while at least keeps my spirit up.
"THE COURT: I note that you approve of the groans of the client in open court.
"MR. KUNSTLER: I approve of those groans, your Honor, when your Honor does not admonish Mr. Schultz.
"THE COURT: I note them. I note them, sir.
"MR. KUNSTLER: What can I do?
"THE COURT: You can continue with your argument." Official Transcript, Page 17,195. **21 days**

Specification 16: On January 22, the Court was again

engaged in a colloquy with Mr. Weinglass. After making a ruling and after indicating directly that the Court did not wish to hear any more argument on that point, Mr. Kunstler then rose and engaged the Court in the following colloquy:

> "THE COURT: I don't want to hear anything further. I have overruled the objection.
> "MR. KUNSTLER: He makes it appear like some startling singular fact, which isn't true.
> "THE COURT: Did you hear me, sir? Did you hear me or must I again have the marshal order you to sit down?
> "MR. KUNSTLER: The marshal has never ordered me to sit down. I have sat down when you said so.
> "THE COURT: The other marshal. We have a new marshal sitting right here.
> "MR. KUNSTLER: There was no marshal when I sat down.
> "THE COURT: Oh, yes.
> "MR. KUNSTLER: He only approached me and I have sat down.
> "THE COURT: That is an order.
> "MR. SCHULTZ: May I restate --
> "MR. KUNSTLER: I'm down.
> "THE COURT: Yes. Please remain there." Official Transcript, Pages 17,307-08. **2 months**

Specification 17: On January 23 the Court denied the motion for a mistrial. After the denial Mr. Kunstler continued to attempt to argue the motion. The record appears as follows:

> "MR. KUNSTLER: You haven't even heard the motion.
> "MR. RUBIN: You haven't heard it yet.
> "THE COURT: For a mistrial.
> "MR. KUNSTLER: Yes, but I would like to argue it.
> "THE COURT: Oh, there is no grounds for a mistrial.
> "MR. KUNSTLER: Your Honor knows you have referred to the question of the defendants taking the stand. You have committed the cardinal error of

a court with reference - -
"THE COURT: I ask you to sit down, sir.
"MR. KUNSTLER: But your Honor - -
"THE COURT: I direct the marshal to have this man sit down.
"MR. KUNSTLER: Every time I make a motion am I going to be thrown in my seat when I argue it?
"THE COURT: You may sit down.
"MR. DELLINGER: Force and violence.
"MR. KUNSTLER: If that is the ruling of the Court that we cannot argue without being thrown in our seats.
"MR. DELLINGER: The Judge is inciting a riot by asking the marshal to have him sit down." Official Transcript, Page 17,371.

After this incident there was a loud burst of applause from the spectators' galleries and the marshal determined that several spectators would have to be removed. During the removal and disorder, instead of attempting to maintain order in the courtroom, Mr. Kunstler issued the following running commentary from the lectern, which had the effect of encouraging disorder among the spectators.

"MARSHAL JOHNSON: Will you sit down.
"(Applause)
"THE COURT: Will you continue, please, with the direct examination of this witness.
"MR. DELLINGER: There goes the violence right there.
"MR. KUNSTLER: That's the Government in operation, your Honor, as it has been throughout this trial.
"THE WITNESS: Your Honor, that's my sister they're taking out of the courtroom.
"THE COURT: Even your sister - -
"MR. KUNSTLER: Nobody but the Government has employed violence in this courtroom - - with Bobby Seale, with spectators.
"THE COURT: Since you refer to Bobby Seale, your client, I recall - -
"MR. KUNSTLER: Not my client, your Honor.
"THE COURT: - - I recall being called various kinds

of pigs by that man.
"MR. RUBIN: Bill, they are taking out my wife.
"MR. KUNSTLER: Well, your Honor would not let him defend himself, everybody knows that now.
"(Cries of 'Hey, stop it.')
"MR. KUNSTLER: Your Honor, must we always have this, the force and power of the Government?
"MR. FORAN: Your Honor - -
"MR. RUBIN: They are dragging out my wife - - will you please - -
"THE COURT: We must have order in the courtroom.
"MR. KUNSTLER: They like to strike women, your Honor, we've seen that constantly here." Official Transcript, Pages 17,373-74. **4 months**

Specification 18: On January 23 when the Court determined that it was time to recess the afternoon session, Mr. Kunstler made an argument and insulted the Court in the following manner:

"MR. KUNSTLER: I realize that, but as long as we are going on six days a week now - -
"THE COURT: 9:30 tomorrow.
"MR. KUNSTLER: - - I just don't understand the half hour difference.
"THE COURT: I am not obligated to explain to you, sir, the time for the arrival of the jurors and the parties - -
"MR. KUNSTLER: No, but since we are going to work the extra day - -
"THE COURT: - - and the parties to a lawsuit.
"MR. KUNSTLER: Why shouldn't that be at 10:00 o'clock like any other day?
"THE COURT: Because it is at 9:30.
"MR. KUNSTLER: That is like a child saying, 'Because, because.' I don't think that when we are going an extra day - -
"THE COURT: Let the record show that, in the presence of the jury, Mr. Kunstler compared me to a child.
"MR. KUNSTLER: Oh, your Honor - -
"THE COURT: Now, we will have no more of that,

sir.

"MR. KUNSTLER: Your Honor, I don't think we can come down to the absurd.

"THE COURT: We have had enough of your remarks in this trial.

"MR. KUNSTLER: That is - -

"THE COURT: 9:30 tomorow morning, ladies and gentlemen.

"MR. KUNSTLER: - - absurd.

"THE MARSHAL: Mr. Hoffman, will you keep quiet, please.

"DEFENDANT HOFFMAN: It is funny.

"THE COURT: If the marshals can keep those defendants quiet, I will direct the jury when to return."

Official Transcript, Pages 17,597-98. **1 month**

Specification 19: On January 28, when Mr. Schultz was making his argument concerning the exclusion of Ramsey Clark from the witness stand, Mr. Kunstler engaged in the following disrespectful colloquy:

"MR. SCHULTZ: Mr. Morrill, will you tell the Court, please, what the Attorney General said about the admissibility?

"MR. MORRILL: May I?

"MR.KUNSTLER: May Mr. Morrill be sworn as a witness and take the witness stand, because I was there, and I heard it.

"MR. SCHULTZ: But Mr. Kunstler can't represent anything in its proper perspective.

"MR. KUNSTLER: Have him sworn, your Honor, and then I will question him.

"THE COURT: Oh, don't assume that attitude here, Mr. Kunstler.

"MR. KUNSTLER: I am going to assume it.

"THE COURT: You ought to know that that makes no impression.

"MR. KUNSTLER: Your Honor, that you could sit there and hear a lawyer say - -

"THE COURT: 'I will examine him,' I don't like that.

"MR. KUNSTLER: Your Honor, he has made a representation.

"THE COURT: I don't like that attitude. I never saw that man in my life before.
"MR. KUNSTLER: I ask you to put him on the stand.
"THE COURT: Right now I will do as I think should be done. Please don't order me around, Mr. Kunstler.
"MR. KUNSTLER: Your Honor, a representation has been made. Mr. Morrill is in the courtroom. Let him take the stand and say under oath - -
"THE COURT: You assume a respectful attitude toward the Court. I have been respectful to you. I have tried awfully hard throughout this trial.
"MR. KUNSTLER: I won't even go into that, your Honor.
"THE COURT: Even though when I say a thing like that, I get the guffaws out there." Official Transcript, Page 19096. **1 month**

Specification 20: On February 2, after the Court ruled that Mr. Kunstler would have to abide by his representation the previous Friday, and therefore would not be able to call the Reverend Ralph Abernathy to the stand, Mr. Kunstler made the following speech at the conclusion of his argument:

"THE COURT: There have been several witnesses called here during this trial—I need not mention their names—whose testimony the Court ruled could not even be presented to the jury: singers, performers, and former office holders. I think in the light of the representations made by you unequivocally, sir, with no reference to Dr. Abernathy, I will deny your motion that we hold - -
"MR. KUNSTLER: I want to comment on this, your Honor, because I think what you have just said is about the most outrageous statement I have ever heard from a bench, and I am going to say my piece right now, and you can hold me in contempt right now if you wish to.

"You have violated every principle of fair play when you excluded Ramsey Clark from the witness stand. The New York Times, among others, has

called it the ultimate outrage in American justice.
"VOICES: Right on.
"MR. KUNSTLER: I am outraged to be in this court before you. Now because I made a statement on Friday that I had only a cameraman, and I discovered on Saturday that Ralph Abernathy, who is the chairman of the Mobilization, is in town, and can be here, and because you took a whole day from us on Thursday by listening to this ridiculous argument about whether Ramsey Clark could take that stand in front of the jury, I am trembling because I am so outraged. I haven't been able to get this out before, and I am saying it now, and then I want you to put me in jail if you want to. You can do anything you want with me, if you want to; because I feel disgraced to be here, to say to us on the technicality of my representation that we can't put Ralph Abernathy on the stand. He is the co-chairman of the MOBE. He has relevant testimony. I know that doesn't mean much in this Court when the Attorney General of the United States walked out of here with his lips so tight he could hardly breathe, and if you could see the expression on his face, you would know, and his wife informed me he never felt such anger at the United States Government as at not being able to testify on that stand.
"VOICES: Right on.
"MR. KUNSTLER: You can't tell me that Ralph Abernathy cannot take the stand today because of the technicality of whether I made a representation. That representation was made in perfect good faith with your Honor. I did not know that Reverend Abernathy was back in the country. We have been trying to get him for a week and a half to be the last witness for the defense in this case. And now to tell me that we are going ahead, the Government is ready, after you took Thursday from us to have this argument over whether a man could be presented to a jury, I told your Honor then, and I am telling you now, no American court has ever done what your Honor did - -

"VOICES: Right on.

"MR. KUNSTLER: - - basing it on a case which was inapplicable to the situation. That was done for one purpose only, and the New York Times said it more beautifully than I could say it, and they said, 'It was done to make inadmissible anything that would "interfere" with the Justice Department's intent to prove a conspiracy to incite a riot during the Democratic National Convention.'

"VOICES: Right on.

"MR. KUNSTLER: That was the reason behind your Honor's ruling, nothing short of that.

I have sat here for four and a half months and watched the objections denied and sustained by your Honor, and I know that this is not a fair trial.

I know it in my heart. If I have to lose my license to practice law and if I have to go to jail, I can't think of a better cause to go to jail for and to lose my license for - -

"A VOICE: Right on.

"MR. KUNSTLER: - - than to tell your Honor that you are doing a disservice to the law in saying that we can't have Ralph Abernathy on the stand. You are saying truth will not out because of the technicality of a lawyer's representation. If that is what their liberty depends upon, your Honor saying I represented to you that I had a cameraman, and that was our only witness, a cameraman, whom we can't get, incidentally, then I think there is nothing really more for me to say.

"THE COURT: There is not much more you could say, Mr. Kunstler.

"MR. KUNSTLER: I am going to turn back to my seat with the realization that everything I have learned throughout my life has come to naught, that there is no meaning in this court, and there is no law in this court - -

"VOICES: Right on.

"MR. KUNSTLER: - - and these men are going to jail by virtue of a legal lynching - -

"VOICES: Right on.

"MR. KUNSTLER: - - and that your Honor is

wholly responsible for that, and if this is what your career is going to end on, if this is what your pride is going to be built on, I can only say to your Honor, 'Good luck to you.'

"(There were shouts of 'Right On,' and there was applause in the courtroom.)"

Official Transcript, Pages 19,108-112. **6 months**

Specification 21: After the Court ruled, on February 2, that the Reverend Abernathy would not be permitted to take the stand, the Court entered an order to Mr. Kunstler and the other attorneys and defendants that they may not mention the name of the Reverend Abernathy in front of the jury. Mr. Kunstler not only defiantly indicated that he fully intended to violate that order, but in the middle of the direct testimony of the witness Lynskey, Mr. Kunstler actually brought the witness -- that should be Reverend, he was not a witness -- Abernathy into the courtroom and made a statement to the jury and physically embraced the witness Abernathy in front of the jury. This flagrant violation of the Court's order is reported as follows:

"MR. SCHULTZ: Your Honor, may the defendants and their counsel then not make any reference in front of the jury that they wanted Doctor Abernathy to testify?

"MR. KUNSTLER: No, no.

"THE COURT: I order you not to make such a statement.

"MR. QUNSTLER: We are not going to abide by any such comment as that.

"Doctor Ralph Abernathy is going to come into this courtroom, and I am going to repeat my motion before that jury.

"THE COURT: I order you not to.

"MR. KUNSTLER: Then you will have to send me to jail, I am sorry.

"MR. SCHULTZ: Your Honor, it is our position we are ready to go ahead now. If Doctor Abernathy were here, if he were here, it would be our position that they could put him on, but he is not here. We are ready to go ahead. We would like to proceed

with the case.
"THE COURT: Bring in the jury, Mr. Marshal.
"MR. KUNSTLER: We have a right to state our objection to resting before the jury.
"THE COURT: Don't do it.
"MR. KUNSTLER: I am going to have to put my liberty in your hands on that score.
"MR. SCHULTZ: Mr. Kunstler is simply inviting it.
"MR. KUNSTLER: Oh, of course, I am inviting it because what your Honor is doing is a disgrace in this court.
"THE COURT: He did more than invite.
"MR. KUNSTLER: He will be here in five minutes. Your Honor, what is an honest man to do when your Honor has done what he has done? What am I to do? Am I to stand here and say, 'Yes, yes, yes'?
"THE COURT: I will ask you to sit down. I have heard enough from you along this line this morning, sir. I have never as a lawyer or a judge heard such remarks in a courtroom made by a lawyer.
"MR. KUNSTLER: Your Honor, no one has heard of such conduct as is going on in this courtroom from the bench. The New York Times is not alone in that respect, and this is the ultimate outrage -- and I didn't say -- the editorial writers of the New York Times said that.
"MR. SCHULTZ: May we proceed, your Honor?
"THE COURT: Yes. I have ordered the jury brought in." Official Transcript, Pages 19,140-42.
"MR. KUNSTLER: Your Honor, if I can interrupt, Doctor Ralph Abernathy has just arrived.
"THE COURT: Let him sit down.
"MR. KUNSTLER: I would like to put him on the stand for the defense.
"THE COURT: Let him sit down.
"MR. KUNSTLER: I would like to move to reconsider to put him on the stand as a witness for the defense. It is now just 11:37.
"THE COURT: Let him sit down, please. You may continue with your examination, Mr. Foran.
"MR. KUNSTLER: Does your Honor deny my motion?

"THE COURT: I do, sir.

"You may continue with your examination.

"MR. KUNSTLER: Your Honor it is only 16 minutes after the Government said they would have no objection to having Doctor Abernathy testify. He was flown here from Atlanta to be a witness for the defense.

"THE COURT: I do not interpret what the Government says to mean that, and the Government is not running this courtroom.

"MR. KUNSTLER: Your Honor - -

"THE COURT: Will you continue?

"MR. KUNSTLER: Is the truth to be deprived from this jury because of 16 minutes?

"MR. FORAN: Your Honor, the Government is in the middle of the examination of a witness.

"MR. KUNSTLER: We have tried to get the few minutes delay so we could bring Doctor Abernathy here.

"THE COURT: I ask you to sit down, sir.

"BY MR. FORAN:

"Q What was the noise level at that time?

"MR. KUNSTLER: Your Honor, before this goes on, would your Honor permit an application for Doctor Abernathy to testify after this witness has testified?

"THE COURT: I ask you to sit down.

"MR. KUNSTLER: Otherwise we are going to excuse him.

"THE COURT: Mr. Marshal, have that lawyer sit down.

"MR. KUNSTLER: Can you give me an answer to my question? We want to excuse Doctor Abernathy.

"THE COURT: If you will please sit down - -

"MR. KUNSTLER: I am going to be forced in a minute so I have no alternative.

"THE COURT: Yes.

"MR. KUNSTLER: Can I get an answer sitting down to my question?

"MR. FORAN: Your Honor, the interruption in the midst of the questioning of a witness in the

presence of the jury is unheard of, your Honor. I wish he would - -
"MR. FROINES: So is not putting on a witness.
"A VOICE: - - going to walk out of the courtroom because we can't put a man on the stand - -
"A VOICE: Can't put on our witness - -
"THE COURT: Did you hear what I asked you to do, sir?
"MR. KUNSTLER: I am down.
"THE COURT: Please continue with your examination.
"MR. KUNSTLER: I am going to ask Doctor Abernathy to leave, your Honor. It is obvious he is not going to testify.
"MR. FORAN: Your Honor, the proper procedure is to discuss such matters outside the presence of the jury, not in the midst of the questioning of the witness.
"THE COURT: I ordered him not to discuss that witness in the presence of the jury before the jury came in. He violated my order.
"MR. FORAN: Your Honor, may I wait? May I await Mr. Kunstler returning to counsel table?
"MR. KUNSTLER: I will be back, your Honor.
"THE COURT: Yes. You may wait.

"Let the record show the hug of counsel for the defendant.

"MR. FORAN: Your Honor, the discussion of whether or not the witness should be called as a witness would properly await the finishing of the examination of this witness and the demonstration - -
"THE COURT: Go ahead.
"MR. KUNSTLER: Then I told him to leave, your Honor. He - -
"THE COURT: All right. You have told him to leave.
"MR. KUNSTLER: I can hold him if there is nothing - - we want him to testify.
"THE COURT: You told him to leave and I again direct you to sit down. We have had enough this morning.
"MR. KUNSTLER: May I send one of the defen-

dants out just to ask him to stay, so perhaps - -
"THE COURT: No, you may not send one of the defendants out. You may not send - -
"MR. KUNSTLER: May I go and tell him?
"THE COURT: I ask you to sit down.
"MR. KUNSTLER: Your Honor, just to tell him so that, if the Government is going to permit him to testify - -
"THE COURT: I have had enough of your insults this morning.
"MR. KUNSTLER: Your Honor, this - - I am not being insulting.
"THE COURT: You were this morning.
"MR. KUNSTLER: I was not insulting. I told you the truth this morning. I told you what the New York Times said - -
"THE COURT: All right.
"MR. KUNSTLER: - - about the refusal to put a witness on the stand.
"THE COURT: Sit down, sir, or we will arrange to have you put down." Official Transcript, Pages 19,154-159. **6 months**

Specification 22: On February 4, when the Court determined that the time had come to revoke the bail of the defendant Dellinger, there was a loud outburst in the courtroom. It was essential that marshals forcibly clear people from the courtroom in order to maintain order. When disorder broke out in the spectator benches, Mr. Kunstler blamed the disorder on the Court, and fanned the flames of the disorder with these inciting comments:
"MR. KUNSTLER: You brought this on, your Honor. This is your fault. This is what happened in Chicago. You made the power move. You exerted the power, and I would like to argue the point.
"THE COURT: You won't argue the point.
"MR. KUNSTLER: I will argue, your Honor, that your Honor's action is completely and utterly vindictive, and there is no authority that says because a defendant blurts out a word in court - -
"THE COURT: This isn't the first word, and I won't argue this." Official Transcript, Pages 19,777-

78.
"MR. KUNSTLER: No, you know that if you did that, you would add to reversible error in this case. Why not take them all?"
"MR. KUNSTLER: Your Honor, there is no need for your action." Official Transcript, Page 19,779.
"MR. KUNSTLER: Your Honor, is there no decency left here? Can't we just argue the point?" Official Transcript, Page 19,780. **4 months**

Specification 23: On February 5, after the Court had denied the defendants' motion to reinstate the defendant Dellinger's bond, the Court determined that argument was complete. Once more Mr. Kunstler defied the Court's order to desist arguing and sit down. The incident is reported as follows:

"MR. KUNSTLER: The United States Attorney is trying to get the stenographer to add words to the record.
"THE COURT: And that order to sit down - -
"MR. WEINGLASS: Your Honor, I ask the Court - -
"THE COURT: Mr. Marshal, please have that lawyer sit down - - both of them.
"MR. WEINGLASS: Your Honor will not permit me to continue legal argument?
"THE COURT: You heard what I said. I deny the motion.
"MR. DAVIS: May we defend ourselves if our lawyers can't?
MR. KUNSTLER: I think the marshal is going to have this time to put me in my seat. I am not going to sit down unless I am forced to sit down.
"THE COURT: I direct you to.
"MR. WEINGLASS: Your Honor cited the Fernandez case - -
"THE COURT: I asked you to sit down.
"MR. KUNSTLER: I think we ought to argue the motion.
"THE COURT: I ask you to sit down and there will be no further argument." Official Transcript, Pages 19,800-1. **1 month**

Specification 24: On February 9, Mr. Kunstler engaged the Court in a colloquy concerning certain representations he had made to the Court concerning defendants surrebuttal case. The Court had occasion to take him to task, and he insulted the Court in the following manner:

"THE COURT: I want to read what you said.

"MR. KUNSTLER: All right.

"THE COURT: I will wait.

"But do you" - - and I am addressing you - - "do you give me your assurance, sir - -" - - I am reading from the transcript of evidence, Page 20278, "in the presence of this jury and all those assembled here, the lawyers, the parties, that you will not attempt or offer any additional - - or offer any additional witnesses on Monday? We are conditioning this continuance or I propose to condition it on your representation that will not be the case.

"May I have just a moment to consult?

"Now it takes a witness to identify a document, sir.

"MR. KUNSTLER: No, no. The witness has testified already, your Honor, Your Honor is now proved wrong. I said 'witnesses,' and I stand by that. There are no additional witnesses. I did - - I think your Honor has read the transcript to show that I was right in this instance. Now, your Honor, you are not going to find it, I don't think.

"Your Honor, why don't you just agree for once that perhaps I am right, and I am.

"THE COURT: I will strike the remark of Mr. Kunstler, insulting as it is.

"MR. KUNSTLER: It is not insulting.

"THE COURT: And I direct the jury to disregard it.

"MR. KUNSTLER: Your Honor - -

"THE COURT: I sat here patiently for five months, sir, pretty nearly.

"MR. KUNSTLER: I have been here patiently for five months.

"THE COURT: I want to tell you that for you to say 'Why don't you agree for once' is about as rotten a thing as I have ever had said to me.

"MR. KUNSTLER: With rare exceptions you have

not agreed with me on anything throughout this trial. It is not meant to be insulting, your Honor. You are poring" -- the records says -- "through the transcript --

"THE COURT: I take it as an insult.

"MR. KUNSTLER: Because you want to find that I am wrong.

"THE COURT: I have given all my judicial time to this case.

"MR. KUNSTLER: I have devoted all my legal time. We have all devoted our time. The jury devotes its time and you do.

"THE COURT: I will not hear you further in connection with that exhibit.

"MR. KUNSTLER: Will you then just for the record admit that you were wrong, that I did not say documents?

"THE COURT: No, I will not admit that I was wrong because I am not wrong. If you will read the transcript -- and I don't propose to take the time --

"MR. KUNSTLER: You have read it to us, your Honor.

"THE COURT: Not all of it.

"MR. KUNSTLER: It is quite clear." Official Transcript, Pages 20,324-26.

Mr. Schultz then spoke. He cited explicit sections of the transcript which conclusively demonstrated that the Court had been correct in its understanding of Mr. Kunstler's representations. Mr Kunstler's accusations were demonstrated to be erroneous. Even Mr. Kunstler recognized that he had erred, and he apologized.

"MR. KUNSTLER: In the light of that, your Honor, I will make the admission and be quite candid and frank that then I was wrong and I will not offer 109 although I think it ought to go in. When I am wrong, I think it is proper to admit it.

"THE COURT: You were pretty sure, though, when you said that I was mistaken. You didn't use the charitable word that you just used.

"MR. KUNSTLER: Your Honor, I admit when a man is wrong, I think he has an obligation to say it and I am saying it." Official Transcript, Page

20,327.

One minute later Mr. Kunstler directly violated an explicit order of the Court by mentioning once more the name of the Reverend Abernathy before the jury. When the Court challenged him to justify his conduct, he attempted to do so by citing previous violations of that order, as if past misconduct by defendants and their attorneys could some way justify this violation.

> "MR. KUNSTLER: I only do it, your Honor, because it has been discussed ten times in front of them (the jurors)." Official Transcript, Page 20,329.

2 months

THE COURT: Do you wish to be heard, Mr. Kunstler?

MR. KUNSTLER: Yes, your Honor. First of all, I make for myself the same motions that I have made for the other clients whom I have represented, with reference to your Honor's powers or lack of power and jurisdiction to impose summary contempt after the trial is over, and I make that with the same force I made it for my client.

THE COURT: I deny the motion.

MR. KUNSTLER: Then I just have a few words, your Honor.

Your Honor, I have been a lawyer since December of 1948, when I was first admitted to the bar in the state of New York. Since that time, I have practiced before, among other courts, the Supereme Court of the United States, the United States Court of Appeals for the Frist, Second, Third, Fourth, Fifth, Sixth, Seventh, Tenth, District of Columbia Circuits, Federal District Courts throughout a great deal of the United States, and the United States Court of Military Appeals.

In addition I have practiced in the State Courts of Texas, Tennessee, Virginia, Georgia, Louisiana, Maryland, New Jersey, Vermont, North Carolina, Florida, Mississippi, Alabama, South Dakota, Kentucky, Pennsylvania, and many others.

Until today I have never once been disciplined by any judge, federal or state, although a large part of my practice, at least for the last decade, has taken place in hostile southern courts where I was representing black and white clients in highly controversial civil rights cases.

Yesterday, for the first time in my career, I completely lost my composure in a courtroom, as I watched the older daughter of David Dellinger being rushed out of the room because she clapped her hands to acknowledge what amounted to her father's farewell statement to her.

I felt then such a deep sense of utter, futility that I could not help crying, something I had not done publicly since childhood.

I am sorry if I disturbed the decorum of the courtroom, but I am not ashamed of my tears. Neither am I ashamed of my conduct in this court, for which I am about to be punished.

I have tried with all of my heart faithfully to represent my clients in the face of what I consider -- and still consider -- repressive and unjust conduct toward them. If I have to pay with my liberty for such representation, then that is the price of my beliefs and my sensibilities.

I can only hope that my fate does not deter other lawyers throughout the country, who, in the difficult days that lie ahead, will be asked to defend clients against a steadily increasing governmental encroachment upon their most fundamental liberties. If they are so deterred, then my punishment will have effects of such terrifying consequences that I dread to contemplate the future domestic and foreign course of this country. However, I have the utmost faith that my beloved brethren at the bar, young and old alike, will not allow themselves to be frightened out of defending the poor, the persecuted, the radicals and the militant, the black people, the pacifists, and the political pariahs of this, our common land.

But to those lawyers who may, in learning of what may happen to me, waiver, I can only say this, stand firm, remain true to those ideals of the law which even if openly violated here and in other places, are true and glorious goals, and, above all, never desert those principles of equality, justice and freedom without which life has little if any meaning.

I may not be the greatest lawyer in the world, your Honor, but I think that I am at this moment, along with my colleague, Leonard Weinglass, the most privileged.

We are being punished for what we believe in.

Your Honor, I am ready, sir, to be sentenced, and I would appreciate it if I could be permitted to remain standing at this lectern where I have spent the greater part of the past five months, while you do so.

Thank you.

(Applause.)

THE COURT: The marshals will remove those who have applauded from the courtroom. Remove them from the courtroom. This circus has to end sometime. Please remove everybody who has applauded. This is not a theater. Mr. Ginsberg just did not perform, nor did any of the other singers. All of those who applauded, exclude them, please.

Mr. Kunstler, you have heard me say here, I think, on at least two occasions that not only have I never had occasion to impose a sentence for contempt of court on a lawyer, never on a witness or a party in this court, except one, and that sentence was merged, made concurrent with the sentence in the main case. So that I approach what I perceive to be my responsibility here just as unhappily as you indicated you are. I, too, have been at the bar for a long time, many years longer than you. I have practiced in the various state and federal courts throughout the land, not all, of course, but many.

I have to repeat what I have said in substance, that I have never heard a lawyer say to a judge in substance the things that you have said to me during this trial. I know you are going to say -- if I permitted you to reply -- you would say that I deserved them.

Well, only the record can reveal what has gone on here. You mentioned there has been mention here in this transcript, observations about the testimony of Mr. Clark. Mr. Clark wasn't kept from the witness stand. We permitted the Government to conduct a voir dire examination, which was proper procedure under existing competent authorities, and I have to repeat here what I said this morning. If Mr. Clark is upset with me, I regret it, not because of him, because I know him only casually, but because of his father, who has been my dear friend for many years, and who, as you know, has been -- has served on the Supreme Court of the United States for many years now, serving as a senior justice. I hold his mother in greatest esteem.

We decided questions here according to the law, as we perceive the law to be. As I indicated this morning, to one of the defendants, if a lawyer or a party perceives that a ruling is erroneous, you certainly, as a lawyer, know there are courts where you can proceed to have error corrected. We don't correct error doing it the way you have done.

Now, I know you, from some of the things you said here, tie in your own personal beliefs with those of your clients, and you live your clients' cases as though they are your own. Nobody disputes that anyone under the Constitution of the United States charged with a crime has a right to counsel of his choice, and if he hasn't the money to employ a lawyer, just about every state and the Government, itself, provide counsel at no cost to them. Certainly, that is the constitutional right of any citizen, or anybody who comes in here charged with a crime. But a man charged with a crime has a right only to a defense properly made, and that does not include what has gone on, the sort of thing that has gone on in this courtroom.

We hear a lot of discussion by men in high political places about crime in this country. I am going to make a rather unorthodox statement. First of all, there is a lot of crime, I know, because I have a lot of criminal cases to try, and I have tried many criminal cases. I am one of those who believes that crime, if it is on the increase, and I don't have the statistics before me, in any jurisdiction, state or federal, it is due in large part to the fact that waiting in the wings are lawyers who are willing to go beyond, to go beyond professional responsibility, professional rights, and professional duty in their defense of a defendant, and the fact that a defendant or some defendants know that such a lawyer is waiting in the wings, I think, has rather a stimulating effect on the increase in crime.

You have quoted newspapers. I have had occasion to tell you that I don't try cases in the newspapers. I don't send letters to newspapers when they praise me, and they have; and I don't send letters of criticism when they criticize me adversely. Certainly a judge's decision must be criticized. A man who takes a public place exposes himself to fair comment, but that comment should be honest and it should be in accordance with the facts as they appear from the official record.

Now, I saw, in fact it was dropped on the Clerk's desk, a xeroxed copy of an editorial in one of the great newspapers of the country -- at least I have so regarded it -- devoted to the Ramsey Clark incident. There was no mention of the fact in that editorial that a voir dire examination of Mr. Clark was conducted, and the Court after carefully listening to it -- I wouldn't expect them to have said "carefully" -- but the Court after listening to it concluded that it was not proper that he be called as a witness, but the impression given was that he wasn't allowed to come to the witness stand. He was five feet away from me, as you know. But I don't complain. That is the sort of thing that men in public place, whether they are an alderman in a big city ward, or the President of the United States, they just don't have the time to write a "Letter to the People," as some of these columns are entitled, and say, "You lied about me," or "You omitted to tell the facts."

I recall seeing quoted somewhere something spoken by Abraham Lincoln who said, "Never argue with a newspaper unless you own the newspaper."

Well, I have never argued with a newspaper.

In this case, you seem to have wanted to rely on editorial comment.

I have literally thousands of editorials back there in my chambers -- I know you won't believe this -- that are complimentary about decisions I have made over the years, over the many years I have served both on the state and federal bench. And for you, the kind of lawyer you say that you are, to have sat through that Bobby Seale incident, for example, and not lifted an arm, of your chair, not lifted your hand, not lifted an arm, not spoken a word, and he could have been spoken to because he was spoken to before he assumed the witness stand as a witness after he came back to this jurisdiction to testify as a witness, not a word from you to him, and your appearance was on file as his lawyer, you spoke for him as a defendant, even if I were wrong, if I were wrong, even if the many times he called me the vile names that he called me -- I don't know how it could be proven that a man of my faith was a pig; that would be very difficult -- but there is a man who never saw me, I believe, before he came into this courtroom, but to have described me as he described me, and for you, and you represent yourself to be a leader at the Bar, and you have practiced in all of these courts that you have mentioned, you have never, never made an attempt to say something like this to him, "Bobby, hush. Cool it. Sit down now." You let him go on.

That is not going to be in my contempt certificate, because there are some things that cannot be proven as direct contempt committed in the presence of the Court. Someday, someday, I hope that his conduct, or the reason for his conduct will be demonstrated clearly, and you can't disassociate yourself from him. He was your client. I know you dispute the fact that he is now, but he was. Even in the way you describe it, he was your client at one time, and you made no effort, no effort, to have him keep from calling a Judge of the United States District Court a pig, a fascist pig, a racist pig. There wasn't any element of racism in this case except that there was one defendant, if you call that racism, who was a member of the black race. You let him continue speaking and repeating. If that is being a great lawyer, I do not share your view. I do not share your view, sir.

MR. KUNSTLER: Your Honor, I just want to say --

THE COURT: The only reason I mention the Seale episode is that I didn't want anyone here to get the impression that I was obtuse and didn't know what was going on. I didn't want any one of the ladies and gentlemen of the press to get the impression that I didn't know what was really the time of day.

MR. KUNSTLER: Your Honor, I am glad your Honor spoke because I suddenly feel nothing but compassion for you. Everything else has dropped away.

THE COURT: All right, Now, as I said earlier, in conformity with Rule 42(a) of the Federal Rules of Criminal Procedure, Title 18, United States Code, Section 401, I certify that I saw and heard the incidents and conduct which I have read here today during the trial of the case of United States of America vs. David Dellinger and others, 69 CR 180, which commenced on September 24, 1969, and continued for about four and a half months thereafter. I find that the acts, statements and conduct of Mr. William Kunstler specified by me each constituted a separate contempt of this Court and that each constituted, and by "each," I mean those as they have been numbered in my oral observations, that each constituted a deliberate and wilful attack upon the administration of justice in an attempt to sabotage the functioning of the federal judicial system, that this misconduct, especially in a lawyer, was of so grave a character as to continually disrupt the orderly administration of justice. To maintain the dignity of the Court and preserve order in the courtroom under these circumstances has been a task of utmost difficulty. Warning after warning, and admonition after admonition were given to you, Mr. Kunstler. Instead of heeding them, you characterized them as attempts to intimidate you.

I have dealt with many thousands of lawyers both as a lawyer and judge over the many years. Nobody has ever charged me with trying to intimidate, but nobody.

Isolated questions from or references to the transcript can give but a partial view of the acts, statements and conduct which I referred to orally here this morning.

I hereby, Mr. United States Attorney, make the entire record part of these proceedings.

With respect to punishment, have you finished everything you want to say to me?

MR. KUNSTLER: Yes, your Honor, I have nothing further.

THE COURT: All right. With respect to *Specification* 1, Mr. Kunstler will be committed to the custody of the Attorney General of the United States or his authorized representative for a period of one month; *Specification* 2, 14 days; *Specification* 3, 3 months; *Specification* 4, 14 months, or 14 days, I beg your pardon; *Specification* 5, 14 days; *Specification* 6, 3 months; *Specification* 7, 3 months; *Specification* 8, 6 months; *Specification* 9, 21 days; *Specification* 10, 14 days; *Specification* 11, 7 days; *Specification* 12, 14 days; *Specification* 13, 14 days; *Speci-*

fication 14, 1 month; *Specification* 15, 21 days; *Specification* 16, 2 months; *Specification* 17, 4 months; *Specification* 18, 1 month; *Specification* 19, 1 month; *Specification* 20, 6 months; *Specification* 21, 6 months; *Specification* 22, 4 months; *Specification* 23, 1 month; *Specification* 24, 2 months.

Mr. Kunstler, because you are counsel of record for the defendants here or some of them, on the court's own motion, the execution of the judgment of conviction entered on these several specifications will be stayed until Monday, May 4, at 9:00 o'clock in the morning, at which time, I order you to report to the United States Marshal for the Northern District of Illinois whose office is in this building.

Mr. United States Attorney, I order you to prepare the proper documents, judgment and commitment specification in accordance with what has been done here today.

MR. KUNSTLER: Your Honor, for the record, may I apply for bail pending appeal?

THE COURT: I haven't the authority to grant you bail pending appeal in the case of direct contempt committed in the presence of the court. If you want bail, they may grant it to you, I don't know, but I don't have the authority.

MR. KUNSTLER: Then there is a denial on the record? That is what I really want.

THE COURT: What did you say?

MR. KUNSTLER: I guess you are denying my motion?

THE COURT: Yes, I am denying it because I don't have the authority to grant you bail.

I am saying to you that I have stayed the execution here of the judgment until Monday, May 4, at nine o'clock.

MR. KUNSTLER: I was taking the legal position.

THE COURT: The reason for it is I think you possibly might have some matters, I don't know. I haven't heard that the jury has come in.

MR. KUNSTLER: I was thinking that I am in constructive custody. That is why I was raising the question regarding it. That is why I was making the motion.

THE COURT: I can't go any further than I have gone. I can't grant bail in a case of this kind. I have no authority.

WEINGLASS

THE COURT: Now we come to the matter of Leonard Weinglass. I will wait until those who wish to leave the courtroom do so.

With respect to Mr. Leonard Weinglass, in conformity with Rule 42(a) of the Federal Rules of Criminal Procedure, Title 18 of the United States Code, Section 401, I certify that I saw and heard the conduct which I am about to describe here orally, which conduct took place in the actual presence of the court during the trial of the case entitled United States of America vs. David Dellinger and others, 69 CR 180, which commenced on September 24, 1969, and has continued and did continue for about four and a half months in that Leonard Weinglass was of counsel for three of the defendants.

Specification 1: Mr. Weinglass has consistently ignored the orders of the court to discontinue argument or to sit down. The first occasion upon which this occurred was on September 24, during motions made prior to the voir dire of the jury panel. The incident is thus reported:

> "MR. WEINGLASS: Mr. Birnbaum and Mr. Bass have withdrawn from the case as trial counsel. Mr. Seale is not represented here in court.
>
> "THE COURT: Mr. Weinglass, I direct you to sit down.
>
> MR. WEINGLASS: If the Court please, I would like to know - -
>
> THE COURT: I would like you to sit down, or I will ask the marshal to escort you to your chair.
>
> MR. WEINGLASS: I will sit down, but I do so under protest.
>
> THE COURT: Then do so."

Voir Dire Transcript, Page 24. **2 days**

Specification 2: On October 1, during the cross examination of the witness Stahl, Mr. Weinglass continually asked questions that were beyond the scope of the direct examination. The court sustained the objections but he persisted in asking the questions, over objection, again and again. In an effort to enlighten him, the court sent out the jury and directed some remarks concerning cases on contempt to Mr. Weinglass who virtually ignored the court while the court was addressing him. The incident is reported in Pages 555 through 565 of the official transcript as follows:

"MR. WEINGLASS: The last document should be marked identification No. 7, Defendants' Exhibit, and we can mark this Defendants' Exhibit 8.

(Said documents were thereupon marked Defendants' Exhibit 7 and 8 for identification.)

BY MR. WEINGLASS:

Q. I show you your handwritten notes of the August 12 meeting marked Defendants' No. 8.

Is that your handwritten note, a copy of it?

A. Yes, these are a copy of my notes of the meeting August 12.

Q. August 12. Directing your attention to the first page, did you state right at the beginning that the National Mobilization Committee made it clear to you at the outset that they wanted to avoid unnecessary tensions, is that correct?

A. Mr. Dellinger made that statement and immediately followed with a statement that he believed in civil disobedience, that he just returned from Paris where he studied street riots. I think that he would say violence and then say non-violence and then say --

Q. Is that correct? Well, does that statement appear in your notes?

A. Yes, the statement about civil disobedience does.

Q. Yes. Would you read to the jury, after having said that, what your notes reflect Mr. Dellinger said about civil disobedience?

MR. FORAN: Object to that.

THE COURT: I sustain the objection.

BY MR. WEINGLASS:

Q. Is it not a fact that Mr. Dellinger said, according to your notes, that he believes in civil disobedi-

ence, but that he does not intend to disrupt delegates at the convention? Isn't that what he said, Mr. Stahl? Isn't that what your notes reflect him saying?
MR. FORAN: Your Honor, I object to that.
THE COURT: I sustain the objection.
BY MR. WEINGLASS:

Q. I ask you to look over that entire first page, and I ask you whether or not there are any notations indicating that Mr. Dellinger had been to Paris or that he had studied riot techniques on that first page?
MR. FORAN: Your Honor, I object to this. There is a clearly proper way to establish that if it is true.
THE COURT: Of course. I sustain your objection.
MR. FORAN: The same type of objection, your Honor, has been sustained a number of times, and I wish counsel would be directed that there is a proper way to go into those matters if he would use it, and it is not this way.
BY MR. WEINGLASS:

Q. Do you further recall Mr. Dellinger saying to you in the course of that meeting that he didn't want to interfere with the police, business or traffic? I am referring to page 2 of your notes.

A. Yes, he made that statement.

Q. He made that statement. Did he also make the statement to you that he wanted to meet with the police?

A. He said he may want to meet with the police.

Q. I refer you to the middle of the page. That was the second request to meet with the police. His first request appears in the middle of the page. Does it qualify -- does he say he wants to meet with the police?

A. My notes say, 'Want to meet with police.'

Q. Yes. Did Mr. Dellinger also make known to you, as reflected in your notes, that denying of the permits is a denial of the rights?

A. Yes.

Q. At the August 12 meeting who appeared there on behalf of the City besides yourself?

A. Assistant Corporation Counsel, Richard Elrod, was there. I believe that's all. There may have been others.

Q. Was there any understanding between you and Mr. Simon or someone else on behalf of National Mobilization that you were to have other department heads there so that this matter could be resolved in one meeting?

A. No, there was no such understanding.

MR. FORAN: I object.

BY MR. WEINGLASS:

Q. There was no such under- - -

THE COURT: Do you persist in your objection, or do you let the answer - -

MR. FORAN: I will withdraw.

THE COURT: Let the answer stand.

BY MR. WEINGLASS:

Q. Did you ever have an understanding with Mr. Dellinger or Mr. Davis that you would bring before them at one meeting heads of the Park District and the Department of Sanitation and Streets for resolution of the problem?

MR. FORAN: I object to that now.

THE COURT: I sustain it.

BY MR. WEINGLASS:

Q. Was it your understanding, Mr. Stahl, at that August 12 meeting that you were to have other people there from the City who did not appear?

MR. FORAN: Object, your Honor.

THE COURT: I sustain the objection.

BY MR. WEINGLASS:

Q. Were you ever able to bring together in a single meeting Rennie Davis and Mr. Dellinger and the head of the Park District or the head of the Department of Streets and Sanitation?

MR. FORAN: Your Honor, I object.

THE COURT: I sustain the objection.

BY MR. WEINGLASS:

Q. Were you ever requested to bring together - - were you ever requested by Mr. Davis and Mr. Dellinger to bring together in a meeting himself and other persons from City Government?

MR. FORAN: Your Honor, I object.

THE COURT: I sustain the objection.

MR. FORAN: May I ask that the jury be excused for a moment?
THE COURT: On request of the United States Attorney, ladies and gentlemen of the jury, I will excuse you.

Before you go into the jury room, my usual orders that you are not to read the newspapers, not to listen to television or radio, not to talk about this case with anybody or let anybody speak with you about it. Do not discuss the case among yourselves. I think I omitted to say, don't look at television, although I don't think our great Government has provided a television in the jury room in any event. But I am obligated to make that order.

You are excused for a few moments.

(The following proceedings were had in open court, out of the presence and hearing of the jury:)
MR. FORAN: Your Honor, I find it a little unusual to conduct or attempt to conduct a class in basic legal procedure, but where counsel constantly asks questions that are outside the scope of the direct examination, I cannot expect that it is for any reason except to generate some erroneous impression in the jury because it generates objections from counsel. There is a perfectly proper way to put in matters other than those covered on direct examination. It is not by trying to put facts into questions that if they are denied sound as if they are in the record. That is the reason that Wigmore, that common law since the beginning of time designated a trial technique, and I ask your Honor to direct counsel to comply with what is the proper conduct of examination of a witness.
THE COURT: Since the jury is out, I do direct counsel to confine his cross-examination to matters brought out on direct.

The objections of the government were valid, and they have all been sustained.

And by the way, Mr. Weinglass, this morning I referred Mr. Kunstler to two cases --
MR. WEINGLASS: Am I being addressed on this?
THE COURT: What did you say?
MR. WEINGLASS: Am I being addressed or Mr.

Kunstler?
THE COURT: No, I said, 'By the way.' I am addressing you. I do mention his name because I referred to two cases this morning, the Sacher case in the 343 Supreme, Sacher and others against the United States, and 343, page 1, and the case of United States, of America vs. Schiffer, reported in 351 F. 2d 91, (1965).

Mr. Kunstler said he was familiar with those cases, but I fear that he misunderstood the names because when he said he understood them, he didn't.

I do want to call your attention to those cases.

I will wait until you get through reading your papers. Have you finished?
MR. WEINGLASS: Am I being questioned on what my co-counsel --
THE COURT: I am telling you something. I am trying to enlighten you. I am trying to do something for you. Haven't you been listening to me?
MR. WEINGLASS: I frankly thought these remarks were addressed to counsel who cited the cases, not to myself. I had no part of that dialogue.
THE COURT: Well, then I tell you, sir, and I am addressing you now --
MR. WEINGLASS: Yes.
THE COURT: I am not accustomed to having lawyers turn pages while I address them. I don't turn pages up here when you address me, sir.

I commend to you for your examination the case of Sacher and others against the United States, 343 U.S., page 1, and United States of America vs. Schiffer, 351 F. 2d, page 91.

I shall not take the time to read those cases to you, but they are quite opposite, I think, when a lawyer persists in asking questions that are beyond the scope of the direct examination after repeated objections have been sustained.

Mr. Marshal, will you please bring in the jury."
Official Transcript 555-65. **4 months**

Specification 3: On October 30 when the court was making an evidentiary ruling, Mr. Weinglass engaged in the following colloquy with the Court indicating his belief that the Court had been prejudicial in its rulings on evidence:

"THE COURT: What do the lawyers say about that, they open the door? Is that what you lawyers all say?

"MR. WEINGLASS: We do not open the door to a prejudicial question. I very carefully avoided any mention of any section of a code.

THE COURT: That is the reason for the open-the-door rule.

MR. WEINGLASS: Well, the door has been --

THE COURT: Very often it kicks back in your face.

MR. WEINGLESS: The door in this courtroom seems to swing in one direction. Many times I have attempted to --

THE COURT: Miss Reporter, please make note of that.

The Court admonishes counsel to be cautious in his observations, in the observations he makes such as he just completed." Official Transcript 4925. **14 days**

Specification 4: On November 26, during the cross-examination of the witness Schaller, Mr. Weinglass engaged the court in the following colloquy:

"THE COURT: In justice to my own position here, I must reveal, sir, that prior to the jury coming in, you said you would need the tape recorders --

MR. WEINGLASS: Because the --

THE COURT: -- on your motion, and I made it of record -- I gave leave to the gentlemen of the government who had those devices in charge to take them out. Now, isn't that true?

MR. WEINGLASS: That is correct, because your Honor -- your Honor must give me a chance to answer that. That's most unfair. That is most unfair, and I object to that.

THE COURT: That is not unfair, sir, and please be careful about your language.

MR. WEINGLASS: Your Honor --

MR. KUNSTLER: We couldn't play those --

MR. WEINGLASS: I couldn't play 40 because it was not in evidence.

THE COURT: I can't listen to two shouting lawyers

at the same time.
MR. WEINGLASS: Because it's the only way we can be heard at times. Those documents were not in evidence. The government excluded - -
THE COURT: Please read that last statement of Mr. Weinglass.
MR. WEINGLASS: It was, because there are times we can't be heard unless we shout.
THE COURT: All right.
MR. WEINGLASS: And that is what I said. I will stand by that.
THE COURT: I just wanted to be sure I heard that statement." Official Transcript, Page 8,286-87. **14 days**

Specification 5: On January 13 Mr. Weinglass engaged the Court in the following colloquy, when the Court made the reasonable request that Mr. Weinglass stop repeating his argument after an extensive statement.

MR. WEINGLASS: Your Honor, Wigmore, the Seventh Circuit Court of Appeals, McCormick on Evidence - -
THE COURT: Don't repeat.
MR. WEINGLASS: - - Judge Learned Hand - -
THE COURT: Don't repeat. I have listened very carefully to you. You are repeating the judges and the authors and - -
MR. WEINGLASS: I am summarizing.
THE COURT: If you have anything additional to say, I will hear you.
MR. WEINGLASS: I am exercising an attorney's right to summarize in argument.
THE COURT: Not in the middle of a trial. I don't think you have that right where the Court has already made a ruling and I have listened to you most attentively.

If you have anything additional, I will be glad to let you put it into the record.
MR. WEINGLASS: Well, all of the authorities I have cited, all of the legal writers who have written on the subject, Judge Learned Hand and the Seventh Circuit Court of Appeals, all agree - -
THE COURT: You are doing precisely what I asked

you not to do.
MR. WEINGLASS: I am doing what I feel I am permitted to do.
THE COURT: I forbid your repeating right in the middle of a trial here. And you haven't even stated your motion. You haven't even stated your motion. That is how carefully I have been listening to you, sir.
MR. WEINGLASS: I will state my motion after my summary conclusion.
THE COURT: Most lawyers when they address the court announce what their motion is. You haven't told me what your motion is yet.
MR. WEINGLASS: Your Honor, I don't think it is very much in doubt that I am moving to put these documents in evidence.
THE COURT: It should not be in doubt at all. A lawyer standing at the lectern to make a motion should state his motions.
MR. WEINGLASS: Well, your Honor, this has happened time and again in the course of the case, the substance of a legal argument has been compromised by your Honor's insistence of pure form." Official Transcript, Page 15,233 to 15,234. **1 month**

Specification 6: On January 13 during the redirect examination of the witness Simons, Mr. Weinglass again in front of the jury attempted to make an invidious comparison between the treatment the Court afforded the witnesses called by the defendant as opposed to the treatment afforded witnesses called by the government. This event is recorded at Pages 15,308 and 15,309 of the transcript as follows:

"THE COURT: Oh, wait at least until he gets through law school.
MR. WEINGLASS: But Mr. Foran - -
THE COURT: Mr. Weinglass - -
MR. WEINGLASS: I didn't go into it. Mr. Foran asked that. I did not go into this on direct examination.
THE COURT: Did I hear an objection to the question?

MR. FORAN: Yes, your Honor.
THE COURT: I think you stood. I sustain the objection.
MR. WEINGLASS: Your Honor, he was asked his opinion about ordinances, laws, what is a responsible act of a public official on cross-examination, so it was opened by the government.
THE COURT: Continue with your redirect examination.
MR. WEINGLASS: Is only one side able to use this witness' expertise and not the other? The government has asked - -
THE COURT: There will be no more of that type of observation. I have tried to make that clear to you all through this trial, Mr. Weinglass.
MR. WEINGLASS: Well, I make that observation reluctantly but I make it only when I think it is based in fact.
THE COURT: You should not succumb to your desire to make that kind of observation, sir, and I can understand why you make it reluctantly.
MR. KUNSTLER: I didn't hear the last remark, your Honor.
MR. WEINGLASS: If your Honor means something derogatory in that reference, I make that observation because I think it is based in fact and I think as a matter of fact it is incorrect. I say that respectfully to the Court. And I don't understand your Honor's observation.
THE COURT: Continue with the redirect examination of this witness, please." **1 month**

Specification 7: On January 13 during the direct examination of the witness Misner, the attorney Weinglass made the following sarcastic comments about the Court's rule on an evidentiary matter:

"MR. WEINGLASS: Oh, if your Honor please, an expert is called to Court by a party to assist the jury in interpreting evidence that has been put before the jury. An expert is needed to assist the jury in that role in order to help the jury draw conclusions, and you can only do that with an expert from testimony or facts already related.

Now your Honor knows that doctors are regularly called as expert witnesses. A jury cannot from hearing a temperature chart or the symptoms of illness draw conclusions as to what is wrong with the patient; that is why you call a doctor.

THE COURT: Oh, this is an eye witness. He has testified that he got hit on the back and even he disagreed with the diagnosis of the doctor. His diagnosis as a criminologist differed from that of the medical man.

So I will sustain the objection.

MR. WEINGLASS: No, your Honor. That is evading the issue.

MR. SCHULTZ: Your Honor - -

THE COURT: Oh, please, sir. I am not evading the issue.

MR. WEINGLASS: It is just evading it. It is getting us off into a little diversion about medical testimony.

THE COURT: Don't say so a third time.

MR. WEINGLASS: I say it most respectfully. This man came here as an expert criminologist. He talked to Chief Nolan - -

THE COURT: Ask another question. I sustain the objection." Official Transcript, Pages 15,1441-42.

14 days

Specification 8: On January 16 Mr. Weinglass once more continued an argument after the Court had ruled and after the Court had directed him to desist in his argument. The incident is reported as follows:

"BY MR. WEINGLASS:

Q. Who did you speak with?

A. I called the office to talk to both Tom Hayden and Rennie Davis.

Q. Did you speak to either or both?

A. I talked to Tom.

Q. Do you recall that conversation at that time?

A. Yes. I told Tom that I had just been in a meeting called the Coalition for an Open Convention at which a number of people who were supporters of Bobby Kennedy, which was what I was, were supporters of Gene McCarthy, who were - -

MR. SCHULTZ: Your Honor, I object. This conversation is wholly irrelevant, and simply because it's a conversation with the defendant does not make it admissible, and I object.
THE COURT: I sustain the objection.
MR. WEINGLASS: Your Honor, it is another telephone conversation which Mr. Schultz apparently has some information on, and I would like again --
THE COURT: Which candidate this witness was supporting, whether it was the late Senator Kennedy or anybody else, is immaterial and irrelevant here.
MR. WEINGLASS: No, your Honor will recall --
THE COURT: I direct the jury to disregard the last statement.
MR. WEINGLASS: Your Honor will recall during the cross-examination --
THE COURT: Ask another question, sir, or if the witness will answer the question without referring to these irrelevant matters -- perhaps he can -- I will let him answer, but there will be none of this stuff about whom he campaigned for, who his candidate was --
MR. WEINGLASS: Your Honor will recall that during the cross-examination of the witness Mark Simons by Mr. Foran, Mr. Foran on cross-examination indicated in his questions that perhaps the people who were coming here were irresponsible people who should not be given permits. The fact of the matter is that a sizable number of McCarthy delegates and Kennedy delegates who were elected and certified representatives to the convention had joined with the National Mobilization in an effort to seek permits in the city.
THE COURT: I will hear no further argument.
MR. WEINGLASS: And that is --
THE COURT: I will let my ruling stand, sir.
MR. WEINGLASS: That is why it is relevant, your Honor, and that is why I am trying to get into it.
THE COURT: No, it is not.
MR. WEINGLASS: These persons are cast as being persons who wanted to create an irresponsible situation.

THE COURT: Will your discontinue your argument, because I have ruled, sir." Official Transcript, Pages 16,063-64. **1 month**

Specification 9: On January 17 Mr. Weinglass once more continued an argument after the court had ruled.

"THE COURT: It is not relevant or material, and there is so much in that that has nothing to do with this case that I just couldn't take it in.

MR. WEINGLASS: Well, the document encompasses Miami and Chicago.

THE COURT: I have heard the argument. I have looked at the document, read it carefully, and that is my ruling, sir.

MR. WEINGLASS: Well, then, I re-offer as Defendants' Exhibit 310 Page 7 of that document.

THE COURT: I remember Page 7. I don't - -

MR. WEINGLASS: Page 7 deals exclusively with Chicago and the status of negotiation.

THE COURT: Do you want to look at Page 7?

MR. SCHULTZ: No, I have read Page 7. I prefer, your Honor, the witness testifies to what occurs rather than introduce a document. Objection.

THE COURT: It is not proper to take that page in, any more than it is to talk about other things to which I shall not here refer.

In order that the record is complete, I sustain the objection of the government to Defendants' Exhibit 310 for identification.

MR. WEINGLASS: Well, your Honor, this documents contains an assessment - -

THE COURT: I have ruled, sir. You must learn - - you mustn't keep on arguing after I rule. I have tried to make you understand that, that I have never had so much difficulty. That is good trial practice, and I have tried to make you understand it, but I haven't been able to.

BY MR. WEINGLASS:

Q. Mr Pomeroy, in preparing this document, whose assistance did you have, if anyone's?

MR. SCHULTZ: Objection. This document has been ruled inadmissible.

THE COURT: I sustain the objection." Official Transcript, Pages 16,298-99.

Shortly later on January 17, also during the testimony of the witness Pomeroy, Mr. Weinglass repeated his conduct. He once more argued after the court had made a ruling. This came within minutes of the court's admonition just quoted, not to argue after rulings.

"THE COURT: I sustain the objection.

MR. KUNSTLER: Your Honor, he just said to ask Mr. Weinglass to say what he saw. Why are they trying to keep hidden what happened here?

MR. SCHULTZ: If they want to bring in the plans of the Chicago Police Department, whatever the witness saw, let them bring in the person who says, 'These are the plans that we enforced. Here's what we did.'

THE COURT: I have ruled. There will be no further argument.

MR. WEINGLASS: He knows - -

THE COURT: I sustained the objection. No further argument.

MR. WEINGLASS: He was liaison officer for the Attorney General of the United States.

THE COURT: Did you hear me, sir? You continue day after day to persist in arguing after ruling has been made." Official Transcript, Page 16,332.

1 month

Specification 10: On January 20 the Court specifically directed Mr. Weinglass not to refer to a document, objection to which had been sustained. Mr. Weinglass continued to argue after this relatively simple ruling had been made. He continued to argue after told to desist. He was insulting to the Court and indicated that the Court had acted dishonestly. The incident is set forth in the record as follows:

"MR. WEINGLASS: After Mr. Schultz says that, Mr. Wilkins went back to Washington and told the Attorney General - -

MR. SCHULTZ: Now, Mr. Weinglass - -

THE COURT: Just a minute, Mr. Schultz.

I direct you, sir, not to refer to a document objection to which has been sustained.

MR. WEINGLASS: He wouldn't have if Mr. Schultz didn't object - -
THE COURT: I order you not to refer to that document.
MR. WEINGLASS: But he replied that this witness- -
THE COURT: There will be no 'but' about it. You will not refer to that document.
MR. WEINGLASS: But it contains the evaluation to rebut just what Mr. Schultz said.
THE COURT: Mr. Weinglass - -
MR. WEINGLASS: It's most unfair, your Honor. You must see that. You have read the document yourself.
THE COURT: I order you to refrain from further discussion of a document where objection has been sustained out of the presence of the jury.
MR. WEINGLASS: But how can you permit this dishonesty? He's read the document - -
MR. SCHULTZ: Dishonesty?
MR. WEINGLASS: It is dishonest, absolutely dishonest.
MR. SCHULTZ: Your Honor, I ask that that statement be stricken from this record and Mr. Weinglass admonished to conduct himself in a professional way in this courtroom."
"THE COURT: I direct the jury to disregard the remarks of Mr. Weinglass, and I strike them from the record, those referring to dishonesty.
MR. SCHULTZ: May I proceed, your Honor?
THE COURT: You may proceed, sir.
MR. WEINGLASS: Will your Honor also direct the jury to disregard the remarks of the Court that I need a defense? And I would like to get an explanation from the Court as to what the Court means by it.
THE COURT: No, I will not - -
MR. WEINGLASS: I would like to know why I need a defense in this particular case.
THE COURT: If you don't understand them, I am sorry, sir. Your lawyers there - -
MR. WEINGLASS: I am afraid I do understand them. I think they are improper." Official Transcript, Pages 16,662-666. **3 months**

Specification 11: On January 22, during the direct examination of the witness Buff, Mr. Weinglass continued to make statements from the lectern rather than question the witness. He was directly ordered to continue the examination and was forbidden to make such statements. He defied that order, and the incident is set forth in the record as follows:

"THE COURT: I direct you, sir --

MR. FORAN: You are supposed to ask a question.

THE COURT: I direct you, sir, to proceed with the direct examination of this witness, and forbid the making of a statement.

MR. WEINGLASS: In order to protect Mr. Rubin's rights in the state court prosecution --

MR. FORAN: There is no necessity of arguing legal questions that are not the obligation of a jury to decide. That is what he is attempting to do, to try to get the jury to violate its obligation.

THE COURT: I forbid you to make any statement during this direct examination other than to ask questions. You may ask any questions you like.

MR. WEINGLASS: These questions are being asked, your Honor, under protest in light of Mr. Rubin's state court prosecution.

THE COURT: I strike that statement because you did it, you made the statement after I gave you my direction not to.

MR. WEINGLASS: I can't compromise the man's rights in this courtroom.

MR. FORAN: There is no compromise of rights. The jury is a factual finding body. It has nothing to do with the legal questions.

THE COURT: I direct the jury to disregard the last statement.

MR. FORAN: That is the law.

MR. KUNSTLER: Your Honor --

THE COURT: I will not hear from you.

MR. KUNSTLER: -- he said I said something that is improper. It is not improper. I have heard this in court after court.

THE COURT: I will not hear from you while your associate is examining this witness.

MR. KUNSTLER: It has nothing to do with this witness.
MR. FORAN: The reference was to Mr. Weinglass.
MR. KUNSTLER: He said I said something that was improper. It was not improper.
THE COURT: I ask you to sit down, sir. And you may continue.
Mr. Marshal, have that man sit down.
You may ask a question. You may ask any question of this witness you like.
Defiantly, you made a statement after three times I directed you not to.
Please don't do it again.
MR. WEINGLASS: I did not make that statement defiantly. I have an obligation.
THE COURT: You made it in derogation of the Court's order.
MR. WEINGLASS: There was nothing improper about the statement.
THE COURT: It is improper if the Court ordered you not to make it. I wish you could continue with the examination now.
MR. WEINGLASS: The effect of the order is to compromise the rights of Mr. Rubin.
THE COURT: Will you continue with the direct examination of the witness. Otherwise, I will ask the witness to leave the stand." Official Transcript, Pages 17,087-89. **1 month**

Specification 12: On December 24, during the direct examination of the witness Davis, Mr. Weinglass continued to argue after a ruling had been made and he had been directed to complete his argument. He openly defied the order of the Court and refused to continue with the examination when told to do so. The incident is set forth in the transcript as follows:

"THE COURT: I will let my ruling stand.
MR. WEINGLASS: Your Honor - -
THE COURT: I said I'd let my ruling stand, sir.
MR. WEINGLASS: Your Honor must permit us the opportunity of responding to that.
THE COURT: I have permitted you. I have per-

mitted Mr. Kunstler to speak, and now you may ask another question of this witness.

MR. WEINGLASS: Reverend Abernathy was mentioned as an officer of the National Mobilization.

THE COURT: Mr. Weinglass - -

MR. DELLINGER: He was co-chairman.

THE COURT: I direct you not to - -

MR. WEINGLASS: He was national co-chairman.

MR FORAN: Your Honor, there were seven individuals who are still in this case as part of this indictment. There is no national - -

THE COURT: Will you continue with the examination - -

MR. WEINGLASS: Your Honor, I would like to ask Mr. Foran what relationship the unidentified speaker had with the National Mobiliaztion. His speech was - -

THE COURT: I order you to continue with his examination, sir.

MR. WEINGLASS: I understand your Honor's sensitivity to what Reverend Abernathy said at that particular time.

THE COURT: And I direct that that remark go out.

MR. WEINGLASS: And Senator McCarthy also spoke.

THE COURT: And I direct the jury to disregard it.

MR. WEINGLASS: Two witnesses referred to what Senator McCarthy had to say, and he is not a defendant here.

MR. FORAN: On cross-examination, your Honor. On cross-examination by these men, not in direct examination by the government.

MR. WEINGLASS: On direct examination - -

THE COURT: Will you comply with my order?

MR. KUNSTLER: Your Honor. I am going to answer the second part of the argument.

MR. WEINGLASS: Richard Goodwin, when he was called as a witness by us, referred to the exact words by Senator McCarthy.

THE COURT: Will you comply with my order?

MR KUNSTLER: What about the second part of the argument that the mule train was mentioned on

direct?
THE COURT: I will ask you to sit down.
MR. KUNSTLER: Your Honor, but that is not -- your Honor ruled that was irrelevant.
THE COURT: I cannot let two lawyers conduct an examination and handle the objections.
MR. KUNSTLER: I am not conducting the examination. I raised the second argument and that was not answered, that the SCLC Mule Train, if the mule train was afraid of the demonstrators, why did Ralph Abernathy speak to them the next day?
THE COURT: Will you comply with my order?
MR. WEINGLASS: If your Honor will not permit the jury to hear what Reverend Abernathy said --
MR. FORAN: Listen to that, your Honor. Just listen to that. Isn't that classical?
THE COURT: I will strike that last remark, and don't make it again. I direct the jury to disregard it.
Mr. Marshal, anyone who laughs aloud at the rulings of the court will please -- other than the defendants -- be asked to leave the courtroom.
MR KUNSTLER: Your Honor, am I entitled to an answer to my objection?
THE COURT: I have heard you.
MR. KUNSTLER: Well, the prosecutor has not responded. He has ignored it.
THE COURT: I have heard you.
MR. WEINGLASS: I just want the record to show that Reverend Abernathy was an officer of the National Mobilization.
THE COURT: Oh, Mr. Weinglass. Mr. Weinglass. I am sorry --" Official Transcript, Pages 17,805-806.

5 months

Specification 13: On December 26, during the cross-examination of the witness Davis, Mr. Weinglass made an objection. When his objection was overruled he again argued the question, and made a citation to the Canon of Judicial Ethics. He was instructed not to make such a statement again during the trial, and he defiantly immediately thereafter made the statement again. The incident is reported at Pages 18,056-18,057 as follows:

"MR. WEINGLASS: Your Honor, I object to that because they are two different conversations. Mr. Froines made a presentation at which the defendant Davis indicated he said that. Mr. Bock was referring to a later time, he said. We are talking, again, about confusion in Mr. Foran's question.

MR. FORAN: When did you structure that, Mr. Weinglass? It wasn't testified to.

THE COURT: I will overrule the objection and let the witness answer if he can.

MR. WEINGLASS: If the Court please, will the Court indicate some admonition to Mr. Foran to my objection?

THE COURT: If it has offended you, I strike it, I direct the jury to disregard it.

MR. WEINGLASS: It didn't offend me. It violated the rules of evidence and Canon of Ethics 47 which prohibits such conduct which they have been engaging in all through this trial and which the court has countenanced. That is why I object.

MR. FORAN: Your Honor, the hypocrisy of Mr. Weinglass' statement - -

THE COURT: I do strike the last statement or comment of Mr. Weinglass, and I direct the jury to disregard it, and direct you not to make such a statement again.

MR. WEINGLASS: I have read that Canon of Ethics, your Honor.

MR. FORAN: - - is monumental.

MR. WEINGLASS: I refer to the Canon of Ethics.

THE COURT: Don't make that statement during this trial again.

MR. WEINGLASS: Well, it is true, and I stand by it.

THE COURT: You did it again.

MR. WEINGLASS: It involves the Canon of Judicial Ethics which indicates the Court must admonish counsel when he refers personally to his adversary, and that hasn't been done on the Government's side."

1 month

Specification 14: On February 5 ,Mr. Weinglass once more defied openly the Court's order to discontinue argument and be seated. The incident is reported as follows:

"MR. WEINGLASS: Your Honor, while Mr. Kunstler is examining the 3500 material, I would want at this time because I sincerely and honestly feel that the Court realizes that its position with respect to the jailing of Dave Dellinger is indefensible in law --

THE COURT: Don't speak for me.

MR. WEINGLASS: That is why I was cut off.

THE COURT: I will not hear you further on that motion.

MR. WEINGLASS: Well, your Honor, you are keeping a man in custody, and you are not permitting a lawyer to make an argument for his freedom. That is unheard of. That is unprecedented in law.

THE COURT: I have considered the matter carefully.

MR. WEINGLASS: You have not considered it because you did not hear the argument.

THE COURT: I ask you to sit down, sir.

MR. WEINGLASS: Your Honor knows -- you cited cases --

THE COURT: I ask you to sit down.

MR. WEINGLASS: -- that you --

THE COURT: Mr. Marshal, will you ask that man to sit down.

MR. WEINGLASS: You have no authority for taking that man's freedom away, and you will not let me make a legal argument in his behalf.

MR. SCHULTZ: That is disgraceful.

MR. WEINGLASS: That is disgraceful.

MR. SCHULTZ: Because Mr. Weinglass --

MR. WEINGLASS: Because I was cut off in the middle of a legal argument.

MR. SCHULTZ: Because Mr. Weinglass would not order his client to be quiet during the argument.

MR. WEINGLASS: Because I wouldn't order Jerry Rubin to be quiet. If Dave Dellinger remains in jail, that is Mr. Schultz' concept on justice.

THE COURT: Will you sit down, sir. Will you have him sit down.

MR. WEINGLASS: If that is the way it is going to apply in this courtroom.

> THE COURT: Mr Marshal, will you have him sit down." Official Transcript, Pages 19,811-13. **21 days**

THE COURT: Mr Weinglass, I will hear from you.
MR. WEINGLASS: If the Court please, I make the motion which both Mr. Kunstler and myself have made before on behalf of the other defendants with respect to the lack of jurisdiction and authority of the Court to impose punishment for contempt at the conclusion of the trial proceedings.
THE COURT: I deny the motion and I say again that the Supreme Court of the United States and the Courts of Appeal have decided otherwise. You may proceed.
MR. WEINGLASS: This trial is my first trial in the federal court. I have never tried a case either in or out of New Jersey in the United States District Court.

As I first came to this courtroom and I realized the nature of the charges against the eight defendants, as well as the personalities and the involvement of my clients, I wondered if it would be possible to exclude from this room all that did go before and all that was occurring outside of this courtroom.

As your Honor heard in the course of this trial, the United States Attorney and - - and I believe he meant it personally and sincerely - - referred to the seven as evil men, and they were equally brief and sincere in referring to the prosecution as fascistic and Nazi-like, and where you have a clash - - your slighting me - - Mr. Feinglass - - some of them referred to me that way - - eventually you become that, but at the outset - -
THE COURT: I don't want you to leave me out.
MR. WEINGLASS: At the outset was the feeling that existed between two adversaries, and I didn't know if these feelings could be kept out of this room or whether or not this trial could proceed as a criminal trial, and I believe this is the constant difficulty and dilemma of what has been referred to in this case often but not accepted by the Court as a political trial.

But even - - even in the midst of all this, even with my hopes that it could be a proceedings disappearing in the midst of what was occurring, I tried and I believe together with Mr. Kunstler, to function as best I could under those circumstances as an attorney and under what I believe, Mr. Kunstler and myself believe, to be the tradition of the law, although we differ greatly on what the tradition of the law is with the court. In every instance in this court, I believe it occurred in excess of 40 times, we have filed extensive legal motions in writing with briefs attached, and memoranda of law, citing case citations. At the outset our motions with which were legal motions were impounded by the court with an indication that we would be punished for filing those legal motions at a later date.

However, we continued to hold our course and do what we felt was our obligation in this courtroom and that is defend 8 men as best we could. And it hasn't been easy for anyone. This has been a long, difficult, highly contested proceeding in which all of us at one time or another have lost their sense of professional control and judgment. I only have to cite to the court Mr. Schultz' reference to the bathroom in front of the jury, for which he later apologized. There were unlawful references to the fact that two of the defendants took the stand and perjured themselves for which he apologized; Mr. Foran's statement that Tom Hayden and Rennie Davis were guilty of a crime for which they had neither been charged nor were before a grand jury, for which he later apologized.

But I have no quarrel with either Mr. Foran or Mr. Schultz. They were attorneys involved in a very difficult adversary proceeding and they are entitled to errors of judgment, to loss of control, which they committed in the course of this four and a half months.

For the same understandable defects, Mr. Kunstler and myself will have to serve time in jail. Your Honor has recited the list of citations, I believe there are 13 or 14 in number—each and every one of those citations without exception occurring in the course of legal argument. I have been called in the course of those legal arguments—and your Honor will recall these words—phony and twofaced. When I attempted to answer Mr. Schultz at one time he called me dishonest. I believe that is one of the citations. I forget which number.

THE COURT: I would wish in this connection that you would confine your observations to matters in mitigation here.

MR WEINGLASS: That is precisely what I am addressing myself to.
THE COURT: No, I am not dealing with anybody here other than yourself. This is a proceeding separate and apart even from the main case. This deals with a matter of direct contempt committed in open court, before the Court, in the presence of the Court, as a separate proceeding.
MR. WEINGLASS: What the Court has chosen to label as direct contempt in the presence of the Court I cite as nothing more than the argument of counsel in the heat of battle and I make the same confession that my brethren have made that at times I have gone beyond -- at times I should have stopped -- at times I argued after a ruling although I submit in almost every instance I was not permitted to argue and what I was doing in effect was asking if I could argue after the court had already ruled, but I submit if your Honor looks through this record with a balanced eye and with a careful eye, you will see on a number of occasions our adversary counsel argued after rulings in several instances. They were even asked to cease their argument by the Court for the very same reasons and if counsel are not permitted that small leeway in the conduct of a defense, then I think you do a disservice to the profession and you unbalance the balance in the adversary proceedings where two parties come before the court as co-equals.
THE COURT: I am not going to permit a lawyer who has had one case in the federal court to tell me that I do a disservice to the profession.

I am accustomed to having lawyers obey the rules and that you consistently failed to do.

I could go into the background of the case as I did with Mr. Kunstler, the matter of the conduct of your clients insofar as they treated the trial judge, but I am not going to do that. You know as well as I do what your obligation was in that regard.

This trial, whatever the result comes to be, could have been conducted fairly and with dignity and without rancor or ill will. I can recall few instances -- Oh, I suppose every judge has a run in with lawyers on occasions, but there have been few instances that I can recall where I have had acrimonious or anything that approached an acrimonious discussion with a lawyer in respect to his conduct. And I have tried cases in this courtroom and in the old court house across the street where the defendants were widely publicized men in the field of crime and we went through trials involving one or two or three months with no rancor or ill feeling. Sometimes there was a conviction, sometimes not. But when a lawyer - - but when the lawyers in the main were told what they had to do, they did it. They did it. That is no matter of arrogance on the part of the judge; it is the way a trial should be conducted, and you heard me use the words of Justice Frankfurter in my charge to the jury, "The judge is the governor of the trial."

If I permit a lawyer to run over me, and I am afraid I did a little bit here, it would be - - it might be unfair even to the defendants, as some defense lawyers have a notion that the plaintiff in this case - - and, as you may now know - - perhaps you don't - - this is the first case in the federal court you just told me - - the United States of America in this case is the plaintiff. The accuser - - Justice Cardozo says "The accuser has some rights."

But there is rapidly growing up a tradition or a belief in this country that the only person on trial is the defendant - - that the only party to the trial is the defendant.

When the United States of America procures an indictment against an individual, the United States of America is the accuser and is entitled as much to the protective rulings of the court as the defendant. But I am sorry to say that procedure isn't always followed.

I guess some judges have gotten to feel that "Oh, maybe the Court of Appeals, maybe the Supreme Court will reverse me."

Several times during this trial I was told by the defense counsel "You know what the Court of Appeals will do to you on that one."

Well, I long ago - - I am going to say now as I said then - - quit trying to second guess what any reviewing court will do. And you will remember my saying I do my honest best, and I know that the Court of Appeals judges, Supreme Court justices will do their honest best.

I don't like to have a lawyer tell me "Don't rule that way; you're going to be reversed."

Here in this very transcript dealing with the termination of the Dellinger bond the statement has been made about how wrong I was and yet within a matter of 48 hours the United States Court of Appeals for this circuit unanimously, citing the very cases I cited to you lawyers here, approved of my order.

Now that doesn't mean that I was brilliant because the Court of Appeals affirmed me; I have been affirmed sometimes when I thought perhaps I shouldn't have been.

But you will get along better -- and I am not -- you haven't asked me to advise you but since you tell me this is your first case in the federal court, you will get along better by being respectful -- and I know you and I differ on what being respectful means. It doesn't mean being obsequious; you don't have to bow and scrape to a judge. But you must be respectful in your manner and when you are ordered to do something -- I don't like the use of the word "order" but that's the way we function in the courts. If it is the court's order, it is my order.

When we restrain a strike on a railroad, it has to be by order, by injunction, and when I direct you to refrain from doing something, I expect you to refrain from doing it. And that would be true if you practiced in the lowest court in the state of New Jersey, your home state. There is no magic in what goes on in the federal courts. We run the whole gamut of the law here. We try a whole lot of unimportant personal injury cases that don't involve a great deal of money merely because the statute requires us to try federal tort claims. I have sat up here for three days to determine that there was $95.00 coming to a plaintiff who sued the government.

So don't feel that because your experience is limited to this one case in the federal court that -- you are much too able a lawyer not to do the right thing.

And I say it militates against a lawyer regardless of the result in this case -- again speaking generally.

MR. WEINGLASS: If I may just be heard for a --

THE COURT: I will hear you now only on the matter -- I took time to digress because of your observations about --

MR. WEINGLASS: If I could just answer that digression for a moment: With respect to our different understandings of respect, I was hopeful when I came here that after 20 weeks the court would know my name and I didn't receive that which I thought was the minimum --

THE COURT: Well, I am going to tell you about that.

MR. WEINGLASS: You have explained it.

THE COURT: I have got a very close friend named Weinruss and I know nobody by the name of Weinrob -- and somehow or other the name of Weinruss stuck in my mind and it is your first appearance here. You have seen lawyers pass before this bar all during your four to five months here whom I know intimately and I scarcely ever forget a lawyer's name even when he hasn't been in for 20 years.

MR. WEINGLASS: My natural instincts are and have always been to avoid, if possible, a protracted fight. I am not as strong a man as Bill Kunstler by far, and I think I am more vulnerable to what I perceive to be intimidation -- whether it is or not. And I have had to fight that instinct here in court, not only because I felt that the rights of other men were involved but because of the inspiration I drew from Bill Kunstler as well as the other persons who have worked with me.

THE COURT: Did you ever feel like tapping one of those defendants, one or more of them, on the hand when they were assailing me with vile epithets to say "Hey, hey, be quiet?"

MR. WEINGLASS: Does your Honor seriously believe that what was in conflict here in this courtroom could have dissipated by an admonishment from Bill Kunstler or myself?

THE COURT: That is not the point.

MR. WEINGLASS: Does the Court seriously believe that?

THE COURT: That is not the point.

MR. WEINGLASS: I submit to this Court that --

THE COURT: It is your duty as an officer of the Court to see to it that the judge is not affronted by your client. I think it is a responsibility under the law. I don't think that a lawyer properly may sit at a table with a client who shouts, calls vile epithets -- I suppose that is as good a name as any. Not once did either you or Mr. Kunstler try to stop them.

MR. WEINGLASS: I only need to point out to you --

THE COURT: I judge your whole attitude toward the Court by your omission to do that. But I am obligated under law to particularize these items of contempt which

I have.

MR. WEINGLASS: I only need point out to the Court one thing in answer to that. Those men are upstairs now, they are serving long prison terms, the Court made it known to them throughout this trial that they would, and your Honor failed in your attempt to silence what they felt was their right to speak out when they just couldn't stand it any more, to sit and be silent.

THE COURT: Well, I can see from that you think a man has a right to speak out before he even knows whether he can stand it.

I was called a fascist pig by somebody who never saw me in his life before, and then one of your clients got up and said "We support him in every respect."

No, I am not --

MR. WEINGLASS: That man was facing a possible ten year prison sentence without his attorney who was in the hospital being present and I with my limited experience --

THE COURT: I don't want to go into that attorney business. I have got a pretty good file on that.

MR. WEINGLASS: I just want to conclude by saying that we have been able to conduct a vigorous defense because of the people who have assisted us.

In order to combat the United States Government and all of the resources available to it in this case, it was necessary for the defense to build a staff and apparatus of equal strength to obtain the materials needed to present the defense.

I came to this city as a stranger and I didn't know these people, but I say to the court that there are people sitting in the front row of this courtroom and in the last row who since September 24 have been sleeping on the floor of my apartment in proximity to the desk; who have been receiving a sum of $20.00 a week for their maintenance and no more; who have worked until three and four o'clock in the morning in going through transcripts and exhibits; who have given up all of the opportunities that are available to them, and, like the defendants, America's best was before them, they merely had to seize it.

THE COURT: I think I would have paid out of my own

pocket for a good bed in a respectable place if you had set them a good example by at least trying to get these men to refrain from the personal epithets hurled at the Court.

MR. WEINGLASS: Well, I am off that subject for a moment.

THE COURT: They would have respected you even more than they do now.

A VOICE: There is no man in this courtroom I respect more than Leonard Weinglass.

MISS LEANER: And you are a racist and a fascist and a pig and I stand with my brothers Weinglass and Kunstler in this courtroom.

THE COURT: Now see what you have? She is your chief staff member. She has been in here more than anyone else -- probably a very competent person. That is an example of the insults I have had to suffer.

You say you are a sensitive person. I have practiced law and been on the bench many years. I can take it. I can take an average amount. But can you imagine a young woman whose people I have befriended to the extent that a judge can -- "you are a racist and a fascist."

Can you imagine that.

After you just got through praising the staff, saying how wonderful they were.

I shall proceed with the disposition --

MR. WEINGLASS: If I may say one sentence in conclusion --

THE COURT: All right. One thing you may say.

MR. WEINGLASS: It might be more than one sentence but it is one thought and it will be brief.

I face what I am told will be punishment and I don't mean to undermine whatever punishment means by saying this but I welcome the opportunity of whatever the Court does which will enable me to once again rejoin the defendants and Bill Kunstler wherever they are and what has been for me the warmest and the richest association of my life.

THE COURT: All right.

As I say, in conformity with Rule 42(a) of the Federal Rules of Criminal Procedure, Title 18, United States Code,

Section 401, I find the statements and acts and conduct of Leonard Weinglass which I have set forth in my oral observations each constitute a separate contempt of this court; that each constitute a deliberate and wilful attack upon the administration of justice in an attempt to sabotage the functioning of the federal judicial system; that this misconduct was of so grave a character as to continue to disrupt the orderly administration of justice.

To maintain the dignity of the Court and to preserve order in the courtroom under these circumstances has been a task -- under these circumstances and the other circumstances here -- has been a task of utmost difficulty.

An excellent example of what I have been confronted with in this case were the observations of your chief staff member. I think she was Miss Leander, the black girl who just went out -- who has been treated with the utmost deference by the members of my staff. All of the time she has been shown the utmost courtesy that she is entitled to have, and for her to make an outrageous statement like that and walk out of here seems to me clear evidence of the thinking of those who have been around the defendants and their counsel.

As I say, I find that the acts, statements and conduct of the defendants -- or not the defendants but of Mr. Weinglass, each constitute a separate contempt of this court.

With respect to *Specification* 1, the court directs that Mr. Weinglass be committed to the custody of the Attorney General of the United States or his authorized representative for imprisonment for a period of 2 days; with respect to *Specification* 2, for a period of 4 months; with respect to *Specification* 3, for a period of 14 days; with respect to *Specification* 4, for a period of 14 days; with respect to *Specification* 5, for a period of 1 month; with respect to *Specification* 6, a period of 1 month; with respect to *Specification* 7, 14 days; with respect to *Specification* 8, a period of 1 month; with respect to *Specification* 9, a period of 1 month; with respect to *Specification* 10, a period of 3 months; with respect to *Specification* 11, a period of 1 month; with respect to *Specification* 12, a period of 5 months; with respect to *Specification* 13, a period of 1 month; with respect to *Specification* 14, a period of 21 days; all of these periods to run cumulatively and consecutively.

I extend the same courtesy to you as I did to Mr. Kunstler, I stay the execution of the judgment of conviction in this situation to and including Monday morning, May 4, at ten o'clock, because I believe that between now and then it is conceivable that you might have occasion to serve those defendants whose lawyer you are in the case out of which these contempts arise.

Mr. Marshal - -

MR. KUNSTLER: Your Honor, there is one further matter that we just want to take up.

There are counsel here for all of the defendants as well as Mr. Weinglass and myself who will be handling these matters, and I would like to introduce them to the court. You know one of them already, Mr. Thomas Sullivan, who has approached the lectern.

THE COURT: Yes, I do know Mr. Sullivan.

MR. KUNSTLER: With him is Mr. Morton Stavis.

THE COURT: I don't perceive that in this kind of a situation, though, that I will hear from counsel with respect to contempt matters. This is a direct contempt. You, of course, have the right of appeal on it.

MR. SULLIVAN: I wonder - -

THE COURT: I have directed the United States Attorney to prepare the necessary papers.

MR. SULLIVAN: Judge Hoffman, I just wondered whether you would hear me briefly on this question of appeal bonds and your authority to enter such bonds.

THE COURT: I have no authority to fix bonds. In any event, in view of the findings, if I had the authority, I would not fix bail.

MR. SULLIVAN: Thank you very much.

THE COURT: Is there anything else?

MR. SULLIVAN: No.

THE COURT: The court will be in recess then.

(Whereupon court adjourned.)

THE PEOPLES Ancient and Just LIBERTIES ASSERTED, IN THE TRYAL OF *William Penn*, and *William Mead*,

At the Sessions held at the *Old-Baily* in *London*, the first, third, fourth and fifth of *Sept.* 70. against the most Arbitrary procedure of that Court.

Isa. 10. 1, 2. *Wo unto them that Decree Unrighteous Decrees, and write Grievousness, which they have prescribed; to turn away the Needy from Judgment, and to take away the Right from the Poor*, &c.

Psal. 94. 20. *Shall the Throne of Iniquity have fellowship with thee which frameth mischief by a Law.*

Sic volo, sic jubeo, stat pro ratione volantas.

Old-Baily, 1st, 3d, 4th, 5th of *Sept.* 1670.

London, Printed and Sold by *T. Sowle*, next Door to the *Meeting-house* in *White-Hart-Court* in *Gracious-street*, and at the *Bible* in *Leaden-hall-street*, near the *Market*.

Conspiracy, contempt, and the question of respect for established institutions are not new phenomena in our culture. To see how far we have progressed in 300 years the reader will find the following summary and excerpts of another trial both interesting and relevant.

The Publishers

The transcript excerpts are taken from and the summary is adapted from two articles originally published in the *American Bar Association Journal:* "The Jury That Tried William Penn," by Barry R. Nager (February 1964); and "Hugh Latimer's Candle and the Trial of William Penn," by Eberhard P. Deutsch (July 1965). Grateful acknowledgment is made for permission to reprint portions here.

On August 14, 1670, Penn had come to the Quaker meeting hall in Gracechurch Street in London. He found that it had been surrounded by soldiers who prohibited any of the assembled Quaker group from entering. In protest Penn began preaching to the people in the street, and he and William Mead were arrested.

On September 1 an indictment was brought in at the Old Bailey charging

> That *William Penn,* Gent.[leman], and *William Mead,* late of *London,* Linen-Draper, with divers other Persons to the Jurors unknown, to the Number of 300, the 14th Day of *August* in the 22nd year of the King, about Eleven of the Clock in the Forenoon, the same Day, with Force and Arms, &c. in the Parish of St. *Bennet Grace-Church* in *Bridge-Ward, London,* in the Street called *Grace-Church Street,* unlawfully and tumultuously did Assemble and Congregate themselves together, to the Disturbance of the Peace of the said Lord the King: And the aforesaid *William Penn* . . . then and there, in the open Street, did take upon himself to Preach and Speak . . . unto the aforesaid *William Mead,* and other Persons . . . by Reason whereof a great Concourse and Tumult of People in the Street aforesaid, then and there, a long time did remain and continue, in contempt of the said Lord the King, and of his Law . . . to the great Terror and Disturbance of many of his Liege People and Subjects, to the ill Example of all others in the like Case Offenders, and against the Peace of the said Lord the King, his Crown and Dignity.

Present on the bench as justices when the indictment was returned and read by the clerk, were Samuel Starling, Lord Mayor, and John Howell, Recorder, of the City of London; five aldermen; three sheriffs; and twelve jurors.

Called on by the clerk to plead to the indictment, Penn addressed the court:

> I am unacquainted with the Formality of the Law, and therefore, before I shall answer directly, I request two Things of the Court. First, that no Advantage may be taken against me, nor I deprived of any Benefit, which I might otherwise have received. Secondly, that you will promise me a fair hearing, and

> liberty of making my Defence.

In response, Penn was assured: "No advantage shall be taken against you; you shall have Liberty; you shall be heard." Each then pleaded "Not Guilty in Manner and Form."

Penn and Mead Have Hat Trouble

When the two prisoners entered the court on the morning of September 3, they kept on their hats, pursuant to a Quaker custom which forbade "hat honour" to superiors. A bailiff accordingly pulled off their hats, and the Mayor immediately exclaimed: "Sirrah, who bid you put off their Hats? Put on their Hats again." The record states that "one of the Officers putting the Prisoners Hats upon their heads . . . brought them to the Bar." The Recorder thereupon asked Penn: "Do you not know there is Respect due the Court?" To which Penn responded in the affirmative, and

> RECORDER: Why do you not pull off your Hat then?
>
> PENN: Because I do not believe that to be any Respect.
>
> RECORDER: Well, the Court sets forty Marks a piece upon your Heads, as a Fine for your Contempt of the Court.
>
> PENN: I desire it might be observed, that we came into Court with our Hats (that is, taken) off and if they have been put on since, it was by Order from the Bench; and therefore not we, but the Bench should be fined.

The Crown's case against Penn and Mead consisted of the testimony of three witnesses who stated that they had seen from three to five hundred persons present at the meeting in Gracechurch Street, and that they had seen Penn speaking but could not hear what he said. A sharp volley of words came when one of the witnesses testified that he had not seen Captain Mead at the meeting. Howell, the Recorder, then asked Captain Mead if he was at the meeting, to which Mead replied:

> MEAD: It is a Maxim in your own law, *Nemo tenetur accusare seipsum,* which if it be not true Latin, I am sure it is true English, *That no Man is bound to accuse himself*. And why dost thou offer to insnare me with such a Question? Doth not this show thy Malice? Is this like unto a Judge, that ought to be

Counsel for the Prisoner at the Bar?

RECORDER: Sir, hold your Tongue, I did not go about to insnare you.

Next, Penn demanded that "to the End the Bench, the Jury, and my self, with these that hear us, may have a more direct Understanding of this Procedure, I desire you would let me know by what Law it is you prosecute me, and upon what Law you ground my Indictment":

RECORDER: Upon the Common-Law.

PENN: Where is that Common-Law?

RECORDER: You must not think that I am able to run up so many Years, and over so many adjudged Cases, which we call Common-Law, to answer your Curiosity.

PENN: This Answer I am sure is very short of my Question, for if it be Common, it should not be so hard to produce.

* * *

RECORDER: You are an impertinent Fellow, will you teach the Court what Law is? It's *lex non scripta,* that which many have studied thirty or forty Years to know, and would you have me to tell you in a Moment?

* * *

PENN: I design no Affront to the Court, but . . . you do at once deny me an acknowledged Right, and evidence to the whole World your Resolution to sacrifice the Privileges of *Englishmen* to your sinister and Arbitrary Designs.

RECORDER: Take him away. My Lord, if you take not some Course with this pestilent Fellow, to stop his Mouth, we shall not be able to do anything to Night.

MAYOR: Take him away, take him away, turn him into the Bale-dock.

Mead, who had been a captain in the Commonwealth army, being left at the bar, then addressed the jury, emphasizing the Quaker tenet of peace and nonresistance, which forbade tumult: "Time was when I had Freedom to use a carnal Weapon . . . but now I fear the Living God, and . . . am a peaceable Man. . . . You Men of the jury, who are my Judges, if the Recorder will not tell you what makes . . .

an unlawful assembly, *Coke,* he that once they called the Lord *Coke,* tells us what makes a Riot, a Rout, and an unlawful Assembly . . . A Riot is when three, or more, are met together to beat a Man, or to enter forcibly into another Man's Land, to cut down his Grass, his Wood, or break down his Pales."

At this point, according to the transcript, *"the Recorder interrupted him and said,* I thank you, Sir that you will tell me what the Law is; *scornfully pulling off his Hat."* One of the other justices remarked: "He talks at random, one while an Independent, another while some other Religion, and now a Quaker, and next a Papist." The Lord Mayor said, speaking to Mead: "You deserve to have your Tongue cut out."

But Mead insisted: "Thou didst promise me, I should have fair Liberty to be heard. Why may I not have the Privilege of an *Englishman?* I am an *Englishman,* and you might be ashamed of this dealing." To this the Recorder replied vehemently: "I look upon you to be an Enemy to the Laws of *England,* which ought to be observed and kept, nor are you worthy of such Privileges as others have." Mead, too, was taken away into the bale-dock, and the Recorder charged the jury:

> You have heard what the Indictment is. It is for preaching to the People, and drawing a tumultuous Company after them, and Mr. *Penn* was speaking; if they should not be disturbed, you see they will go on; . . . Now we are upon the Matter of Fact, which you are to keep to, and observe, as what hath been fully sworn, at your Peril.

From the bale-dock, Penn cried out:

> I appeal to the Jury, who are my Judges, and this great Assembly, whether the Proceedings of the Court are not most Arbitrary . . . I say, it is directly opposite to, and destructive of the undoubted Right of every *English* prisoner, as *Coke,* in the 2 *Instit.* 29, on the Chap. of *Magna Charta,* speaks.

At this, the Recorder remarked: "Why, ye are present, you do hear, do you not?" And he ordered: "Take them away into the Hole." According to Penn's record: *"The Jury were commanded up to agree upon their Verdict, the Prisoners remaining in the stinking Hole."*

The jury then retired to reach their verdict. After an hour and a half they came back, saying that they stood eight to four with no hope of a verdict.

Jury Refuses To Find an Unlawful Assembly

After receiving more threats from the court, the jury was sent back to reach a verdict. When they returned their verdict was that William Penn was guilty of speaking at Gracechurch Street. The court asked if that was all and the foreman was asked by the Lord Mayor, "Was it not an unlawful assembly? You mean he was speaking to a tumult of people there?" To which the foreman replied, "No, my Lord, this was all I had in commission."

The court, after hurling further insults at the jury, told the jury that they would not be released until they reached a verdict. The jury retired again and a half hour later they came back with their verdict, which was that William Mead was not guilty as charged in the indictment and that William Penn was guilty of speaking or preaching to an assembly on Gracechurch Street on August 14, 1670.

Upon this, the Recorder addressed the jury angrily:

> Gentlemen, you shall not be dismisst till we have a Verdict, that the Court will accept; and you shall be lock'd up, without Meat, Drink, Fire, and Tobacco; you shall not think thus to abuse the Court; we will have a Verdict, by the help of God, or you shall starve for it.

To this Penn countered:

> My Jury, who are my Judges, ought not to be thus menaced; their Verdict should be free, and not compelled; the Bench ought to wait upon them, but not forestal them. I do desire that Justice may be done me, and that the Arbitrary Resolves of the Bench may not be made the Measure of my Jury's Verdict.

When the Recorder shouted, "Stop that prating Fellow's mouth, or put him out of the Court", Penn called after the jury: "You are *Englishmen,* mind your Privilege, give not away your right." Bushel called back to him: "Nor will we ever do it."

The jury was detained all night "without so much as a chamber pot" and when they reconvened the next morning the verdict was still as before: "that William Penn was guilty of speaking in Gracechurch Street".

> MAYOR: You are a factious Fellow, I'll take a Course with you.
> BLOOD[worth]: I knew Mr. *Bushell* would not yield.
> BUSHELL: Sir *Thomas,* I have done according to my Conscience.
> MAYOR: That Conscience of yours would cut my Throat.
> BUSHELL: No, my Lord, it never shall.
> MAYOR: But I will cut yours as soon as I can.

Penn thereupon asked the recorder whether he would "allow of the Verdict given of *William Mead*", to which the Recorder replied: "It cannot be a Verdict, because you were indicted for a Conspiracy, and one being found Not guilty, and not the other, it could not be a Verdict."

To this Penn responded: "If Not guilty be not a Verdict, then you make of the Jury and *Magna Charta* but a meer Nose of Wax"; and he submitted that if William Mead "be Not guilty, it consequently follows, that I am clear, since you have indicted us of a Conspiracy, and I could not possibly conspire alone".

After further "passages . . . between the Jury and the Court, [t]he Jury went up again, having received a fresh Charge from the Bench", and returned for the fifth time with the same verdict:

> RECORDER: [to Bushell] I will set a Mark upon you; and whilst I have any thing to do in the City, I will have an Eye upon you.
> MAYOR: Have you no more Wit than to be led by such a pitiful Fellow? I will cut his Nose.
> PENN: It is intolerable that my Jury should be thus menaced: Is this according to the Fundamental Laws? Are not they my proper Judges by the great Charter of *England?* What hope is there of ever having Justice done, when Juries are threatened, and their Verdicts rejected? . . .
> MAYOR: Stop his Mouth; Jaylor, bring Fetters and stake him to the Ground.
> PENN: Do your Pleasure, I matter not your Fetters.

And the Recorder in his exasperation disclosed the real basis of the prosecution and fitted the proceeding expressly into the history of religious intolerance in Europe: "Til now", he said, "I never understood the Reason of the

Policy and Prudence of the *Spaniards,* in suffering the Inquisition among them: And certainly it will never be well with us, till something like unto the *Spanish* Inquisition be in *England*"*!*

The Recorder Continues To Threaten the Jury

Addressing himself once more to the jury, the Recorder went on:

> Gentlemen, we shall not be at this trade always with you; you will find [that at] the next Sessions of Parliament there will be a Law made, that those that will not conform shall not have the Protection of the Law. . . . Your Verdict is nothing, you play upon the Court; I say you shall go together, and bring in another Verdict, or you shall starve; and I will have you carried about the City, as in *Edward* the Third's time.
>
> FOREMAN: We have given in our Verdict, and all agreed to it; and if we give in another, it will be a Force upon us to save our Lives.
>
> MAYOR: Take them up.

Upon this, the jury retired for the sixth time.

Again the jury was detained all night without any physical comforts and when they returned the next morning they announced to the court that they had changed their verdict. With high hopes the clerk asked them, "How say you, is William Penn guilty or not guilty?" the foreman, Thomas Vere, replied, "Not guilty".

Upon this, the Recorded addressed the jury as follows:

> I am sorry, Gentlemen, you have followed your own Judgments and Opinions, rather than the good and wholesome Advice, which was given you; God keep my Life out of your Hands; but for this the Court Fines you forty Marks a Man; and imprisonment till paid. . . .
>
> PENN: I demand my Liberty, being freed by the *Jury*.
>
> MAYOR: No, you are in for your Fines.
>
> PENN: Fines, for what?
>
> MAYOR: For Contempt of the Court.
>
> PENN: I ask, if it be according to the Fundamental Laws of *England,* that any *Englishman* should be Fined or Amerced, but by the Judgment of his Peers or Jury; since it expressly contradicts the fourteenth and twenty-ninth Chapters of the great Charter of

> *England,* which say, No Free-man ought to be amerced, but by the Oath of good and Lawful Men of the Vicinage.
>
> RECORDER: *Take him away, . . . Take him out of the Court.*
>
> PENN: I can never urge the Fundamental Laws of *England,* but you cry, Take him away, take him away. But it is no wonder, *since the* Spanish *Inquisition hath so great a place in the* Recorder's *Heart. . . .*

Eight of the jurors soon capitulated and paid their fines, but the remaining four—Edward Bushell, John Hammond, Charles Milson and John Bailey—resolved to become a test case and remain in prison. After two months their attorneys were able to move the Court of Common Pleas for a writ of habeas corpus. Common Pleas granted bail, but it was more than a year before the case could be heard. The justices in a unanimous opinion ruled that the jury had been illegally fined and imprisoned and that a jury could not be punished for its verdict. The opinion, written by Lord Chief Justice Sir Robert Vaughn, declared in part:

"Is any thing more frequent in the controversies of religion", asked the eminent Chief Justice, "than to press the same text for opposite tenets? How then comes it to pass that two persons may not apprehend with reason and honesty, what a witness, or many, say, to prove in the understanding of one plainly one thing, but in the apprehension of the other, clearly the contrary thing: must therefore one of these merit fine and imprisonment, because he does that which he cannot otherwise do, preserving his oath and integrity? And this often is the case of the Judge and Jury."

And this portion of the opinion concluded "that this return, charging the prisoners to have acquitted Penn and Mead, against full and manifest evidence . . . without saying that they did know and believe that evidence to be full and manifest against the indicted persons, is no cause of fine or imprisonment".

As to "the next part of the retorn, viz. that the jury acquitted those indicted against the direction of the Court in matter of law, openly given and declared to them in Court", the Chief Justice asked rhetorically, "what use can be fancied of juries, or to continue tryals by them at all", if the judge, "from the evidence, shall by his own judgment first resolve upon any tryal what the fact is, and so knowing the fact, shall then resolve what the law is, and order the jury penally to find accordingly?"